The Other Within

feminist constructions

Series Editors: Hilde Lindemann,
Sara Ruddick, and Margaret Urban Walker

Feminist Constructions publishes accessible books that send feminist ethics in promising new directions. Feminist ethics has excelled at critique, identifying masculinist bias in social practice and in the moral theory that is used to justify that practice. The series continues the work of critique, but its emphasis falls on construction. Moving beyond critique, the series aims to build a positive body of theory that extends feminist moral understandings.

The Other Within

*Ethics, Politics, and the Body in
Simone de Beauvoir*

Fredrika Scarth

ROWMAN & LITTLEFIELD PUBLISHERS, INC.
Lanham • Boulder • New York • Toronto • Oxford

ROWMAN & LITTLEFIELD PUBLISHERS, INC.

Published in the United States of America
by Rowman & Littlefield Publishers, Inc.
A wholly owned subsidiary of The Rowman & Littlefield Publishing Group, Inc.
4501 Forbes Boulevard, Suite 200, Lanham, Maryland 20706
www.rowmanlittlefield.com

PO Box 317
Oxford
OX2 9RU, UK

British Library Cataloguing in Publication Information Available

Library of Congress Cataloging-in-Publication Data

Scarth, Fredrika, 1965–
    The other within : ethics, politics, and the body in Simone de Beauvoir /
Fredrika Scarth.
        p. cm. — (Feminist constructions)
    Includes bibliographical references and index.
    ISBN 0-7425-3475-8 (hardcover : alk. paper) — ISBN 0-7425-3476-6
(pbk. : alk. paper)
    1. Beauvoir, Simone de, 1908– 2. Beauvoir, Simone de, 1908– Deuxième sexe.
3. Feminist theory. 4. Feminist ethics. 5. Body, Human—Social aspects. 6. Body,
Human—Political aspects. 7. Sex role—Philosophy. I. Title. II. Series.
HQ1190.S293 2004
305.42'01—dc22

                                                                        2004011722

Printed in the United States of America

♾™ The paper used in this publication meets the minimum requirements of
American National Standard for Information Sciences—Permanence of Paper for
Printed Library Materials, ANSI/NISO Z39.48-1992.

To Matthew

~

Contents

~

Preface

Simone de Beauvoir's *The Second Sex* is a founding text of second-wave feminism. And Beauvoir, as an independent woman, an intellectual, and a feminist, was both symbol and model for many women in that movement. Beauvoir's personal or private life was in fact remarkably public—she acted as a witness to her times in her memoirs and also presented her life story and her long-term relationship with Jean-Paul Sartre as a model for other women. The text and its author together have acquired an iconic status in second-wave feminism. It is not surprising, then, that a common feminist response to Beauvoir is the sense that we are all her daughters, that she is "the mother of us all."[1]

But relationships between mothers and daughters, as Beauvoir herself noted, are both rewarding and difficult, and feminists' relationship to both Beauvoir and her text have been complex and fraught with ambivalence. After all, the model Beauvoir presents for feminists is an equivocal one. She is at once a powerful founding mother figure, a model of an emancipated woman, yet one who insists on her intellectual subservience to a man and thus suggests also her loyalty to the philosophical tradition he represents. Nowhere is this ambivalence more marked than in feminist responses to Beauvoir's writing on the female body. Beauvoir's writing on maternity, in particular, has been controversial. While some have hailed what they read as her uncompromising refusal of maternity—really a refusal of the ideology that expects every woman to have children and the circumstances in which they have had to raise them[2]—others have found, in the language with which she describes pregnancy and motherhood, a horror and repudiation of motherhood—and even the female body itself—that echoes the denigration of the feminine in the philosophical tradition.

It is this apparent horror that led to a dismissal of Beauvoir by feminists in the 1970s and 1980s as a first-generation and male-identified feminist. By the time I first began my work on Beauvoir in the early 1990s, it seemed *The Second Sex* had the ambiguous status of an oft-cited but generally unread classic. I began with the aim of doing a reading that would take Beauvoir seriously as a philosopher and be a corrective to the dismissals of her work as masculinist. As I continued my work on Beauvoir, I realized that I had become Beauvoir's defender. Only what I had thought of as a solo defense of Beauvoir was actually part of a collective project—a renaissance of Beauvoir studies that is also a revisionist project.

One strand of this revision has taken up the personal and philosophical relationship between Beauvoir and Sartre. Beauvoir's recently published letters and journals show her to be more intellectually independent of Sartre than her public statements had suggested and reveal an intellectual relationship that was more often a collaboration than a relationship of teacher and disciple.[3] The consideration of Beauvoir as intellectually independent of Sartre has also opened a space for examining the other intellectual influences on her thought. Rather than read Beauvoir as simply Sartrean, current writing takes her seriously as a philosopher, investigating her intellectual roots in the tradition of European philosophy but also recognizing the ways in which her work is critical of that tradition.[4] And, having situated her thought in the continental philosophical tradition, some feminist writing is now identifying her original philosophical contributions: her development of the phenomenological concept of the situated subject, her ethics of ambiguity, and her distinctive approach to philosophy.[5]

My reading of *The Second Sex* builds on this recent work. I read *The Second Sex* as an ethical text, driven by Beauvoir's preoccupation with what possibilities have been closed off to women by patriarchal structures, oppression, and inequality and also driven by her preoccupation with what possibilities of individual agency and collective action are possible in women's futures. But in contrast to many of Beauvoir's feminist readers, I see Beauvoir's writing on the female body, and particularly on maternity, as an important piece of this puzzle: Maternity, long an important locus of women's oppression, can also open up, I argue, new possibilities of embodied subjectivity and agency and can found a truly ethical relationship with the other.

To see this, I focus on a set of ideas that thread through Beauvoir's writing but are only now becoming the focus of feminist critical attention: ambiguity, conversion, risk, and generosity. When we read Beauvoir's work attuned to these ideas, it becomes immediately and clearly related to more recent feminist writing on embodied subjectivity that takes female embodiment, in its specificity, seriously. She is revealed then as not just a neglected foremother, but as someone whose analysis is still relevant. Her analysis of eroticism and carnal love bears striking similarities to more recent writing on the topic by Luce Irigaray, and her writing on pregnancy prefigures Julia Kristeva's treatment of it in certain respects, as well as, from another perspective, Iris Marion Young's.[6] But perhaps more important than recognizing the sometimes unacknowledged influence and sources of current feminist thinking such as these quite disparate examples is the extent to which Beauvoir's analysis of women's lived subjectivity can animate and provide insight into current feminist debates on subjectivity and broader debates within political theory.

Though I began as Beauvoir's defender, I came to discover points in her texts where Beauvoir was unable to fully develop the implications of her own analysis. The book that emerged from my encounter with Beauvoir is less a straight reading of her texts than a reading of Beauvoir that thinks with her in directions her thought points toward and in directions it opens up for us. It's difficult in this sense to say where Beauvoir leaves off and I begin. As Andrea Nye writes about her study of Rosa Luxembourg, Simone Weil, and Hannah Arendt, while I was writing this book it was not always clear to me "whose thought was in question, mine or the woman whose words I was reading."[7] The ideas that drive this book—maternal subjectivity, generosity, the risks of giving oneself as flesh, and assuming otherness within the self—are neither simply Beauvoir's nor fully my own. To the extent that I am drawing on a few scattered passages in Beauvoir's work—though passages that are key to understanding her work in a new light—and elaborating on their significance, Beauvoir herself might not fully recognize the thinker revealed in this book. But to the extent that this book is able to open up Beauvoir's thinking for another feminist generation, I think she would applaud.

And so I return to the question of what kind of relationship we as feminist philosophers want or need with our feminist foremothers. As Beauvoir reminds us, it is as mother that women have been most definitively cast as Other, losing their individuality, losing themselves in cultural imperatives of self-sacrifice and devotion. And the authority we bestow on mother figures can lead to resentment—casting us as eternal daughters, either dutiful or rebellious ones. Can we separate Beauvoir from the layers of meaning wrapped up in the mother image, liberate her and ourselves? I hope with this book I have been able to leave behind the position of the daughter—with her expectations, her resentments—and been able to engage generously with Beauvoir as someone whose thought reaches out into the future, as someone who risked writing as an engagement in the world that would be taken up by others and used to found new projects. I hope that I have been able, in Romand Coles's words, to balance my obligation to accuracy to the texts with my obligation to think generously with Beauvoir in directions she richly suggests but does not fully pursue.[8] This way of relating to her work, neither as dutiful nor resentful daughter but as someone recognizing in it its promise for the future, is in the end something I think Beauvoir would have appreciated. As she wrote in one of her earliest philosophical essays:

> We depend upon the freedom of the other: she may forget us, misrecognise us, use us for ends which are not our own. . . . What the other creates starting with me will belong to her and not to me. I act only when I assume the risks of this future; they are the inverse of my finitude and in assuming my finitude I am free.[9]

Notes

1. This phrase is from a feminist article that appeared in France shortly after Beauvoir's death in 1986. It is cited as emblematic of a general feeling by Yolanda Patterson, "Simone de Beauvoir and the Demystification of Motherhood," *Yale French Studies* 72 (1986): 90. See also chapter 2, note 22.

2. As Beauvoir told Alice Schwarzer in an interview in 1976. Schwarzer, *Simone de Beauvoir Today: Conversations 1972–1982*, trans. Marianne Howarth (London: Hogarth, 1984).

3. Michèlle le Doeuff has long analyzed the Beauvoir–Sartre relationship, focusing particularly on Beauvoir's insistence on her status as Sartre's disciple. See, for example, le Doeuff, *Hipparchia's Choice: An Essay Concerning Women, Philosophy, etc.* (Oxford: Blackwell, 1991). Kate and Edward Fullbrook have portrayed the relationship as a collaborative one and have revealed Beauvoir's contributions to Sartre's thought. See Fullbrook and Fullbrook, *Simone de Beauvoir and Jean-Paul Sartre: The Remaking of a Twentieth Century Legend* (Hertfordshire: Harvester Wheatsheaf, 1993).

4. For example, Sonia Kruks reads Beauvoir (and Sartre) as part of the French phenomenological tradition. See, for example, Kruks, *Situation and Human Existence: Freedom, Subjectivity and Society* (London: Unwin Hyman, 1990); Debra Bergoffen focuses more specifically on Husserl's influence on her thinking. See Bergoffen, *The Philosophy of Simone de Beauvoir: Gendered Phenomenologies, Erotic Generosities* (New York: SUNY Press, 1997); and Eva Lundgren-Gothlin notes the influence of Heidegger. See Lundgren-Gothlin, *Sex and Existence: Simone de Beauvoir's The Second Sex* (London: Athlone Press, 1996).

5. On the concepts of situation and ambiguity in Beauvoir, see, for example, Kruks, *Situation and Human Existence*. Kristana Arp, *The Bonds of Freedom: Simone de*

Beauvoir's Existentialist Ethics (Chicago: Open Court, 2001), and Debra Bergoffen, *The Philosophy of Simone de Beauvoir*, both interpret Beauvoir as primarily an ethical thinker, though they understand her ethical project in differing terms. And Karen Vintges and Nancy Bauer both argue that *The Second Sex*, rather than simply applying existentialist ideas, presents a distinctive mode of doing philosophy. See Vintges, *Philosophy as Passion* (Bloomington: Indiana University Press, 1996) and Bauer, *Simone de Beauvoir, Philosophy and Feminism* (New York: Columbia University Press, 2001).

6. See, for example, Luce Irigaray, *To Be Two*, trans. Monique M. Rhodes and Marco F. Cocito-Monoc (New York: Routledge, 2001); Julia Kristeva, "Stabat Mater," in *Tales of Love*, trans. Leon S. Roudiez (New York: Columbia University Press, 1987), 234–63, and "Motherhood According to Giovanni Bellini," in *Desire in Language: A Semiotic Approach to Literature and Art*, ed. Leon S. Roudiez (New York: Columbia University Press, 1980), 237–70; Iris Marion Young, "Pregnant Embodiment," in *Throwing Like a Girl* (Bloomington: Indiana University Press, 1990), 160–76.

7. Andrea Nye, *Philosophia* (New York: Routledge, 1994), viiii.

8. Romand Coles, *Rethinking Generosity* (New York: Cornell University Press, 1997), ix.

9. Beauvoir, *Pyrrhus et Cinéas*, (Paris: Gallimard, 1947; reprinted in *Pour une morale de l'ambiguïté, suivi de Pyrrhus et Cinéas*, 233–370. Paris: nrf, Gallimard, 1965), 365.

~

Acknowledgments

This book has had a long gestation and a correspondingly long list of friends and colleagues who have helped in its creation. During this time, I have also seen my own transformation into a political theorist, and for this, I want to thank Charles Taylor, for the generosity of his responses to my first work in the discipline, and James Tully, who first encouraged my interest in feminist theory and held me to exacting standards of scholarship. I also want to thank my friends at McGill University, particularly Gopal Sreenivasan and Duncan Ivison, for creating a community in which political theory mattered.

The book that has emerged owes much to the capable hands and minds of several women. I owe most of all to Jennifer Nedelsky and Kathryn Morgan who, as my dissertation advisors, guided this project in its earlier incarnation as my Ph.D. dissertation; Linda Zerilli, whose work inspires me as a model of what feminist political theory can be and whose enthusiastic response to the dissertation encouraged me to transform it into this book; and Sara Ruddick, a most sensitive and discerning reader, who shaped it in its latter stages.

Teachers and colleagues in the Political Science Department at the University of Toronto provided support and feedback, particularly Ed Andrew, who first suggested I might work on Simone de Beauvoir, who helped me focus my ideas in innumerable conversations, and who was invariably generous with his time and knowledge, and Alkis Kontos, who commented on many early drafts. Students in the Ph.D. program also provided support, encouragement, and insightful responses to early versions, particularly Alice Ormiston, Sandra Clancy, and Peter Lindsay. My thanks also go to the students in my women in Western political thought seminar who allowed me to learn along with them and may discern the results of that exploration in the first chapter of this book. Participants in the Canadian Women's Studies Association and Canadian Political Science Association meetings also gave me valuable feedback on earlier versions of chapters 4 and 5.

Friends and housemates sustained me through the long and all-consuming process of writing a thesis and then a book and created an atmosphere where philosophy could be discussed around the dinner table. I want to thank in particular Bruce Alcock, Darin Barney, Richard Bingham, Katherine Bruce, Lesley Byrne, Stephen Gregory, Tish O'Reilly, Russell Smith, Dave Smythe, and Mary Stone. My parents and family provided unflagging support and—most of the time—tactfully refrained from asking when the book would be finished. And finally, I owe much more than I can repay to Matthew Lella, my best critic, sharpest editor, and most loving partner, and to Astrid Scarth-Lella, whose arrival while this book was being written taught me, in an intense and undeniable way, about the ambiguity of otherness within.

CHAPTER ONE

~

Rethinking the Body

The Body in Political Thought

Much of Western political thought expresses a profound ambivalence toward the body. The body has often figured, in this tradition, as a threat to the freedom of the self. Its desires are an unwelcome reminder of our animality, a sign of the species undermining our autonomy; its vulnerability and inevitable decay haunt us, mocking our projects and proclaiming the vanity of our individual aims. Politics—the creation of a shared public world of speech and action—has a complex and ambivalent relationship to this embodied condition. While the creation of a political community is conditional on the satisfaction of the corporeal needs of its members, the political realm also transcends bodily life. In transcending bodily life, politics serves both to contain the threatening desires and needs of the body and at the same time to create a second body, the body politic, which, by outlasting the individuals that compose it, will provide them with continuity as a bulwark against the fragility of their individual lives.

Feminist theorists, looking retrospectively at this tradition, have not failed to notice that the body in question is gendered.[1] Though the relation of the body to the realm of the political has admitted of much variation, a deep connection between the feminine and the bodily has been a constant thread running through Western culture and thought. Women have been associated with the body, with the realm of nature and of necessity, while masculinity is associated with cultural achievement.[2] Women have been associated, not

1

only historically but also symbolically, with the household as a realm of privacy and of the body's needs. Seen as intimately connected to natural cycles of birth and death,[3] and as naturally destined for the private sphere, women have been associated with those aspects of embodiment that seem to signal a submission to the demands of the species—particularly the reproductive body—while men, as citizens, are dissociated from the body to the extent that they find and fulfill themselves in the public realm. The body's desires and needs are coded as feminine, while the male citizen in effect sheds his own fallible body as he becomes part of the larger social body. The feminine is what must be contained or controlled, its powers channelled, within civilization, and politics is the art of this containment.

These are, of course, Western cultural ideals of masculinity and femininity, ideals that have not always held for all men and women. It is one of the central paradoxes of Western thought that central ideals of masculinity and femininity have coexisted with large groups of people to whom they were held not to apply. In the history of political thought, female slaves, for example, have not always been considered women in certain respects, as laboring men have not always been considered men.[4] However, Western conceptions of citizenship and agency have developed enmeshed in this relation of the feminized private realm to the masculine public world, in these perhaps unrealizable ideals, and if we interrogate what the body has meant in Western political thought, we also gain insight into ways in which our conceptions of freedom and autonomy are linked to certain assumptions about the body.

In ancient political thought, the realm of true human freedom is beyond the merely bodily. Virtues, including citizen virtues, are revealed in a particular kind of relationship to the body; virtue is expressed in moderation, the moderating of appetites or even in their denial. There are two senses in which the body in Greek thought is antithetical to freedom and political life, insofar as it is through politics that freedom can be manifested and expressed. In one sense, it is the desires of the body itself—erotic and appetitive—that pose a threat to political order. In Plato, for example, we find images of the body as the dungeon of the mind and rule of reason over the body and its appetites as an analogy to rule in the city. While it is clear that the body is a threat to political order for Plato, it is less clear that that body, in his thought, is gendered.[5] For Aristotle, in contrast, the differences between male and female bodies are significant, as they are the corporeal sign of one's place in a natural hierarchy.[6] The life of the body, embodied in the household as the realm of necessity, is the foundation for political life. Those consigned to labor in the household—women and slaves—are necessary conditions for political life, but not integral parts of the *polis*. In this sense, the needs of the body, while not posing a threat to the political order, are what the political must transcend. In either case, politics is something beyond the life of the body.

In modern political thought the explicit associations with gender have been transmuted into a pervasive but less obvious set of associations and a broad metaphorical structure. The sense of politics as "beyond" the body is not found in the thought of early modern thinkers such as Hobbes and Locke, but there is still implicitly a very specific kind of relationship to the body that one must have to be a subject or citizen. While politics isn't explicitly divorced from the realm of necessity, the social contract does express a kind of second birth for the subject into a rational and nonfeminine realm.[7]

This relationship can be seen to have its origin in Descartes. His sharp and clear distinction between mind or consciousness and its body drew on the earlier mind–body distinction, but for Descartes this is not just a mind–body distinction, division and hierarchy but an epistemological difference: The mind is the basis of knowledge and the body and its sense perceptions unreliable, not an aspect of knowledge but only a known object.[8] Cartesianism is to some extent the conceptual frame in which we have come to see the body and that has come to dominate modern thought.[9] Descartes's images still hold sway: The body is an object of knowledge for the natural sciences or the possession of a subject who is thus to some extent dissociated from carnality. We need only think, for example, of Hobbes's metaphor of the body as a machine and politics as ensuring the smooth peaceful functioning of these machines or of the Lockean conception of individuals as owners of their labor power.[10] What is emphasized in both is the separateness of mind and body and control of the body by the mind.

While the abstract equality of the Enlightenment would thus seem to promise equality for both sexes, since the knowing consciousness has no connection to sex, in fact, a set of exclusions was in place.[11] Joan Landes argues persuasively that in the democratic public space created by the French Revolution, citizenship was premised on a particular relationship to the body of containment and control; the subject was "one capable of subjecting (his) individual passions and interests to the rule of reason." Women's bodies were conceived of as uncontrollable in important respects, their emotionality and sexuality excessive, unruly, and a threat to the public sphere.[12]

If a citizen is one who possesses his body, either as an owner of his body and its labor power, or in a more general sense of controlling its passions, his body must be one seen as capable of being possessed—bounded, impermeable, and controlled. Individual rights are most easily envisioned as rights over a clearly bounded body. As Carole Pateman has written, the social contract that founds the modern polity can be seen as a contract among men that depends on a previous assumption of ownership over women's bodies—an ownership that women themselves are not capable of realizing:

> The body of the "individual" is very different from women's bodies. His body is tightly enclosed within boundaries, but women's bodies are permeable, their contours change shape and they are subject to cyclical processes. All these differences are summed up in the natural bodily process of birth . . . women lack neither strength nor ability in a general sense, but, according to the classical contract theorists, they are naturally deficient in a specifically *political* capacity, the capacity to create and maintain political right.[13]

The reproductive body, then, isn't one that fits easily into the model of the body as possession. If women aren't in possession of their bodies, they can't be full subjects; if women aren't in possession of their bodies, they by definition lack self-control, independence, autonomy, and integrity. All this suggests that the difficulty of integrating women as full citizens of the political order may have much to do with an idea of the requirements of citizenship that is implicitly based on a masculine relation to the body, or rather a cultural idealization of the masculine relation to the body.

Feminism as a political movement grew out of the Enlightenment ideals of abstract equality, and in it the dilemmas and difficulties of this model of equality are manifested. On the model of abstract equality, feminists claimed citizenship for women on the basis of sameness or likeness to men. Mary Wollstonecraft's argument that virtue does not have a sex is the pioneering example,[14] but more recent egalitarian and liberal feminism rest on similar arguments. In liberal feminist analysis, women are like men in as much as they are rational agents, and women are, or ought to be, considered proprietors of their own persons in the same way that men are.[15] But feminist arguments for equality based on sameness often seem to be stymied by the female body and its reproductive capacity. Citizenship for women often seems to require a repudiation of female biology and reproduction and an attempt to quiet the disorderly desiring body in favor of egalitarian relationships of friendship.[16]

Women's relation to the political realm thus remains profoundly ambiguous: The political realm as a realm of male agency and freedom both excludes and depends on women and the feminine, in ways both practical and symbolic. While excluding women as agents, the political regime depends on their labor in the private, social, and civil realms. Perhaps more important, and more difficult to transform, is the way in which masculine conceptions of freedom and agency implicitly depend on the feminine as that which is excluded, repressed, and not acknowledged.[17] In examining the Western political canon we are led astray if we concentrate solely on the distinction between ancient and modern political thought. We would miss the fundamental and underlying continuity, which is that the freedom guaranteed by and manifested in the political sphere, the citizen's freedom, whether conceived of as action or as production, is conditional on having a body that is possessed, contained, under control, bounded, and separate—a body that can serve to express individuality or virtue, rather than a body that, whether in its emotionality, its subordination to necessity, or its unboundedness, is a body out of control.

Simone de Beauvoir: A Difficult Legacy

Seen in the light of this theme and debate, Simone de Beauvoir's work has a very curious place. Her pioneering feminist analysis of patriarchal culture in *The Second Sex* reveals the history of "Woman" as man's Other, a masculine creation, mystery for man. It reveals the history of the social construction of femininity in its association with Nature, with necessity, and with the body. It is largely for this descriptive analysis that Beauvoir has been praised.

However, the prescriptive side of her argument has come under much criticism. If Beauvoir's analysis of women's situation reveals that women's Otherness is the crucial support for the masculine Absolute Subject, the whole force of that analysis is dedicated to arguing that women should become subjects in their own right. Beauvoir argues that for women to concretely express their freedom, or subjectivity, their human capacity to initiate and to transcend, the debilitating pattern of feminine dependence and confinement to the domestic sphere must end. To this end, Beauvoir largely focuses on the conditions necessary for women's access to the public world.

Becoming subject, on this model, is equivalent to transcendence—projecting oneself into the future through action—a conception of freedom or subjectivity that Beauvoir shares with Sartre. In *The Second Sex*, Beauvoir, like Sartre, distinguishes transcendence, the capacity of all humans to initiate, act, and project themselves into the future, from the realm of immanence, or being subject to given conditions, creating nothing new.[18] The problem, from the perspective of many of Beauvoir's feminist critics, is that the categories of transcendence and immanence map all too readily onto the historical patterns of associations outlined above—mind is to body as male is to female—particularly when Sartre's associations between the feminine and the in-itself are considered.[19] These patterns suggest that freedom is threatened by a feminine in-itself that is associated with the body.

These problems are compounded when another of Beauvoir's theoretical sources is considered: Hegel's dialectic of master and slave. In a particularly infamous passage describing the origins of patriarchy, Beauvoir writes that "the worst curse that was laid upon woman" was that she was excluded from the hunt in early nomadic societies, "for it is not in giving life but in risking life that man is raised above the animal; that is why superiority has been accorded in humanity not to the sex that brings forth but to that which kills."[20] This suggests to Beauvoir's critics not only that the female body is a hindrance, a threat to freedom (she seems to equate reproduction with submission to the cyclical time of the species rather than with free projection into the future), but also, troublingly, that subjectivity is inevitably linked to hostility toward and domination of others. To some of Beauvoir's feminist readers, her commitments to this philosophical tradition severely limit the emancipatory potential of her thought.[21]

The most potent sign of this is what is seen by many feminist critics as her repudiation of the female body. To many, Beauvoir's description of feminine embodiment inadvertently replicates traditional masculine patterns of thought that mark the female body as Other and a threat to freedom.[22] Her descriptions of women seem to bespeak an ambivalence, contempt, even horror of the female body mirroring that of the Western philosophical tradition and marking her work as emblematic of an early, now-transcended stage or "first generation" of feminism.[23] Thus Beauvoir's feminism, in its vision of equality as sameness, is said to be masculinist. She is said to identify with masculine values, devalue feminine difference, and advocate that women take up masculine values of transcendence and autonomy without reenvisioning these values. As some authors write, she asks women to be just like men.[24]

Beauvoir's work would, then, seem a perverse place to look to find a way to change or re-vision the gendered metaphors about the body that underlie our political thought. I would argue, however, that labeling Beauvoir's work as "first generation" is a reductionist and limiting move, and one that blinds us to the richness of The Second Sex (and indeed of Beauvoir's work in general) and to its transformative potential. Far from simply replicating masculine values and advocating that women become just like men, The Second Sex undermines and challenges the masculine subject.

Many of Beauvoir's feminist critics have been able to miss this transformative potential of The Second Sex because they read it in isolation from Beauvoir's other works and read it not only in the context of Beauvoir's presumed personal problem with the body but also in terms of the public image of (and her own portrayal of) her relationship with Sartre, on whom she is assumed to be philosophically dependent. When Beauvoir's work is under-

stood to have a range of influences beyond Sartre, and her languag
are not simply reduced to a personal problem (that is, when she i_
riously as a philosopher), then the place of the body in her thought becomes
much more complex and revealing.

A reading of Beauvoir as "masculinist" misses one of the central arguments
of *The Second Sex*: that the female body that Beauvoir is describing is one
women live out in the context of the masculine mythology and social norms
that are patriarchy, and so her negative depiction of the female body is thus
part of her indictment of the social oppression of women. But perhaps more
importantly this reading also obscures another portrayal of the body in *The
Second Sex*: Beauvoir's lyrical and intensely evocative portrayal of the erotic
potential of the embodied self. As I show, Beauvoir reveals the lived body,
and particularly the erotic body, as the locus in which the subject's illusions
of mastery and self-containment break down. The potential of the erotic
body is only made explicit in *The Second Sex* in brief passages; however, when
The Second Sex is read in the context of Beauvoir's broader ethical and political project, these passages stand out as crucial. I both consider the broader
ethical and political project of Beauvoir's writing and elaborate on these few
brief passages in *The Second Sex*.

I read *The Second Sex* in the light of the ethics that Beauvoir began developing during the Second World War. *The Second Sex* is philosophically
grounded in the ethics that Beauvoir developed in *Pyrrhus et Cinéas* and particularly in *The Ethics of Ambiguity*.[25] It is also driven by her insistence, con-
tra Sartre, that ethical relationships with others are possible and that relating to others ethically will require the acceptance of our ambiguity as
situated and embodied subjects. Beauvoir wrote the ethical essays as a way of
demonstrating that existentialism (or more precisely, Sartrean existentialism) could provide the basis for an ethics. However, it would be wrong to
read these essays only in the context of Sartre's thought, or even to assume
that in them Beauvoir remains entirely consistent with Sartre's thought in
Being and Nothingness. One of the ways in which these essays show Beauvoir's
thinking diverging from Sartre's is in the relation between situation and freedom. The concept of freedom that founds *The Second Sex* isn't Sartrean absolute ontological freedom (the *pour-soi*) but is a conception of concrete freedom that Beauvoir developed in the essays: freedom that requires concrete
opportunities, an open future, and the recognition of others. For Beauvoir,
freedom isn't the spontaneous upsurge of our consciousness, but is the extent
to which we can establish real, concrete actions and projects on the basis of
this upsurge. Freedom requires certain material conditions for its realization;
it is conditioned, and can even be denied by our situation. There are social

and economic situations that are so restrictive that they are experienced as natural, as given. Individuals in these situations are not only denied concrete opportunities to express their freedom, but in a sense their ontological freedom has also been denied.

Beauvoir describes the human condition of being a freedom-in-situation as ambiguity. As we read her ethical essays, it becomes apparent that this ambiguity is complex: As a freedom/consciousness (*pour-soi*), we are solitary and separate, but since that freedom requires concrete expression and the recognition of others, we are also interdependent. As a situated freedom our freedom is always made manifest through our body, and this too is an aspect of our ambiguity. Since our body is our grasp on the world, it is the instrument through which we express our individuality, but it is also as embodied that we are enmeshed in a species. As it involves us in a species-being, our body doesn't express our individuality but contests and undermines it. Beauvoir insists, in these essays, that we must assume this ambiguity in a "conversion" that moves us beyond oppressive and dominating relations with others and allows for the possibility of generosity as we take on the real risks of human freedom.

In *The Second Sex*, Beauvoir's focus on women led her to see that embodiment was not the same experience for women as it was for men. She began to see that the experience of embodiment was enmeshed in a web of social and material conditions. Indeed, she developed a very pointed thesis: that in patriarchal culture, men are very easily able to identify their bodies with freedom and transcendence and that women are led, almost inevitably, to identify their own bodies with immanence. This realization merged with her ethics and her growing awareness of the importance of material conditions and concrete freedom to make up the main argument of *The Second Sex*: that men have defined themselves as the Absolute Subject by creating women as the Other, and that a crucial aspect of this is the identification of women's very embodied being with a lack of freedom.

When we read *The Second Sex* in the light of the essays, we can see that not only have men closed off women's concrete opportunities for freedom in defining them as Other, but that this definition of women as Other rests on a denial of the ambiguity of the human condition. The dynamic of masculine Absolute Subject and feminine Inessential Other is one in which men are able to avoid the difficult tension of living out their ambiguity as situated freedoms by projecting the troubling aspects of that ambiguity onto women. Men are able to avoid conversion, to avoid the real risks of human freedom, and to experience themselves as solitary pure freedoms (pure constituting consciousnesses) by identifying their embodied existence with transcen-

dence and by projecting onto women the body as immanent, the body enmeshed in species-being, the body-as-flesh. It is not the body itself that is a
problem for women, but what the female body has come to mean—pure
immanence—in a culture that refuses ambiguity and instead defines freedom
or subjectivity as transcendence.

Is Beauvoir herself committed to the vision of freedom or subjectivity as
pure transcendence marked by hostility toward and attempts to master the
other? That is, is she suggesting that women should become subject on the
same model as men? At times she seems to be: At the beginning of *The Second Sex*, she writes about the inherent hostility of consciousness, which can
only posit itself by creating vaguely hostile others. But if we recognize her
theoretical independence from Sartre, and take seriously the direction she
was heading in her ethical essays, where hostility is only one possible response to the ambiguity of our human condition as both solitary and bound
to others, then the thrust of her argument must be seen to lead her to a different position. While she values transcendence as what distinguishes us
from animals, she argues against a vision of transcendence that forgets its in-
tertwining with immanence. When we "forget" that the correlative of our individuality is our immersion in a collectivity or species (and we do this by experiencing our body as an instrument and "forgetting" that it is also flesh),
then our transcendence becomes implicated in domination, since we can
only maintain this forgetfulness, or bad faith, at the cost of projecting our immanence outside and creating an Other.

Beauvoir seems to provide two answers to the problem of how women are
to claim their status as subjects. On the one hand, women must claim their
status as subject and experience their transcendence and capacity to initiate.
They must enter the master–slave dialectic and force men to recognize the
reciprocity of otherness, on the model of black men, and men in other oppressed groups.[26] This suggests a perpetual tension between two transcendent
freedoms who must each recognize each other and be in a material position
to respond to each other's appeals. To be able engage in freely chosen projects, and respond to others' appeals, women would need material independence, need access to education, and need to learn the lessons of bodily risk
that would allow them to challenge the givens of a situation constructed by
others in order to initiate new meanings themselves.

This alone (women being given the opportunities to challenge the given,
to risk themselves through initiating meaning in the world), however,
doesn't address the problem that Beauvoir suggests has made the dialectic of
masculine Subject and feminine Other so tenacious—the identification of
women with the body as immanent and as flesh. If all that is recognized in

Beauvoir's prescriptions is a demand to allow women to engage concretely in projects—and the implications of her stress on ambiguity are ignored—then Beauvoir seems to create an untenable situation for women, requiring them to engage freely in projects while weighed down by flesh and in bondage to the species in reproduction. If she is severing the connection between women and the flesh or body as immanent, without challenging the meaning of the flesh within patriarchal culture, then she may be liberating women from Woman as Other (as immanent, as flesh) but the flesh itself remains Other. It will remain a difficult aspect of the self for both men and women and will still be projected and rejected. This model of subjectivity still seems to depend on an excluded and rejected Other and on mastery, even if that Other isn't identified with Woman. That is, it still implicitly depends on the body experienced as an instrument rather than as flesh.

The model of the project, however, is not all that Beauvoir provides. She also insists that we live our "existence made body" as an ambiguity or tension of immanence and transcendence at once, that is, as body-subjects.[27] When she is being most attentive to this, her model of subjectivity is not pure transcendence, and it puts the idea of the existentialist project, as she has drawn it from Sartre, into question. It is at this point that the importance of the erotic in The Second Sex really comes into focus, for the erotic is a privileged moment in which we are able to recognize the other as subject and the self as ambiguously embodied and thus in some sense other: a moment of accepting otherness and letting difference be that gets us past the damaging dynamic of Absolute Subject and Inessential Other. The meeting in the erotic embrace Beauvoir describes at the end of The Second Sex isn't precisely a project for either party but an abandonment, a giving, a gift and risk of self.[28] It is a relationship of mutual generosity. In the erotic embrace both participants are both freedom and flesh, but for once the two don't stand opposed. The partners in the erotic embrace can't experience the body, at this moment, as active and expressive without also experiencing it as passive and receptive. This moment is privileged because in it we can see freedom not in tension with flesh, but freedom as revealed through flesh. The meaning of the flesh, and the meaning of risk, in this vision of equality, has subtly changed. Flesh is no longer alienating; it is revelatory, and risking has lost its connections with domination and control. Otherness is no longer hostile, as we have learned to acknowledge and accept the otherness within—our own fleshiness, that within us that contests and undermines our individuality in drawing us into the great cyclical repetitions of species life. It is only in the short section on the erotic embrace that Beauvoir is able to fully grasp the implications of her analysis of patriarchal culture and fully do justice to her own vision of the ambiguity of our human condition as immanence and transcendence entwined. It is this passage that truly fulfills the promise of the conversion she demands: the recognition of the other within.

It is also this passage, I argue, that provides the key to reading Beauvoir's controversial writing on pregnancy and motherhood. Free motherhood, *maternité libre*, becomes in Beauvoir's text a kind of litmus test of the project. It is an example of a project that seems to confront most directly the limits of our subjectivity and in doing so points toward another model of subjectivity. With Beauvoir, we can explore the possibility of maternity as a generous gift and a risk of self and as an assumption of the other within.

Reading Simone de Beauvoir as a Political Theorist

Beauvoir's most obviously political writing—her analysis of women's oppression—is thus rooted in a broader ethical project. While the oppression of women that Beauvoir explores in *The Second Sex* cannot simply be reduced to an interpersonal relationship, because it is mediated through institutions, it still has as its emotional core a symbiotic but deadly relationship between men and women in which women are cast as Other/body so that men can maintain an illusion of absolute freedom. This is why we miss much of the richness and importance of Beauvoir's work when all we see of her political thought is her insistence on economic independence for women, her insistence that women gain reproductive choice and control and that they have access to a public world of freely chosen projects—that women, in short, have all the same opportunities as men. What we miss is the way that these demands require, for both men and women, a shift in our relationship with others and with our own embodiment.

When seen in the light of Beauvoir's ethical concerns, the politics of *The Second Sex* takes on new meaning. Politically, *The Second Sex* is asking us to create the conditions for relations of generosity between men and women. Rather than reading her prescriptions for women's economic independence and involvement in the public world as simply asking women to become like men, we can see how *The Second Sex* seeks to end a dynamic in which both men and women, in fleeing their ambiguity, are trapped in different forms of bad faith: men in the illusion of the Absolute Subject, and women in the role of the Other.

The path from ethical demand to political prescription in *The Second Sex* is not explicit. Rather, Beauvoir's ethics implies political tasks and responsibilities. At the heart of Beauvoir's existentialist ethics is the recognition that freedom is interdependent, and thus that to will oneself free is to will others free: freedom is unthinkable apart from community. Once we recognize that our freedom can exist only in a world populated by other freedoms, that freedom is not simply ontological but requires concrete opportunities for action and can be denied or "consumed" by hunger and want, we should recognize our responsibility to widen the sphere of others' freedom in concrete ways. As we will see, Beauvoir analyzes not only patriarchy but also colonization and totalitarianism as structures of systemic violence to those designated as Other, as violence that also lessens the oppressors.

What does it mean to will others free? As an ethical demand, it means to recognize others as subjects as one recognizes otherness within the self. As a political demand, it means to work to create situations in the world in which others will have the opportunity to exercise their subjectivity, to experience, as Beauvoir writes, their adolescence. In this sense Beauvoir's ethical demand is also a political demand. She recognizes that some groups of people—slaves, women, subjects of colonial regimes—have never, in a sense, experienced their own adolescence, because they have been confined in a child's world. Her demand that we cease projecting otherness, that we recognize otherness within ourselves, is also a political demand to end structures of political and economic exploitation. But beyond this, if freedom is not only situated but embodied, then Beauvoir's ethical demand is for us to assume our own embodiment by ceasing to project the body-as-flesh onto the other. The political and social inequalities of patriarchal society have made this projection credible. The moral coming of age that Beauvoir calls for, while enacted individually, is not isolated from the society that helps to construct and sustain the illusions that uphold oppression. If, in her account of this conversion, Beauvoir doesn't provide a roadmap for collective action, she does provide a vision of what subjectivity in equality could be and an account of embodied subjectivity that has relevance today. *The Second Sex* provided a groundbreaking analysis of the body as a site of oppression, and it was this that made it so influential for the women's movement. Its value in the future, I believe, will lie more in its elucidation of the ethical potential of the ambiguous body to divest us of our illusions of a freedom that is a freedom from the flesh—freedom from its limitations and frailties, but also from its capacity for connection and communication.[29]

Notes

1. Diana Coole, *Women in Political Theory: From Ancient Misogyny to Contemporary Feminism* (Boulder, Colo.: Lynne Reinner, 1993); Elizabeth Grosz, *Volatile Bodies: Toward a Corporeal Feminism* (Bloomington: Indiana University Press, 1994), 13–14.

2. See, for example, Genevieve Lloyd, *Man of Reason: Male and Female in Western Philosophy*, 2d ed. (London: Routledge, 1993).

3. See, for example, John Seery, *Political Theory for Mortals* (Ithaca: Cornell University Press, 1996), 122–24.

4. See Elizabeth Spelman, *Inessential Woman: Problems of Exclusion in Feminist Thought* (Boston: Beacon Press, 1988), for an astute analysis, and Peter Riesenberg, *Citizenship in the Western Tradition* (Chapel Hill: University of North Carolina Press, 1992), 29–30.

5. See Plato, *The Republic*, trans. G. M. A. Grube (Indianapolis, Ind.: Hackett Publishing Co., 1974), 533d; and Plato, *Symposium*, trans. with introduction and notes by Alexander Nehamas and Paul Woodruff (Indianapolis, Ind.: Hackett Publishing Co., 1989). Elizabeth Spelman argues that Plato's comments on emotion link women more closely to the body and its threats than men. Spelman, "Woman as Body: Ancient and Contemporary Views," *Feminist Studies* 8, no. 1 (Spring 1982): 109–31. However, see Grosz, *Volatile Bodies*, for an argument that Plato's "somatophobia" applies to *all* bodies, male and female.

6. Aristotle, *The Politics*, trans. Ernest Barker (London: Oxford, 1958), Bk. I and Bk. III, ch. V. For Aristotle, the distinction between form and matter is explicitly aligned with the male and female roles in reproduction (following Greek tradition from Hesiod, Plato's account of reproduction in Timaeus, and drawing on a host of associations from Pythagoras) and hierarchically ordered, underpinning women's broad exclusion from public life. See Coole, *Women in Political Theory*, ch. 1. Aristotle was perhaps not explicitly trying to justify the exclusion of women from the polis (which would not have been contentious to his contemporaries), but the exclusion makes sense philosophically in the context of the symbolic associations outlined here.

7. See Moira Gatens, *Feminism and Philosophy: Perspectives on Difference and Equality* (Bloomington: Indiana University Press, 1991), 123–28.

8. See Grosz, *Volatile Bodies*, 6–10.

9. While mind–body dualism is the main motif in Descartes's thought, some of his writing is more ambiguous on the relation between mind and body. It is perhaps more accurate to use the term *Cartesianism* to indicate the way in which his thought has been taken up in the philosophical tradition. See Amelie Oksenberg Rorty, "Descartes on Thinking with the Body," in *The Cambridge Companion to Descartes*, ed. John Cottingham (Cambridge: Cambridge University Press, 1992).

10. Thomas Hobbes, *The Leviathan*, ed. C. B. Macpherson (London: Penguin, 1985) and John Locke, *Second Treatise of Government*, ed. C. B. Macpherson (Indianapolis, Ind.: Hackett, 1980).

11. See Adriana Cavarero, "Equality and Sexual Difference: Amnesia in Political Thought," in *Beyond Equality and Difference*, ed. Gisela Bock and Susan James (London: Routledge, 1992).

12. Joan Landes, "The Performance of Citizenship: Democracy, Gender and Difference in the French Revolution," in *Democracy and Difference*, ed. Seyla Benhabib (Princeton: Princeton University Press, 1996), 296. See also Landes's discussion in

Women and the Public Sphere in the French Revolution (Ithaca: Cornell University Press, 1988) and Geneviève Fraisse, *Reason's Muse: Sexual Difference and the Birth of Democracy*, trans. Jane Marie Todd (Chicago: University of Chicago Press, 1994).

13. Carole Pateman, *The Sexual Contract* (Stanford: Stanford University Press, 1988), 96.

14. Though Wollstonecraft also argued for specific duties for female citizens—republican motherhood—and so her work can't be fully contained within the Enlightenment tradition. See Virginia Sapiro, *A Vindication of Political Virtue: The Political Theory of Mary Wollstonecraft* (Chicago: University of Chicago Press, 1992), for a good analysis of Wollstonecraft's political thought. Alternative arguments for female citizenship based on special skills or duties, or on claims of women's moral superiority or peacefulness, have also defined the tradition. See the articles in Gisela Bock and Susan James, eds., *Beyond Equality and Difference* (London: Routledge, 1992), for feminist attempts to get beyond the impasse created by the equation of equality with sameness.

15. The egalitarian feminism of Harriet Taylor and John Stuart Mill is an early example. Taylor, "The Enfranchisement of Women," in *Essays on Sex Equality: John Stuart Mill and Harriet Taylor Mill*, ed. Alice Rossi (Chicago: University of Chicago Press, 1970), 89–122; Mill, *The Subjection of Women*, ed. Susan M. Okin (Indianapolis, Ind.: Hackett, 1988).

16. Mill's conception of marital friendship is an example of this attempt. See Mary Lyndon Shanley, "Marital Friendship and Slavery: John Stuart Mill's 'The Subjection of Women,'" in *Feminist Interpretations and Political Theory*, ed. Mary Lyndon Shanley and Carole Pateman (University Park: Pennsylvania State University Press, 1991), 164–80.

17. Coole, *Women in Political Theory*, 1–3.

18. Simone de Beauvoir, *The Second Sex*, trans. and ed. H. M. Parshley (New York: Vintage, 1989), xxxiv–xxxv.

19. The classic statement of this position is by Margery Collins and Christine Pierce, "Holes and Slime: Sexism in Sartre's Psychoanalysis," in *Women and Philosophy: Toward a Theory of Liberation*, ed. C. Gould and M. Wartofsky (New York: Putnam, 1976), 112–27. See also Karen Green, "Femininity and Transcendence," *Australian Feminist Studies* 10 (June 1989): 85–96.

20. Beauvoir, *The Second Sex*, 64.

21. As Moira Gatens argues in *Feminism and Philosophy*, 48–59. See also the analysis of this passage in Kathy Ferguson, *The Man Question: Visions of Subjectivity in Feminist Theory* (Berkeley: University of California Press, 1993), ch. 2; Catherine Keller, *From a Broken Web: Separation, Sexism and Self* (Boston: Beacon Press, 1986), ch.1; and Genevieve Lloyd, "Masters, Slaves and Others," *Radical Philosophy* 34 (1983).

22. Toril Moi, for example, makes this argument in "Existentialism and Feminism: The Rhetoric of Biology in 'The Second Sex,'" *Oxford Literary Review* 8 (1986): 88–95 and *Simone de Beauvoir: The Making of an Intellectual Woman* (Oxford: Basil Blackwell, 1994).

23. To Julia Kristeva, one of Beauvoir's most fierce critics, this generation is a "sacrificial generation," because the price of entering the public sphere and becoming

subject was the sacrifice of their specificity as women. Julia Kristeva, "Women's Time," trans. Alice Jardine, *Signs* 7, no. 1 (1981): 13–35. Originally published as "Le Temps des femmes" in *34/44: Cahiers de recherche de sciences des textes et documents*, no. 5 (1979): 5–19.

24. See, for example, Susan Hekman, "Reconstituting the Subject: Feminism, Modernism and Postmodernism," *Hypatia* 6, no. 2 (1991): 44–63, 44; Lisa Appignanesi, *Simone de Beauvoir* (London: Penguin, 1988), 96, 97; Kathy Ferguson, *Self, Society and Womankind* (Westport, Conn.: Greenwood Press, 1980), 151; and Tina Chanter, *Ethics of Eros: Irigaray's Rewriting of the Philosophers* (London: Routledge, 1995), 76.

25. Simone de Beauvoir, *The Ethics of Ambiguity*, trans. Bernard Frechtman (New York: Philosophical Library, 1948), and *Pour une morale de l'ambiguïté, suivi de Pyrrhus et Cinéas* (Paris: nrf, Gallimard, 1965). This edition is a reprint of the two essays together; the original French publication dates are 1944 (*Pyrrhus et Cinéas*) and 1947 (*Pour une morale de l'ambiguïté*).

26. This is the interpretation of Eva Lundgren-Gothlin, in *Sex and Existence: Simone de Beauvoir's The Second Sex*, trans. Linda Schenck (London: Athlone Press, 1996). Lundgren-Gothlin argues that Beauvoir analyzes women's position as Other as the result of their being excluded from the struggle for recognition (the master–slave dialectic). On this reading, the route to full subject status for women is entering into the dialectic.

27. Beauvoir, *The Second Sex*, 728.

28. Beauvoir, *The Second Sex*, 728.

29. Throughout this study, I focus mainly on *The Second Sex*, where Simone de Beauvoir's description of female subjectivity and her most clearly elaborated analysis of women's subordination and oppression is to be found. In order to flesh out her work on the body, however, I am making selective use of her other writings, both philosophical essays and criticism and autobiographical writings. Beauvoir crossed disciplinary boundaries with abandon; it seems to me that it would be missing the spirit of her work not to cross them with her and to isolate her ostensibly political writings from the rest of her corpus. A final note on the translation of Simone de Beauvoir's writings. For the most part I make use of readily available English translations of her works. (The exception is *Pyrrhus et Cinéas*, of which there is no complete English translation. I have referred to the selections translated by Jay Miskowiec, "Selections from *Towards a Morals of Ambiguity, According to Pyrrhus and Cinéas*," *Social Text* 17 [Fall 1987]: 135–42, but the responsibility for translation here remains my own.) In a few places I have found the available translation to be inadequate or perhaps slightly misleading, and in these cases I have supplied the original text as well. In the case of *The Second Sex*, however, the American edition, edited and translated by H. M. Parshley, is terribly problematic and I have made my own modifications to the translation where the Parshley version mistranslates key philosophical concepts or makes unmarked deletions from the original text. Where I have done so, I have indicated TA (translation altered) in the

notes; the translation will be Parshley's except as so noted. For good discussions of the problems with Parshley's translation, see Deirdre Bair, "'Madly Sensible and Brilliantly Confused': from 'Le Deuxième Sexe' to 'The Second Sex,'" *Dalhousie French Studies* 13 (1987): 23–35, and Margaret Simons, "The Silencing of Simone de Beauvoir: Guess What's Missing from 'The Second Sex,'" *Women's Studies International Forum* 6 (1983): 559–64. Bair also provides a short history of the writing, publishing, and translation of *The Second Sex*, citing Beauvoir's outline, drafts, and correspondence with Knopf (the original American publishers) in her introduction to the Vintage edition of the book.

~

CHAPTER TWO

Simone de Beauvoir:
A Masculine Mother?

Reading *The Second Sex* as a feminist theorist now is no simple matter. We open not an inconsequential, dusty volume plucked from a library shelf but one whose source and subsequent history crowd in upon our reading of it. It is tempting to imagine a reader happening upon *The Second Sex* without any knowledge of Simone de Beauvoir, without images of a fashionable existentialist couple in a postwar Parisian café or a grandmotherly figure in a 1970s feminist march flitting through her head, but such a reader is unlikely to be found. *The Second Sex* is inextricably linked to the history of second-wave feminism, and its author too much of a public figure of the twentieth century to ignore. It is because of my sense that this history and these images have profoundly affected our reading of it that in considering what *The Second Sex* can offer for feminist theory now, I want to turn first to the question of what it has been and has meant for feminists throughout its history.

Reading the feminist literature on *The Second Sex* is an initially baffling undertaking because what one finds is at once praise of the text's pioneering status and harsh, at times intensely hostile criticism of its theoretical structure, argument, and language. Engaged criticism and disagreement over the argument or implications of a text as significant as *The Second Sex* are not, of course, surprising. Indeed, if there were no criticism of and no disagreement on the text it would no longer be a living thing and would have no more contribution to make. From this perspective, what is most striking—and to my mind unfortunate—about the feminist literature on *The Second Sex* is the extent to which critical opinion has, in fact, solidified around one position on the text: not one or the other of the praise and hostile criticism mentioned earlier but the ambivalence of both at once. It is at once lauded as inspirational and pioneering and also harshly criticized as theoretically flawed. Catherine Rodgers, in an account of its reception among feminists in France, notes "the ambiguity of the relation" feminists maintain with *The Second Sex*; it is felt to be necessary at the same time that it provokes resentment in feminists who feel "forced" to read it.[1]

It is difficult to read the text, and consider the feminist literature that has grown up around it, without being struck by its unique status among texts of feminist theory and the heightened emotional tone of feminist writing on Beauvoir. A feminist theorist now is faced not only with a founding text but also with a founding mother: The text and its author are inextricably linked with the political and conceptual history of second-wave feminism.[2] It is difficult to read *The Second Sex* without considering its symbolic function and historical place within twentieth-century feminism and how these two have intertwined to frame our reading of it.

This chapter reviews the feminist reception of and responses to *The Second Sex* in order to explore its curious status as a feminist "classic" that incites a surprisingly high degree of hostile and ambivalent response from feminist theorists.[3] Though responses to *The Second Sex* have differed somewhat in tone both over time and in different feminist communities, it is generally true that the book has a high symbolic status within feminism but has been engaged with theoretically relatively seldom and even then with distinct ambivalence.[4] I want to explain this phenomenon by exploring the symbolic power of "Simone de Beauvoir" as a public figure and feminist "mother" and the conceptual framework of "generations of feminism": both of these have, I argue, encouraged a method of reading *The Second Sex* that looks to "Simone de Beauvoir" for the source of meaning of the text and led to a reductive reading of Beauvoir as a "first-generation" feminist. Symbolically, Beauvoir has served for feminism as both "the 'good' founding mother of modern feminism [and] the 'bad' phallic perpetuator of humanist rationalism," the "unconscious misogynist."[5] As Rosi Braidotti writes, we need to consider this symbolic function of Simone de Beauvoir for feminism "before we can proceed to an evaluation of her actual theoretical viability today."[6]

The critical focus on Beauvoir's psyche and personal life (which is generally understood as her life with Sartre) has shaped and constrained many feminist readings of *The Second Sex*. Both the argument of the book and its language, rhetoric, and style have been investigated and criticized in terms of their source in Beauvoir's (or Sartre's) personal obsessions. As I describe later, *The Second Sex*'s reception by the feminist community thus ironically echoes in some respects the hostile and dismissive criticism Beauvoir received from her first readership in Paris in 1949.

The Second Sex and "Simone de Beauvoir"

Close to half a century ago, Simone de Beauvoir sat down to write her autobiography and decided that in order to write about her life, she first had to consider what it had meant to her to be a woman. "I wanted to talk about myself, and . . . I realized that in order to talk about myself I needed to understand the fact that I was a woman."[7] The result of this autobiographical impulse, expressed through a detour into theory, was the publication in 1949 of what was to become her most controversial and, arguably, her most important book, The Second Sex, a groundbreaking analysis of the condition of women as one of socially produced alterity. Women, Beauvoir argued, are not born but made, and they are made into the Other, the very ground and condition for the masculine assertion of subjectivity: "He is the Subject, he is the Absolute—she is the Other."[8]

Beauvoir argued, following existentialist precepts derived from Heidegger and Sartre, that the distinguishing characteristic of a human being was the capacity to put the self into question. Human beings constantly reach beyond themselves into an indefinitely open future. We are not determined by biology or history, but create ourselves through our own choices and acts, our projects in the world. We create ourselves as transcendent freedoms. However, throughout history, women have been denied this open future and denied the opportunity to define themselves, since they have been defined by masculine mythology as Other and kept from the experience of their own transcendence.[9]

The first volume of Beauvoir's two-volume work considers, and dismisses, various arguments that women's destiny is inevitably determined by physiological, psychological, or economic forces and goes on to investigate the origin of women's Otherness in history and its function in masculine myth. The first volume is thus an attempt to assess the points of view taken on women in various masculine discourses, both scientific and literary. The second volume, in contrast, switches perspective, describing, from the point of view of women, the world "such as it has been offered to them."[10] It comprises a phenomenological account of women's lived experience,[11] describing, in the voices of many women, both the process of being made into Woman/Other and the daily experience of subordination: the frustrations of being "an autonomous freedom," like all human beings, in "a world where men compel her to assume herself as the Other."[12] As Beauvoir describes women's formation in infancy, childhood, and adolescence and goes on to consider the various situations women live out in maturity, the second volume also becomes a ringing denunciation of the various institutions, among them marriage, romantic love, and "compulsory maternity," that perpetuate masculine dominance.[13]

Though Beauvoir lived at the center of Paris, researching at the *Bibliothèque Nationale*, *The Second Sex* was a book written, in some sense, in the wilderness. Beauvoir neither wrote from within a feminist community nor could assume a feminist readership. Indeed, Beauvoir didn't use the word "feminist" about her own position in *The Second Sex* or publicly identify herself as a feminist when she published the book.[14] *The Second Sex* was written within a literary and intellectual milieu largely hostile to its political project.

The Second Sex emerged onto the Parisian literary scene in a burst of notoriety. Beauvoir was already a well-known figure whose unconventional relationship with Jean-Paul Sartre and leftist politics caused predictable controversy in the French press, but the greater source of scandal was in her description of women's lived experience. Specifically, Beauvoir's analyses of motherhood and women's sexuality proved truly shocking to her first French audience.[15] The publication of the chapter on "Women's Sexual Initiation" prompted the right-wing critic François Mauriac to call for an investigation of pornography and to condemn Simone de Beauvoir's article as a particularly vile example. Linking her name with the Marquis de Sade, he declared that with the publication of Beauvoir's work, France had "reached the limits of the abject."[16] In her memoirs, Beauvoir describes the press indulging in a "festival of obscenity" under the pretext of castigating Beauvoir for her own obscene writings. She was called "unsatisfied, cold, priapic, nymphomaniac, lesbian," reproached with every fault, but above all indecency.[17] Indeed, the operative concept in the criticism of Beauvoir in the popular press was the indecency or "shamelessness" of discussing female sexuality in print. The critics implied that Beauvoir had lost her sense of shame to such an extent that it was as if she had exposed her own body in public.[18]

The notoriety of the book largely overshadowed what little critical attention it received either as a serious analysis of women's condition or as an attempt to conceptualize gender oppression within the theoretical frame of existentialism. It was a "succès de scandale" but was hardly accepted or treated as a serious work, and it received little scholarly attention prior to the second wave of feminism. *The Second Sex* is not discussed in many historical treatments of philosophy; particularly striking is the absence of any discussion of Beauvoir in most critical studies of existentialism, which include only male existential theorists.[19]

The Second Sex gradually found a popular readership, and gained a new life with the second wave of feminism in North America and Europe. Its history became intertwined with the history of the second-wave feminist movement, and the context in which the book was read and critically received changed dramatically from post-war Paris: it took on the status of a foundational feminist text. Far from being experienced in the way Beauvoir herself described it, as a "very objective, very detached study . . . not at all combative,"[20] it came to be read as a battle cry. The Second Sex was inspirational for a whole generation of feminist activists and was taken up as a symbol of the new wave of feminist activism, the "bible of feminism."[21]

As much as The Second Sex is now recognized as a landmark feminist text, one of the founding theoretical texts of second-wave feminism, Beauvoir herself is lauded by feminist theorists as a founding mother: "the mother of us all,"[22] the "prophetess extraordinaire of feminism."[23] Beauvoir is unique among feminists in the extent to which the always uncertain line between life and work has become blurred, her "life" has become a public artifact, and her name has become a symbol. Her very public life as an intellectual woman, and particularly her lifelong relationship with Sartre and other significant lovers, as related (and re-created) in her four-volume memoirs and her semiautobiographical fiction, have become sources for the creation of a "Simone de Beauvoir" of mythic proportions. Indeed, the critical focus on Beauvoir's life is striking in comparison to the relative paucity, at least until very recently, of critical work on The Second Sex itself.[24]

Of course, Beauvoir's own literary production has had much to do with this myth-making. Her texts overlap to create an "intertextual network" of philosophical, fictional, autobiographical, and epistolary writings.[25] Situations analyzed in The Second Sex are fictionalized in her novels and presented as the "truth" of her life in memoirs and letters. We have not only The Second Sex itself as a text, but also Beauvoir's commentary on it in her memoirs and her retrospective evaluation of it in interviews. Her writing enacts both the creation of a public self and a reflective commentary on that self and the writing.

More importantly, Beauvoir's reflective commentary and self-evaluation tended to emphasize not only her lifelong personal partnership with Sartre, which she once famously described as "the one true success" of her life, but also his intellectual leadership within it. Beauvoir wrote that Sartre was the true philosopher of the two, that she took her cue from him philosophically, and, notoriously, that she felt she could only be in a relationship with a man she considered her intellectual superior.[26] As many critics have noted, Beauvoir herself is at least partly responsible for her enduring reputation as Sartre's "most faithful of disciples."[27]

Beauvoir's life as a politically committed intellectual and her relationship with Sartre thus provided a model for many feminists of the 1970s and, more diffusely, for the generation of women who read Beauvoir as a novelist and chronicler of her times. However, the model Beauvoir presents for feminists is an equivocal one. Her decision to forgo traditional marriage and motherhood in favor of a writing career was presented as, and understood as, a model of female independence. Yet while insisting on her independence, Beauvoir also proclaimed her intellectual subservience to a man and thus also her loyalty to the masculine philosophical tradition he represented. Any reading of Beauvoir's writing now takes place in the context of these conflicting images, this public symbol and model that "Simone de Beauvoir" has become of and for feminism.[28]

The Second Sex and Feminist History

How, then, has the symbolic importance of Beauvoir for feminism affected the feminist reception of The Second Sex? A survey of early feminist responses to Beauvoir's work reveals a curious phenomenon: It is more often cited and honored in symbolic fashion than by a close attention to her arguments. When The Second Sex was discovered by North American feminists in the early 1970s, it served more as an inspiration than as a text to study critically. Many groundbreaking early texts reveal Beauvoir's influence: Betty Friedan's The Feminine Mystique, Kate Millet's Sexual Politics, and Shulamith Firestone's The Dialectic of Sex all use Beauvoir's analysis as a starting point, acknowledged or not. However, with the exception of Dorothy Dinnerstein's The Mermaid and the Minotaur, none of these early books inspired by Beauvoir engage with her arguments directly.[29]

Now, its place in the feminist historical canon assured, The Second Sex generally receives only a perfunctory page or two of discussion in English-language surveys of feminist thought, rarely eliciting sustained critical analysis on its own account.[30] One critic, citing the "legend of The Second Sex as the 'Bible' of American feminism," goes on to note that, "like the Bible, The Second Sex seems to have been much worshipped, often quoted and little read."[31] The Second Sex has had, then, in the feminist theoretical community, the ambiguous status of an oft-cited but generally unread classic.[32] It seems to be a book universally praised but not much liked. Beauvoir serves well as a symbolic mother, but something is keeping her "daughters" at a distance.

Perhaps it is precisely the looming figure of Simone de Beauvoir, founding mother, which has contributed to this distancing effect. During the 1980s, as North American feminist critical engagement with The Second Sex increased, it often also took the form of an emotional engagement with Simone de Beauvoir and an engagement that produced not a little ambivalence. Carol Ascher's Simone de Beauvoir: A Life of Freedom is a particularly self-reflexive example of the kind of writing that emerges from such intense emotional engagement. In the middle of her account of Beauvoir's life and work, Ascher inserted an open letter to Beauvoir, which begins thus: "I am in the midst of writing my book about your ideas, and I have been badly troubled by you. . . . Often in the morning as I go to my desk, I feel resentful, begrudging, sick of the lack of reciprocity between us." Later in the letter Ascher, describing a dream in which Beauvoir figures as a mother, writes of her frustrated longing for Beauvoir as a "good mother" and of the ambivalence of her own relationship with Beauvoir's work.[33] Indeed, one of the most remarkable things about the feminist literature on *The Second Sex* is the disappointment and ambivalence, if not clear hostility, on the part of many feminists to both the book and its author. It is rather unusual to find so much energy invested in an author so honored and yet seemingly so disliked.

Much of the North American literature on *The Second Sex* is striking in its personal tone. Judith Okely writes that Beauvoir's books, especially *The Second Sex*, "evoked a curiously intimate relationship between female reader and writer, between reader and text."[34] Some of Beauvoir's feminist critics, in the course of their work, interviewed the author and developed a personal relationship with her, but even those who did not are often very involved with her life in their writing. Most of the feminist critics of the book are women who feel themselves to be personally involved with Beauvoir, as someone who provides a model of a feminist life or as a mother figure. This has led to the "life and work" study as the prevalent model of Beauvoir criticism: neither clearly biography, nor pure textual or philosophical analysis, but an uneasy mix of the two. The life and work study mixes a chapter or two of biographical details of Beauvoir's, and often Sartre's, life with chapters on her novels, memoirs, *The Second Sex*, and, very occasionally, other essays.[35] These studies rest on and subtly promote the notion that Beauvoir's life choices and personal or political commitments not only inform her writing but explain it, an assumption that they leave largely unexamined.

That Beauvoir studies should have taken on this form is significant, because writings of this critical form, even when sympathetic, often come perilously close to using the dismissive tactic Toril Moi describes as "reducing the book to the woman."[36] Moi describes this tactic as a rhetorical strategy employed by hostile mainstream (nonfeminist) critics of Beauvoir, but the effect is the same when the form is used by Beauvoir's feminist critics. The force of Beauvoir's ideas are lessened as they are all explained away as products of her "obsessive personality." The effect is to render both hostile and more balanced accounts of her work equally reductive and dismissive. This can be seen in two studies, both literary criticisms of Beauvoir's writings focusing on the theme of death. Elaine Marks's early study, *Simone de Beauvoir: Encounters with Death*, while thoughtful, reduces the rich theme of death in Beauvoir's philosophical and fictional writings to a projection of her own discomfort with it. Though recognizing that some of the greatest scenes in modern literature are scenes of encounters with death, Marks argues that such encounters in Beauvoir's work inevitably reflect her "obsession" with death, and even descriptions of places in her fiction become "projections of [her] inner, obsessive world." The effect, even in this careful scholarly study, is the same as that produced by Jean-Raymond Audet's very hostile polemic, *Simone de Beauvoir face à la mort*, in which every death in Beauvoir's fiction reflects her own psychological obsession, and every character in her fiction can be understood as a projection of her own personality.[37]

If Beauvoir's position as a symbolic feminist mother in North America was an ambiguous one, her relation to the French second-wave feminism that arose in the wake of the May 1968 student protests was yet more complicated. In North America, the relatively distant Beauvoir could serve as a symbol; in Paris, she was a living presence who, after publicly identifying herself as a feminist in the early 1970s, was actively involved in feminist groups. Braidotti argues that the role of "absent, distant mother" that Beauvoir played for North American feminists, was more productive for them than her active presence was for French feminists.[38] In both cases, the public persona of Simone de Beauvoir has had an extraordinary effect on the interpretation of her central feminist text.[39]

Beauvoir was surprisingly uninfluential as a *theorist* for second-wave feminists in France. As historian Claire Duchen writes: "Given that Simone de Beauvoir was considered the 'mother' of contemporary feminism, and that May '68 was given as the starting point of feminism in France, it is curious to note the almost complete absence of attention to *Le deuxième sexe* either during or immediately after the May events as feminists began to theorize women's oppression."[40] Duchen argues that Beauvoir was important not as a theorist but as a presence: a prestigious figure who was publicly committed to the liberation of women, willing to sign petitions and lend financial support. In short, Beauvoir played a role in feminist struggles, even if as a figurehead. This meant that she was directly involved in feminist politics in France in the early 1970s. She was strongly associated with the "radical" tendency in feminism, represented in print by the journal *Questions Feministes* (later *Nouvelles Questions Feministes*), which she cofounded and edited. Beauvoir's position as a famous intellectual associated with feminist protests and with one current of feminist thinking would make her a magnet for both adulation and hostility in the very stormy feminist politics in Paris in the 1970s.

The materialist feminism of *Questions Feministes* was openly opposed by a group called *Psych et Po*, short for *Psychanalyse et Politique*.[41] This group was the locus of a ferment of poststructuralist theorizing, influenced by the psychoanalytic theory of Jacques Lacan and Derridean deconstruction. Writers such as Julia Kristeva turned away from the analysis of the material conditions of women's lives toward a consideration of language, identity, and the unconscious. Members of *Psych et Po* sought to affirm and celebrate feminine difference; Hélène Cixous did this through practicing *écriture féminine*, or feminine writing.

Feminist politics in Paris were about the very definition of feminism: Was it a movement to integrate women into the public world, a struggle for legal, political, and social equality, or a movement to recover and affirm feminine *différence*? *Psych et Po* members clearly distanced themselves from feminism on the former model. In the early 1970s they defined feminism as a "reformist movement of women wanting power within the patriarchal system" and then marched on International Women's Day carrying signs reading "Down with feminism!" The political–theoretical battles over the "ownership" of feminism took on a symbolic form later in the decade when *Psych et Po* registered a trademark on the initials MLF (*mouvement de libération des femmes*, or women's liberation movement) for their publishing house, *des femmes*.[42] The gesture was telling and eventually proved successful, at least for the perception of French feminism internationally. In North America, judging by the writers who are translated and anthologized, French feminism is often represented by writers once associated with *Psych et Po*.[43]

What was in a sense simply a generational shift in thought—from the humanism of Beauvoir and Sartre's postwar generation to the poststructuralism of Derrida—became, in the context of feminist activism, also a crusade against "Beauvoir-style feminism." As a public figure closely associated with Sartre, she also became a target for polemical attacks and caricatures. One of the most vicious came on the twenty-fifth anniversary of the publication of *Le deuxième sexe*. In its report on a conference being held in New York to mark the occasion, *des femmes hebdo*, the journal of *Psych et Po*, characterized Beauvoir as the Big Bad Wolf in the following exchange with a feminist Little Red Riding Hood: "Oh grandmother, what fine concepts you have!" cries Little Red Riding Hood. "The better to retard you with, my child," responds Beauvoir as the Grandmother/Wolf. The same article criticized the "phallic sons" of Beauvoir's feminism.[44] These attacks were, it would seem, largely successful in discrediting Beauvoir and thus also her theoretical work: There has been very little scholarly work done on *The Second Sex* in France since the 1970s.[45]

The Second Sex and Feminist Generations

It is worth considering in more detail the polemics and politics of French feminism in the 1970s, since the terms of the debate as defined then continue to frame and limit interpretations of *The Second Sex* now. The debates have led to the identification of Beauvoir and thus also *The Second Sex* with a particular "generation" of feminism—moreover, a generation that has been superseded. They also most decisively linked Beauvoir with what came to be termed "phallic" or "masculinist" feminism.

The sense of feminist theorizing as comprising not only temporal but also conceptual "generations" is developed most clearly in Julia Kristeva's influential article "Women's Time."[46] Kristeva's article, written in 1979, is at once a polemical attack on Beauvoir and a theoretical account of feminism in Europe. "Women's Time" is worth dwelling on, not only because it has had enormous influence in how Western feminists have retrospectively constructed our history, but also because in it she at once clarifies and exaggerates the theoretical differences between the generations she outlines.[47]

Kristeva's analysis of feminism is couched in a more general analysis of temporality: of women's relationship to time and thus also to language and subjectivity. "Father's time, mother's species," as she quotes from James Joyce to illustrate men's and women's different relationships to temporality: "when evoking the name and destiny of women, one thinks more of the *space* generating and forming the human species than of *time*, becoming, or history."[48]

Women symbolize space, particularly the maternal space of the womb: "the *chora*, matrix space, nourishing, unnameable," space that is in a sense beyond time, or at least entirely foreign to the linear time of history. Female subjectivity is related instead to time experienced as repetition and eternity: the repetition of "cycles, gestation, the eternal recurrence of a biological rhythm which conforms to that of nature" and a perception of eternity "all encompassing and infinite like imaginary space."[49]

Cyclical and monumental time are thus contrasted with linear time: "time as project, teleology, linear and prospective unfolding; time as departure, progression and arrival—in other words, the time of history."[50] Linear or historical time is also, importantly, the time of language, of the enunciation of sentences, of what Kristeva calls the "symbolic." For Kristeva, access to language is what defines the subject; separation from the mother is the condition of acceding to the symbolic. Speaking requires an identification with the law of the father, which excludes the feminine. Linear time is a temporality that enables the subject–object division; it is also in her view one that leads the subject to an obsessional attempt at mastery: mastery of linear time and its "stumbling block," death.

Kristeva's analysis of feminism in modern Europe is framed in this analysis of temporality and language. She argues that there are three distinct attitudes on the part of feminists toward historical time, "this linear temporality which is readily labelled masculine, and which is at once both civilizational and obsessional"; these are what Kristeva refers to as the three generations of feminism. One might just as easily say that these are three approaches to the project of becoming a historical subject.[51]

In its beginnings, Kristeva writes, "the women's movement, as the struggle of existentialist feminists and suffragists, aspired to gain a place in linear time as the time of project and history."[52] This involved making political demands: "struggles for equal pay for equal work, for taking power in social institutions on an equal footing with men." The first generation's struggle also required "the rejection, when necessary, of the attributes traditionally considered feminine or maternal in so far as they [were] deemed incompatible with insertion in that history."[53] This struggle to enter history is part, Kristeva argues, of a "logic of identification" with the dominant "logical and ontological values of rationality" of the nation-state, and while this identification has achieved certain benefits and successes for women (Kristeva mentions abortion, contraception, equal pay, and professional recognition), her analysis implies that it has also entailed significant losses.[54]

This first generation of feminists, in "the egalitarian and universalistic spirit of Enlightenment Humanism," advocate "a necessary identification between the two sexes as the only and unique means for liberating the 'second sex.'"[55] She goes on to write that given this ideology—which considers human beings only in their relation to production, rather than according to their place in reproduction or in the symbolic order—"the specific character of women could only appear as nonessential or even non-existent."[56] Equality as sameness erases women in their specificity.

The second generation of French feminists is made up of women who came of age politically after the student protests of May 1968.[57] Kristeva characterizes the stance of these feminists as one of refusal of linear temporality and distrust of the political dimension.[58] This generation is qualitatively different from its predecessor in its conception of identity and in its concern with "the specificity of female psychology and its symbolic realizations."[59] In short, "the struggle is no longer concerned with the quest for equality but, rather, with difference and specificity."[60] And since, on Kristeva's reading, the struggles for economic, political, and professional equality have been won, the essential struggle for the second generation is on the terrain of the sexual. Thus sexual difference emerged as *the* problem for feminism and provoked what Kristeva would call "an attempt to give a language to the intrasubjective and corporeal experiences left mute by culture."[61]

Kristeva does not dwell on the third generation of feminism; it is a signifying space in which "the very dichotomy man/woman as an opposition between two rival entities may be understood as belonging to metaphysics."[62] The third generation, one Kristeva endorses, would refuse to recognize either identity or difference and would undermine oppositional masculinity and femininity in favor of diversity or differences. These generational differences are crucially differences in women's relation to temporality and language: about what it means for a woman to become a subject. And what is most at issue is the place of the body and sexual specificity or "sexual difference" in subjectivity.

The struggle of the "existentialist feminists" Kristeva writes about also translates into language more familiar in North America: it would be described as a struggle or political program based on a conception of equality as sameness. In the same way, Kristeva's second generation is comparable in some respects to the "difference feminism" of such North American feminists as Carol Gilligan and Nancy Chodorow.[63] But to identify the French and North American debates too quickly is to risk losing the specificity of the French context that provides particular insights into the reading of Beauvoir. Though she does not refer to Beauvoir by name in "Women's Time," Kristeva's comments about the first-generation "existentialist feminists'" strategy for liberating the "second sex" are quite pointed. "Women's Time," for all its rather detached, meta-level criticism and analysis, is also a rhetorical broadside against Simone de Beauvoir, within a highly charged political context.[64] The political project for women of entering into history is indeed Beauvoir's project: Woman should, Beauvoir suggested, enter the time of becoming and history. A recurrent theme in *The Second Sex* is that women have had no history, no collective story or myth of their own; her aim is certainly for women to take the historical stage. The question at issue is what costs this will involve.

Kristeva's targeting of Beauvoir as emblematic of the first generation of feminism is most pronounced when she begins to discuss maternity. The desire to be a mother was, she writes, "considered alienating and even reactionary" by the first generation of feminists, who, Kristeva implies, advocated the refusal of maternity as a "mass policy" and foreclosed the question of maternal desire.[65] Thus the first generation of feminists is, on Kristeva's reading, a sacrificial generation: one that has sacrificed femininity, specificity, and difference and made a symbolic identification with the father, by promoting the "mass policy" of refusing the maternal role. This generation, she suggests, has become implicated in the masculine relation to temporality and thus subjectivity: an obsessional attempt to master time and mortality.

What needs to be asked now is not only Kristeva's question of whether Beauvoir's feminism forecloses maternal desire and feminine specificity, but also the question of what Kristeva's construction of feminist generations forecloses in the reading of *The Second Sex*. The identification of Beauvoir with one style of feminism, and particularly with one generation, closes off rather than opens up the text to new readings in new contexts and obscures the complexity of the text. What has emerged is a reading of Beauvoir as a rather naive thinker, one who addresses the three struggles Kristeva describes— economic, political, and professional—but does not engage with sexuality, or the connections among sexual difference, subjectivity, and power.

A Feminist Mother with Masculine Values?

The feminist writing critical of Simone de Beauvoir is both framed by Kristeva's generational analysis and shaped by the public image of Beauvoir. The interpretation of *The Second Sex* as articulating typically first-generation demands for access to historical time is quickly reinforced by the image of Beauvoir herself, closely linked in the public imagination with Sartre, and a woman who refused both marriage and motherhood in favor of a career as a writer. The result is a body of literature in which the criticism of Beauvoir's text is very closely linked to criticism of her own life choices.

What makes Beauvoir emblematic of the first conceptual generation of feminism for many feminist critics? Membership in this generation would be marked by an insistence on women's entrance into historical time, with women becoming historical subjects through achieving economic, political, and professional equality with men. However, it would also be marked by a particular stance toward femininity (and, by implication, the female body): one of refusal and repudiation. Beauvoir is found by her critics to be of the first generation in both senses. Her call for women to become historical subjects is seen as intimately tied to and conditional upon a refusal of femininity, and the maternal role in particular.

The description of Beauvoir's political project as one involving women becoming historical subjects by demanding political, social, and economic equality is one that Beauvoir would of course not contest. *The Second Sex* issues a call for women to cease accepting the role of the Other and to take up their role as subjects who realize their freedom through concrete action, or projects, in the world.[66] Beauvoir insists that freedom must be actualized through concrete possibilities and opportunities and will thus only be realized when women achieve social equality with men and economic independence from them.[67] That freedom, or becoming subject, would also require a repudiation of traditional femininity is, again, a claim that Beauvoir would not contest, since it is precisely in the guise of "proper femininity," which Beauvoir often calls the "Eternal Feminine," that women are cast as the Other.[68] The chapters of *The Second Sex* on marriage, domesticity, and motherhood are a scathing critique of institutions in which women are trapped as dependents, living vicariously through their husbands and children, waging a war on dirt in lieu of any involvement in a broader project.[69]

The problem, as many see it, is that the subject that Beauvoir is urging women to become is a specifically modern, masculine construct. Urging women to become subjects, without recognizing the partiality of that conception of subjectivity, is thus urging them to become just like men: to embody the masculine subject of modernity. Thus critics complain that Beauvoir's work is masculinist, that her painstaking analysis of the social construction of femininity, and of the damage inflicted on women in this process, amounts to little more than a repudiation of femininity itself and leads her to imply that women, to be free, to be subjects, should be just like men. The charges of "masculinism" and "acceptance of patriarchal values" are ones that are repeated frequently in the feminist literature on *The Second Sex*.

Mary Evans, for example, concludes that Beauvoir's feminism is shaped by "patriarchal habits and values." Beauvoir, Evans writes, counsels "the adoption by women of male habits and values," and in fact places major importance on living like a "childless, rather singular employed man." Beauvoir's feminism, on this reading, is entirely uncritical of traditional masculine values or activities; it is a simple repudiation of traditional femininity. Evans's mode of reasoning is instructive: She relies heavily on an interpretation of Beauvoir's life choices to explain her prescriptive arguments and her vision of freedom. Because Beauvoir herself led a nontraditional life, choosing to avoid marriage and motherhood and to support herself through her teaching and writing, because she identified herself with Sartre and valued the intellectual interests that cemented their personal bond, her writing shows a "lack of engagement with and experience of the subjectivity of femininity" and could almost be called misogynist.[70] Not only is this an outrageously oversimplified, almost caricatured portrayal of the kinds of choices Beauvoir made and the constraints she faced as a woman in the context of postwar France, but also its logic isn't clear: Why would Beauvoir's lifestyle lead her to a lack of experience of femininity? Surely she still appeared, to her contemporaries, to be a woman, and feminine, and, even if she was not a mother, experienced the "subjectivity of femininity." Surely it was a different thing for her, as a woman, to live out the life of an intellectual and a writer than it was for Sartre?[71] But the most significant point about Evans's analysis for my purposes is that it reveals the dangers of reading Beauvoir's work through her life in a reductive and dismissive way: If Beauvoir's life choices are read simply as the refusal and repudiation of traditional feminine activities and her choice of an intellectual life seen as a desire to be just like Sartre, then the demand made in *The Second Sex* for woman's access to concrete opportunities is easily removed from its place in a complex and critical argument about the lived experience of femininity and understood as a demand that women be "just like men."[72]

The "Body Problem" in *The Second Sex*

I have, in this chapter, focused on the circumstances surrounding the text that constrained its reading and led to the charges of masculinism and complicity in mastery. In what follows I want to look more closely at the arguments of *The Second Sex* to explore how this masculinism comes to be understood as Beauvoir's own "body problem" and how Beauvoir's feminism becomes read both as an attempt to disavow the body and an attempt to master others. Even many sympathetic accounts of *The Second Sex* assume that the explanatory keys of the work are Beauvoir's personal and philosophical loyalty to Sartre and that both the argument and the language of the text can be traced back to their source in Beauvoir's psyche.

The claim of the feminist critics who charge Beauvoir with masculinism is that she has mistaken a partial, masculine form or conception of subjectivity, autonomy, and freedom for a universal one. She has idealized a modern subject that is in fact a masculine subject. The modern subject targeted by Beauvoir's critics is autonomous, or self-governing, and independent: a self-choosing, creative being. The existentialist subject, as a "becoming" who unfolds through his own acts, projects, and decisions, is conceived in terms of a divide between consciousness and facticity, which identifies the self with the mind in opposition to the body. This picture of the autonomous subject evokes an ideal relation between self or mind and body of containment and control.[73] This is a particularly masculine vision of subjectivity, autonomy, agency, and freedom to the extent that it draws on traditional associations of masculinity with mind or reason and femininity with the body and values the former at the expense of the latter.[74] To the extent that subjectivity and freedom are conceived of as freedom from the body, and women are associated with the body, bodily necessity, and uncontrolled desire, they are therefore associated also with a lack of freedom.[75]

What is peculiar about these criticisms of The Second Sex is that Beauvoir's analysis of women's Otherness highlighted just these associations: The ways in which "Woman" as a masculine construction has come to embody everything that the masculine subject is not. In contrast to the freedom of the subject, Woman as Other symbolizes limitation and necessity. In contrast to culture she is (though ambiguously) Nature itself, and in contrast to his transcendent consciousness, Woman is identified with immanence, a lack of freedom, and the body.[76] Most critics agree that Beauvoir is at her best when outlining the multitude of myths, customs, and practices that create and maintain Woman as the Other and when analyzing the long history of body-loathing in Western culture: the way in which actual women have been made into reflections of Woman or the Eternal Feminine and have had to bear cultural responsibility for being embodied creatures.

However, Beauvoir's emphasis on the harm involved in the identification of women in their concrete multiplicity with Woman as masculine construction has been read by her critics as simply a denigration of the body itself. Many authors, following Kristeva, see her analysis as predicating women's liberation not only on the disruption of this identity but also on a refusal of the female body itself. In practical terms, this is seen as requiring a refusal of reproduction and more broadly, as requiring freedom from the work of the body and necessity and from all the deprivations of the private realm. Beauvoir's writing is, on this analysis, simply replicating the negative valuation placed on the body and its needs in the masculine philosophical tradition, seeking to end only the pernicious association and identification of women with the body rather than the association between the body and the lack of freedom itself.[77]

I want to consider more closely these charges of masculinism, which have come to constitute almost a critical consensus on The Second Sex.[78] The body problem of The Second Sex is seen as having its source in both the philosophical framework of the book and in Beauvoir's own psyche.

The Body as a Philosophical Problem

The root of the problem is seen by most commentators, then, to be the body: Beauvoir reflects in her thought the "body trouble" of masculine thought, specifically Cartesian or Enlightenment thought, or existentialist thought (as a particularly extreme example of modern masculine thought). The issue then becomes The Second Sex's relationship to this philosophical framework: Does Beauvoir accept and reproduce it uncritically or does she transform it?

The philosophical problem is said to be that Beauvoir recognizes but repro-duces a series of dualisms, common in philosophical thought and particularly clear in Sartre's, which associate activity, freedom, the project, and transcen-dence with mind and masculinity and, correspondingly, passivity, unfreedom, necessity, and immanence with the body and femininity.[79] In fact the claim is more specific than this. It is that Beauvoir is reproducing two key dualisms: a distinction between body and mind, in which consciousness and freedom are identified with mind, and a distinction between nature and culture, in which the body is consigned to nature. And finally, that subjectivity—or human free-dom and agency—becomes transcendence as disembodied consciousness, and immanence thus becomes associated with bodily necessity and natural func-tions. This seems to make the female body itself the root cause of women's op-pression.[80] Moira Gatens argues that Beauvoir's use of a Sartrean existentialist philosophical framework led her to "entertain a philosophical dualism of the most orthodox kind that predisposes [her] work toward locating the source of women's inferior status in female biology."[81] On Gatens's reading, Beauvoir's apparently uncritical use of Sartrean existentialism undermines both her criti-cal stance toward patriarchal culture and the liberatory potential of her argu-ment, since

> to fail to take note of the value-laden character of any particular theory is im-plicitly to perpetuate the values that have been constructed by a culture that devalues women and those aspects of life with which they have been especially associated, for example, nature and reproduction.[82]

In "condemning" the maternal role, Gatens argues, Beauvoir "posits the ne-cessity to transcend the female body and its reproductive capacities without questioning the ways in which the significance of the female body is socially constructed and its possibilities socially limited."[83] Gatens locates Beauvoir in a tradition of feminism, beginning with Mary Wollstonecraft, which has connected women's liberation with "the ability to become disembodied and transcend 'mere animal functions' and nature."[84] Gatens thus suggests that Beauvoir, unable to respond critically to the philosophical framework devel-oped by Sartre, was led almost inevitably into biological determinist argu-ments to explain women's oppression.

Other readers of *The Second Sex* have been more willing to give weight to Beauvoir's explicit repudiation of biological determinism. Judith Butler, for ex-ample, recognizes that Beauvoir explicitly contests biological determinist argu-ments about women's nature. On Butler's reading, Beauvoir distinguishes sex (anatomical and biological) from gender (cultural); only the latter determines femininity. Women are not born, they are made, and they are made through a process of cultural construction.[85] However, Butler, like Gatens, also reads Beauvoir as accepting Sartre's vision of freedom and his identification of consciousness with freedom. In the end, in Butler's interpretation, Beauvoir still reinforces the body–mind distinction and consigns the body to "mute facticity," making of it a biological given, albeit one that has no essential connection to gendered femininity. Beauvoir, as Butler understands her, subscribes to a voluntarist theory of gender, and the construction of femininity is reduced to a matter of free choice.[86] Gender, from this perspective, is the product of individual choice. It is simply a situation that I, as a free consciousness, constitute through my choices, actions, and mode of self-presentation in the world. Gender then is entirely unrelated to the sexed body and radically arbitrary.

The arbitrary nature of gender is what Butler takes to be the profoundly liberating insight in Beauvoir's thought: It severs femininity, the lived expression of gender, from the female sex and reveals traditional femininity to be only one of presumably many, even infinite, ways to choose one's corporeal style.[87] But we must also notice that this liberating moment is inextricably linked to what is seen by most critics as the main problem of Beauvoir's work: that it must, since it is based on a Sartrean premise of freedom as the free choice of a detached consciousness, conceive of freedom as a freedom from the body. It is, at the very least, a vision of freedom in which the body has no weight.

Other, more sympathetic readings of Beauvoir also interpret her as subscribing to voluntarism. Le Doeuff identifies Beauvoir as arguing against any form of determinism—not just biological determinism (as Butler noted, Beauvoir explicitly denies biology any determining power) but also psychological and economic determinism.[88] As Le Doeuff writes, Beauvoir's arguments against determinism are so forceful that the subordination of women begins to seem in The Second Sex like a great uncaused scandal.[89] This Le Doeuff, like Butler, takes to be the great strength of the work: If the oppression of women can't be said to have any foundation in biology, anatomy, or the distribution of labor, it begins to appear more and more as a structure without foundations, a house of cards that will be toppled by the quick gust of wind that is feminist activism.

Both Le Doeuff's and Butler's liberating interpretations of Beauvoir as voluntarist, however, depend on dismissing an aspect of her thought that doesn't fit their interpretations and that does point to a foundation for women's oppression: the ontology that Beauvoir appropriated from Hegel and Sartre.[90] Once the ontological structure expressed in the relation of Absolute Subject and Inessential Other is considered, Beauvoir's thought seems to be beset again with masculinist assumptions: that freedom is expressed through the risk of life and not through giving of life and that subjectivity or freedom is predicated on the domination and mastery of others. The Hegelian subject is one that can be posed only in being opposed; Beauvoir cites the "fundamental hostility toward every other consciousness" that characterizes each consciousness.[91] Feminist critics wonder whether this masterful and dominating subject is one that can ever be overcome. Beauvoir's use of Hegel seems to signal that for women, freedom will simply mean a chance to become dominating subjects themselves.[92]

Some critics find Beauvoir's use of Hegel yet more troubling. Mary O'Brien locates Beauvoir's philosophical body problem in her acceptance of Hegelian theoretical categories that reflect a masculine reproductive consciousness: alienation from the birth process and thus from an experience of reproductive continuity. The battle to the death that makes up the master–slave dialectic reflects, according to O'Brien, a profound hostility to life and marks a sharp distinction between truly human consciousness and mere animal life. In Beauvoir's account of primitive life, the "worst curse that could be laid on woman" was her exclusion from hunting expeditions, because "it is not in giving life but in risking life that the human being is raised against the animal; that is why superiority has been accorded in humanity not to the sex which brings forth but to that which kills."[93] O'Brien argues that what Beauvoir referred to as the "key" to the mystery of the origin of woman's Otherness establishes the source of woman's lack of freedom in a reproductive function conceived of as "an intransigent and unalterable biological function."[94]

These criticisms suggest that Beauvoir's analysis of woman's Otherness rests on an assumption about the inherent lack of freedom in women's reproductive role that casts doubt on her explicit rejection of any form of determinism, especially biological determinism. The core of Beauvoir's argument is in the famous statement that "One is not born, but rather becomes, a woman. No biological, psychological or economic fate determines the figure that the human female presents in society; it is civilization as a whole that makes this product, intermediate between male and eunuch, which is described as feminine."[95] However, critics contend that her discussions of prehistory and biology weaken or contradict this antiessentialist position, leading to either confusion or a "secondary" or "inadvertent" biologism in her analysis.[96] Catriona Mackenzie finds that these tensions and contradictions in Beauvoir's account of the body in *The Second Sex* stem from her use of the dualistic Sartrean–Hegelian philosophical framework. On Mackenzie's reading, Beauvoir presents the feminine body both as a social construction and as a natural thing oppressive in itself at different points in the text.[97] Mary Lowenthal Felstiner also concludes that Beauvoir relied on both cultural and physical explanations for the strain of living in a woman's body, writing that "behind Simone de Beauvoir's social explanation [for women's subordination] lurk images of a female physiology inherently formed for intrusion." Lowenthal Felstiner cites two passages from *The Second Sex* describing reproduction that give this impression: A female, Beauvoir writes, "is like an enclosure that is broken into," she is "tenanted by another, who battens upon her substance" during pregnancy.[98]

"Horror" of the Body

Lowenthal Felstiner's reference to the images with which Beauvoir describes the female body is instructive. Many of Beauvoir's feminist readers cite the sexist or masculinist imagery and language with which Beauvoir describes the female body and see personal aversion or distaste as the source of the body trouble implicit in the philosophical framework of the book. What is it that discomfits and dismays Beauvoir's readers in her language? It is particularly evocative: Images and metaphors of darkness, softness, passivity, and viscosity abound in her descriptions of female sexuality and reproduction.[99]

As I argued in chapter 1, the philosophical tradition has long associated man with the mind and woman with the body, has valued mind over body, and has figured embodiment in metaphors that evoke the mind trapped in the body. References to the body as tomb and prison, as darkness or murkiness connote an entrapment and engulfment of the mind by the body. Beauvoir's imagery regarding women and women's biology echoes that tradition. Her infamous reference to women in the throes of desire as bogs and carnivorous plants echoes Plato's body as a "barbaric bog" or "mire" from which the mind must struggle to free itself,[100] and her language signals to many feminist critics the extent to which Beauvoir remained trapped in the cultural "somatophobia"[101] that she analyzed in *The Second Sex*.

More disturbing still for the feminist critics who read Beauvoir is the similarity of her descriptions—her metaphors and imagery—of the female body to certain passages of Sartre's *Being and Nothingness*. In Sartre's text, the transcendent *etre-pour-soi*, being-for-itself, is associated with masculinity, while the immanence of *etre-en-soi*, being-in-itself, is associated with matter, nature, and flesh and is explicitly feminine. Sartre's "holes and slime," "moist and feminine sucking," viscosity, and stickiness famously depict the free transcendent subject constantly threatened by immanence as by a shadowy, lurking, horrifying feminine monster.[102] Beauvoir's language is thus either read as a sign that she is caught in a cultural hostility to the body or that she was overly influenced by Sartre's particularly marked horror of flesh, and particularly of female flesh. In either case, the horrifying body depicted in *The Second Sex* is seen to reflect Beauvoir's horror of her own femininity, and flesh in general; the body problem is traced to a source in Beauvoir's own psyche.

Toril Moi reads Beauvoir's language as a sign of personal pathology. Beauvoir's "long, harrowing" descriptions of the natural processes—menstruation, pregnancy, menopause, and the like—of the female body turn the female body, in Beauvoir's text, into a "monstrous conspiracy" against the woman herself. Moi judges these descriptive passages to constitute a "denigration of the female body."[103] The female body is, on Moi's account, a problem for Beauvoir personally: The passages in question evince Beauvoir's clear "distaste for female biology" and her own revulsion at the processes of menstruation and lactation. However, if the source of the problem with the female body lies in Beauvoir's own psyche, it is a problem that then goes on to infect the text itself: The female body becomes the "monster which threatens to subvert her discourse" and that resists Beauvoir's efforts to repress it, going on to "haunt her whole essay."[104] Beauvoir tries to slay the monster by confronting it in the first chapter of *The Second Sex* on biology, arguing that biology is not destiny, but the "curiously alarmist intensity" of her description of the female body in the rest of the text reveals that the monster won't die: It undermines Beauvoir's (antibiological-determinist) argument about the nature of freedom in revealing the body to be "a crucially important material structure" of oppression.[105]

In her later re-reading of *The Second Sex*, Moi finds Beauvoir's "troubled relationship to the female body written into the very argument of *The Second Sex*." This troubled relationship Moi again characterizes as a "visceral disgust for the female sexual organs," which "can only be disparaging to women," and reveals Beauvoir's unconscious horror of the female body. In this second analysis, Moi names the "monster" that is the source of Beauvoir's horror: It is "the threatening image of the mother." It is not simply the female body that horrifies Beauvoir and haunts her text, but the mother's body.[106]

Critics also turn to events and choices in Beauvoir's life to explain the imagery in the text. Moi is echoed in her focus on the mother's body by Dorothy Kaufmann, who notes Beauvoir's "consistent hostility to the biological as well as the cultural conditions of maternity," arguing that the language with which Beauvoir evokes maternity reveals this hostility. On Kaufmann's reading, Beauvoir's evocation of "quivering jelly which is elaborated in the womb (the womb, secret and sealed like the tomb)," and her comparison of it to the "soft viscosity of carrion" can only have its source in the author's own hostility to the maternal.[107] Kaufmann goes on to explain this hostility as a product of

Beauvoir's childhood relationship with her parents: her rejection of an emotionally demanding mother, overbearing in relation to Beauvoir herself but clearly lacking in material power and authority, and her identification, as a "dutiful daughter," with her father, "who embodied the Law and worldly knowledge." On this reading, Beauvoir's enduring "fear of maternal engulfment" led her to "repress the feminine" in her writing, leading her to write in a way that is now characterized as masculine.[108]

Evans also finds personal revulsion underlying Beauvoir's description of the female body and turns explicitly to Beauvoir's life as the source for her theorizing. Beauvoir views the functions of biology "with what can only be described as a certain amount of distaste," moreover, a distaste "coloured by the view that women's biology makes her inferior to man." The root of Beauvoir's rejection of femininity is her view of a female biology that dooms women to passivity and alienation and seems to necessitate a repudiation of heterosexual intercourse and child-bearing.[109] Evans argues that Beauvoir's memoirs reveal a "suspicion and dislike of the body" in general and suggests that Beauvoir was thus personally drawn to a rather cerebral, disembodied conception of subjectivity.[110]

Other critics look more specifically to Sartre's influence over Beauvoir to find the source of the troubling imagery. Okely finds that Beauvoir's description of the fetus as "quivering jelly," which evokes the "soft viscosity of carrion," echoes not only Sartre's discussion of viscosity in *Being and Nothingness* but also his own disgust with the sexual body. In aiming to deconstruct the myth of the feminine, Okely writes, Beauvoir instead "naively reproduces her partner's and lover's ideas about the female body, while possibly deceiving herself that these are objective and fixed philosophic truths." She thus "reveals the extent to which she has internalized both the views of her own culture and the extreme reactions of Sartre."[111] Ascher finds the source of Beauvoir's "vilifying language" about motherhood in "Beauvoir and Sartre's revulsion with physicality and particularly with the female body." In her open letter to Beauvoir she berates Beauvoir for her "dislike of women," which she analyzes as a form of self-hatred.[112] And Anne Whitmarsh, in an otherwise quite sympathetic study of political and social commitment in Beauvoir's writing, finds Beauvoir's existentialist arguments about pregnancy to be only "a rationalization of a deeply felt disgust (the equivalent of Sartre's *nausée*) at the thought of pregnancy, the foetus, [and] childbirth." She speculates that this "disgust of the flesh and biological functions" that Beauvoir shared with Sartre "could have its origins in the puritanical attitudes fostered by their upbringing."[113]

These criticisms, repeated often in the feminist literature on Beauvoir, are an ironic and disturbing echo of the first, shocked reaction to *The Second Sex*.

Now Beauvoir is not revealing her own body in print but, through her "un-relentingly savage portrayal of the female body," she reveals her horror and aversion to it.[114] It is not only the shock and discomfort of Beauvoir's first readers that is echoed, however, but also the assumption that the disturbing elements in the text can, and should, be explained away by reference to Beauvoir's presumed pathology.

Conclusion: Beyond the First Generation

In recent feminist criticism of *The Second Sex*, there has been something of reconsideration of both the text and of the familiar image of Beauvoir as Sartre's faithful disciple. This reconsideration has been spurred in part by the posthumous publication of Beauvoir's letters to Sartre and World War II diary, which paint a surprisingly different picture of her emotional ties and loyalties than had her memoirs.[115] The letters and diary add another layer to the already complex public image of Beauvoir. The image of the indissoluble couple has given way to a recognition of the complexity of Beauvoir's emotional and sexual ties, which included lengthy intimate relationships with other women and men.[116] Likewise, the assumption that Beauvoir followed Sartre's philosophical lead has been complicated by the fact that the letters and diary more often show philosophical innovation on the part of Beauvoir and collaboration between the two, rather than a pupil–teacher relationship.[117]

This shift in the image of Simone de Beauvoir has perhaps opened a space for a consideration of *The Second Sex* as a philosophical text not wholly subsumed by its presumed theoretical submission to Sartrean existentialism. Closer attention to the text, as well as attention to the development of Beauvoir's thinking in her other philosophical writings, has resulted in interpretations of Beauvoir's work as a clear, if unannounced, break with Sartre's thought. This has undermined the sense of Beauvoir's subject as an obviously "masculine," masterful or dominating one.[118] The other theoretical influences that shaped *The Second Sex* have become correspondingly clearer: Recent interpretations focus on the influence of phenomenology on Beauvoir's understanding of the body and revise the idea that Beauvoir's thought was dualistic.[119]

In all this reconsideration of Beauvoir's writing, however, there has been surprisingly little attention paid to the style, language, or rhetoric of *The Second Sex*. Linda Zerilli has written suggestively that the structure and narrative voices employed in *The Second Sex* can be read as critical strategies on the part of its author: Just as Beauvoir's text is being shown to be more theoretically independent of the masculine philosophical tradition it sprang from than was previously thought, it can also be recognized as more critical of that tradition.[120] There has, however, been no attempt to re-read Beauvoir's intensely evocative imagery on the female body in the light of this revaluation of her ideas.[121]

In what follows I will add my voice to this reevaluation of Beauvoir's writings. The Second Sex can, and should, be read as critical of the masterful modern subject; the text points beyond this conception of subjectivity as pure transcendence toward a nondualistic conception of selfhood as embodied subjectivity, the ambiguity of transcendence and immanence at once.

Notes

1. Catherine Rodgers, Le Deuxième Sexe de Simone de Beauvoir: Un héritage admiré et contesté (Paris: L'Harmattan, 1998), 10. My translation.

2. Judith Okely, Simone de Beauvoir: A Re-reading (London: Virago, 1986), 70.

3. My consideration here is limited to the French and English (North American and British) feminist literature on Beauvoir, as these are the two major languages of Beauvoir criticism (though the book has also generated some literature in the rest of Europe, particularly Italy and Scandinavia). I have also limited my review to writings that consider Beauvoir's philosophy and political thought, rather than literary criticism of her as a novelist, critical accounts of her memoirs, or purely biographical treatments of her life.

4. Until recently, there were, to my knowledge, only two books (single-authored books, rather than collections of articles) devoted exclusively to The Second Sex, neither by writers engaged in the women's movement: Suzanne Lilar, Le Malentendu du deuxième sexe (Paris: P.U.F., 1970), and Donald Hatcher, Understanding "The Second Sex" (New York: Peter Lang, 1984). Lilar's book is a notoriously hostile attack on both Beauvoir and her book; Hatcher's is a summary aimed at undergraduate students rather than a critical work. The vast majority of books on Simone de Beauvoir are general discussions of her "life and work" with only minimal critical discussion of The Second Sex. (I discuss the implications of this form of criticism later.) Recently, however, there has been a revival of interest in The Second Sex, and a number of feminist authors, among them Nancy Bauer, Debra Bergoffen, Karin Vintges, Toril Moi, and Eva Lundgren-Gothlin, have published critical writings on the book (see later).

5. Rosi Braidotti, Patterns of Dissonance, trans. Elizabeth Guild (Cambridge: Polity, 1991), 170; Deirdre Bair, editor's introduction to The Second Sex (New York: Vintage, 1989), xiii. She cites this as one of the most sustained criticisms of Beauvoir and The Second Sex throughout its history.

6. Braidotti, Patterns, 170.

7. Hélène Wenzel, "An Interview with Simone de Beauvoir," Yale French Studies 72 (1986): 7.

8. Simone de Beauvoir, *The Second Sex*, trans. and ed. H. M. Parshley (New York: Vintage, 1989), xxii.

9. Beauvoir, *The Second Sex*, xxxiv–xxxv.

10. Beauvoir, *The Second Sex*, xxxv, TA; *Deuxième sexe I*, 32: *"Tel qu'il leur est proposé."* Parshley's translation here, the world "in which women must live," misses the sense of the masculine constitution of the feminine situation that is clear in Beauvoir's original text.

11. As others have noted, Parshley's translation of the title of the second volume, *L'expérience vécue*, as "Woman's Life Today" rather than the more literal "Lived Experience" obscures Beauvoir's phenomenological intent. See, for example, Karen Vintges, "The Second Sex and Philosophy," in *Feminist Interpretations of Simone de Beauvoir*, ed. Margaret Simons (University Park: Pennsylvania State University Press, 1995), 57, note 1.

12. Beauvoir, *The Second Sex*, xxxv, TA; *Deuxième sexe I*, 31: *"un monde où les hommes lui imposent de s'assumer comme l'Autre."*

13. Beauvoir, *The Second Sex*, chs. XVI and XVII.

14. However, she did include an extensive history of nineteenth-century feminism in her analysis. Beauvoir's first public assertion of a feminist identity was made in a 1972 interview with Alice Schwarzer in *Le Nouvel Observateur*, reprinted in Schwarzer, *Simone de Beauvoir Today* (London: Hogarth, 1984), 32.

15. It is possible to distinguish, to some extent, between the reaction to Beauvoir's politics and the reaction to her analysis of female sexuality and motherhood because the book was first published serially by chapter in *Les Temps Modernes*. "La Femme et les Mythes" was published first in *LTM* 32–34 (May–July 1948), followed by "L'initiation sexuelle de la femme," "La Lesbienne," and "La Maternité" in *LTM* 43–45 (May–July 1949) respectively. See Claire Laubier, ed., *The Condition of Women in France: 1945 to the Present, A Documentary Anthology* (London: Routledge, 1990), ch. 2, for an account of the reaction.

16. François Mauriac, *Le Figaro*, May 30, 1949. Cited in Rodgers, *Deuxième sexe de Simone de Beauvoir*, 15.

17. Claude Francis and Fernande Gontier, *Les ecrits de Simone de Beauvoir* (Paris: Gallimard, 1979), 154; Beauvoir, *The Force of Circumstance*, trans. Richard Howard (London: Penguin, 1964), 197.

18. Again Mauriac provides a telling example. He wrote to the office of *Les Temps Modernes*, the journal Beauvoir cofounded and edited with Sartre and Merleau-Ponty, that "your employers' vagina now held no secrets from [him]." Cited in Beauvoir, *Force of Circumstance*, 197. Beauvoir and Sartre decided to publish the letter, to force Mauriac into publicly defending his opposition to *The Second Sex* on principled grounds.

19. Jo-Ann Pilardi describes this early notoriety in a review of the critical reception of *The Second Sex*. Pilardi, "The Changing Critical Fortunes of 'The Second Sex,'" *History and Theory* 32, no. 1 (1993): 51–73. Margaret Simons has analyzed the lack of attention to *The Second Sex* in philosophical circles in "Sexism

and the Philosophical Canon: On Reading Beauvoir's 'The Second Sex,'" *Journal of the History of Ideas* 51 (1990): 487–504; see also her editor's introduction to *Feminist Interpretations*, ed. Simons, 6–9. Hazel Barnes's early study *The Literature of Possibility: A Study in Humanistic Existentialism* (Lincoln: University of Nebraska, 1959) is a notable exception to the philosophical neglect of Beauvoir; in it she discusses the philosophical framework of Beauvoir's first novel, *She Came to Stay*, in relation to Sartre, *Being and Nothingness*, trans. Hazel Barnes (New York: Philosophical Library, 1956).

20. Wenzel, "Interview," 7.

21. Schwarzer, *Simone de Beauvoir Today*, 71.

22. See Yolanda Patterson, "Simone de Beauvoir and the Demystification of Motherhood," *Yale French Studies* 72 (1986): 90. This sentiment was expressed by numerous French feminists at the time of Beauvoir's death. Rodgers, *Deuxième sexe de Simone de Beauvoir*, 18.

23. Mary O'Brien, *The Politics of Reproduction* (London: Routledge & Kegan Paul, 1981), 65, emphasis in original. There are many others: Iris Marion Young and Mary Evans describe Beauvoir as the "mother of contemporary feminism," Evans, *Simone de Beauvoir: A Feminist Mandarin* (London: Tavistock, 1985), 59, or "mother of feminist philosophy," Young, "Humanism, Gynocentrism and Feminist Politics," in *Throwing Like a Girl* (Bloomington: Indiana University Press, 1990), 73–91. Elizabeth MacNabb's study of Beauvoir's influence on American feminists, *The Fractured Family* (New York: Peter Lang, 1993), is framed by the mother–daughter metaphor.

24. There have been least eleven full-length biographies or personal memoirs of Beauvoir published to date (listed in the bibliography), four of which explicitly focus on Beauvoir as one half of the Sartre–Beauvoir couple: Claude Francis and Fernande Gontier, *Simone de Beauvoir: A Life, A Love Story*, trans. Lisa Nesselson (New York: St. Martin's Press, 1987); Gilbert Joseph, *Une si douce occupation: Simone de Beauvoir, Jean-Paul Sartre, 1940–1944* (Paris: Albin Michel, 1991); Bianca Lamblin, *A Disgraceful Affair: Simone de Beauvoir, Jean-Paul Sartre and Bianca Lamblin*, trans. Julie Plovnick (Boston: Northeastern University Press, 1966); and Axel Madsen, *Hearts and Minds: The Common Journey of Simone de Beauvoir and Jean-Paul Sartre* (New York: Morrow, 1977). As well, there is one book of images (Claude Francis and Janine Niepce, *Simone de Beauvoir et le Cours de Monde* [Paris: Klincksieck, 1978]) and there have been a number of films. See, for example, Josée Dayan, *Simone de Beauvoir* (Paris: Gallimard, 1979 [film transcript]). Beyond biography and memoir, there are many "life and work" studies that mix biography with criticism. See the section titled *The Second Sex* and Feminist History, and see Karen Vintges, *Philosophy as Passion: The Thinking of Simone de Beauvoir*, trans. Anne Lavelle (Bloomington: Indiana University Press, 1996), for criticism of this genre.

25. See Toril Moi, *Simone de Beauvoir: The Making of an Intellectual Woman* (Oxford: Basil Blackwell, 1994), 4.

26. Beauvoir, *Memoirs of a Dutiful Daughter*, trans. James Kirkup (London: Penguin, 1959), 145, 343; and *The Prime of Life*, trans. Peter Green (London: Penguin, 1965), 220–21; Alice Schwartzer, *Simone de Beauvoir Today*, 109.

27. The phrase is from Robert Cottrell, *Simone de Beauvoir* (New York: Frederick Unger, 1975), 106. Beauvoir's own portrayal of her relationship to Sartre has been a subject of much feminist analysis. It has been the animating preoccupation in Michèle Le Doeuff's writing on Beauvoir: Le Doeuff, "Simone de Beauvoir: Falling into (Ambiguous) Line," in *Feminist Interpretations*, ed. Margaret Simons, 59–66; *Hipparchia's Choice: An Essay Concerning Women, Philosophy, etc.* (Oxford: Blackwell, 1991); and "Simone de Beauvoir and Existentialism," *Feminist Studies* 6, no. 2 (1980): 277–89. See also Dorothy Kaufmann, "Simone de Beauvoir, 'The Second Sex' and Jean-Paul Sartre," *Signs* 5 (1979): 209–33 and Nancy Huston, "Castor and Poulou: The Trials of Twinship," *L'éspirit Créateur* 29, no. 4 (1989): 8–20.

28. Penny Forster and Imogen Sutton attempt to assess this legacy in interviews with women who cite Beauvoir's writing and/or life as a significant model for them. Forster and Sutton, *Daughters of de Beauvoir* (London: Women's Press, 1989). MacNabb's study is likewise an attempt to assess this mixture of literary and personal influence through psychological and literary theory. MacNabb, *Fractured Family*. And Okely also explicitly considers Beauvoir as both a personal and literary influence. Okely, *Re-reading*.

29. Betty Friedan, *The Feminine Mystique* (London: Penguin, 1986; first published in 1963); see also Sandra Dijkstra, "Simone de Beauvoir and Betty Friedan: The Politics of Omission," *Feminist Studies* 6, no. 2 (1980): 290–303; Kate Millet, *Sexual Politics* (New York: Avon, 1970) ; Shulamith Firestone, *The Dialectic of Sex* (New York: William Morrow, 1970) and Dorothy Dinnerstein, *The Mermaid and the Minotaur* (New York: Harper & Row, 1976). See also Mary Dietz, "Debating Simone de Beauvoir," *Signs* 18, no. 1 (1992): 74–88, 79. MacNabb describes some of these early feminist authors as Beauvoir's "disconnected daughters" because of their failure to acknowledge her work. MacNabb, *Fractured Family*, 26.

30. One example is Valerie Bryson's *Feminist Political Theory: An Introduction* (New York: Paragon, 1992). Rosemarie Tong, *Feminist Thought: A Comprehensive Introduction* (Boulder, Colo.: Westview, 1989), rather an exception to this rule, is organized thematically rather than strictly chronologically and devotes a chapter to Simone de Beauvoir and "existential feminism." This neglect is perhaps now ending: see Michèle le Doeuff, *Hipparchia's Choice*, Moi, Vintges, and Bergoffen (see later).

31. Dietz, "Debating," 78. Rodgers notes both an obsession with *The Second Sex* and an evasion of its arguments by French feminists. Rodgers, *Deuxième sexe de Simone de Beauvoir*, 10.

32. Kaufmann describes its "domestication as a generally unread classic," in "Simone de Beauvoir, 'The Second Sex' and Jean-Paul Sartre," 209.

33. Carol Ascher, *Simone de Beauvoir: A Life of Freedom* (Boston: Beacon Press, 1981), 107, 112, 114.

34. Okely, *Re-reading*, vii.

35. Some examples of this form of writing are Lisa Appignanesi, *Simone de Beauvoir* (London: Penguin, 1988); Evans, *Feminist Mandarin*; Ascher, *Life of Freedom*; and Okely, *Re-reading*.

36. Toril Moi, *Feminist Theory and Simone de Beauvoir* (Oxford: Blackwell, 1990), 27–33.

37. Elaine Marks, *Simone de Beauvoir: Encounters with Death* (New Brunswick, N.J.: Rutgers, 1973), 5, 8; Jean-Raymond Audet, *Simone de Beauvoir face à la mort* (Lausanne: Editions l'Age d'Homme S.A., 1979). I must note, however, that Marks's later, and more sympathetic, work on aging in Beauvoir's texts does not rely on this reductive and dismissive tactic. See Elaine Marks, "Transgressing the (In)cont(in)ent Boundaries: The Body in Decline," *Yale French Studies* 72 (1986): 181–202.

38. Braidotti, *Patterns*, 168.

39. Michelle Perrot, commenting on Beauvoir's influence on French feminists in the 1970s, emphasizes the difficulty of isolating the influence of her text from that of her personality and lifestyle. Cited in Rodgers, *Deuxième sexe de Simone de Beauvoir*, 25.

40. Claire Duchen, *Women's Rights and Women's Lives in France, 1944 to 1968* (London: Routledge, 1994), 236 n.33. See also Duchen, *Feminism in France: From May '68 to Mitterand* (London: Routledge, 1986).

41. Perhaps the most well known of the feminists associated with *Questions Feministes* is the sociologist Christine Delphy, currently editor of *NQF*. *Psych et Po* was led by the psychoanalyst Antoinette Fouque and counted Helène Cixous, Luce Irigaray, Julia Kristeva, and Annie Leclerc as members at various times in the 1970s.

42. These events are chronicled in Duchen, *Feminism in France*. See also Anne Tristan and Annie de Pisan, "Tales from the Women's Movement," in *French Feminist Thought*, ed. Toril Moi (Oxford: Blackwell, 1987), 33–69, for a firsthand account of the early 1970s feminist politics, and Moi's introduction to the same collection, esp. 3–4.

43. See, for example, the special edition of *Signs* dedicated to New French Feminism (vol. 7, no. 1, 1981). Moi's collection, *French Feminist Thought*, is somewhat more inclusive of the range of feminist thought existing in France. Kelly Oliver discusses the North American perception of Kristeva, Irigaray, and Cixous as the "holy trinity" of French feminism in *Reading Kristeva* (Bloomington: Indiana University Press, 1993), ch. 7. See also Dorothy Kaufmann-McCall, "Politics of Difference: The Women's Movement in France from May 1968 to Mitterand," *Signs* 9, no. 2 (1983). Christine Delphy analyzes the North American projection of "difference feminism" onto French feminists in general in "L'Invention du 'French Feminism': Une démarche essentielle," *Nouvelles Questions Feministes* 17, no. 1 (1996).

44. *des femmes hebdo*, 1 (November 9–16, 1979): 11–12, cited in Dorothy Kaufmann, "Simone de Beauvoir: Questions of Difference and Generation," *Yale French Studies* 72 (1986): 121–31, 123.

45. Moi notes that in the 1980s, Beauvoir studies shifted decisively away from France. Before 1980, only five out of an estimated twenty-one full-length studies were published in English. In contrast, from 1980 to 1988, ten out of thirteen books

on Beauvoir were written in English. Of the three in French, two were written by French academics living and working in the United States and the third was a memoir by a personal friend of Beauvoir's. Moi, *Feminist Theory*, 25. If Moi's figures are updated through to 1999, the disparity becomes even more striking: An additional thirteen books have been published in English, only one in French. Books from the same period (1980–1999) that consider *The Second Sex* specifically show the same pattern: twenty-one published in English, one in French. (The sole book in French on *The Second Sex* in this period is Le Doeuff's *Etude et le Rouet*, trans. as *Hipparchia's Choice*.) However, it is important to note that a number of feminists in France, though not writing interpretative studies of Beauvoir's writing, continued to do work influenced by her analysis, among them Delphy, Monique Plaza, Elizabeth Badinter, and Monique Wittig.

46. Kristeva, "Women's Time," trans. Alice Jardine. *Signs* 7, no. 1 (1981): 13–35. (Originally published as "Le Temps des femmes" in *34/44: Cahiers de recherche de sciences des textes et documents*, no. 5 [1979], 5–19.)

47. At least two writers on Beauvoir explicitly frame their analysis in terms of Kristeva's generations: Jane Heath, in *Simone de Beauvoir* (New York: Harvester Wheatsheaf, 1989), 3–7, and Irène Pagès, "Simone de Beauvoir and the New French Feminism," *Canadian Women's Studies* 6, no. 1 (1984): 60–62. Many others, such as Iris Marion Young, use Kristeva's analysis implicitly.

48. Kristeva, "Women's Time," 15.

49. Kristeva, "Women's Time," 16.

50. Kristeva, "Women's Time," 17.

51. Kristeva, "Women's Time," 18. She argues that the generations she is describing aren't temporal but are "moments" that may all coincide in time; however, I would argue that the rhetorical effect of the word *generation* remains, connoting the temporal gap between Beauvoir's writing and that of the 1970s feminists. The generation metaphor also implies an attitude that the previous generation has been superseded. One can see this attitude more explicitly in many accounts of Beauvoir. For example, Iris Marion Young describes feminism's move away from and growing disillusionment with humanist (Beauvoirian) feminism as a transition from "childhood to puberty." Young, *Throwing Like a Girl*, 73.

52. Kristeva, "Women's Time," 18.

53. Kristeva, "Women's Time," 19.

54. Kristeva, "Women's Time," 19.

55. Kristeva, "Women's Time," 20.

56. Kristeva, "Women's Time," 21.

57. This locates them in time, but Kristeva also specifies that the second generation is made up of women who have had "an aesthetic or psychoanalytic experience," clearly identifying members of *Psych et Po*.

58. Kristeva, "Women's Time," 21. Though she recognizes that the "sociocultural recognition" of women is still a priority for this second generation, implying continued support for the kinds of political gains won by the first.

59. Kristeva, "Women's Time," 19

60. Kristeva, "Women's Time," 21.

61. Kristeva, "Women's Time," 19. Kristeva is referring perhaps most specifically here to the work of Luce Irigaray, who has argued that sexual difference is *the* problem of our time. Irigaray, *An Ethics of Sexual Difference*, trans. Carolyn Burke and Gillian Gill (Ithaca: Cornell University, 1993), 5.

62. Kristeva, "Women's Time," 33.

63. Hester Eisenstein analyzes North American feminist thought in generational terms similar to Kristeva's. Eisenstein, *Contemporary Feminist Thought* (Boston: G.K. Hall, 1984).

64. Kelly Oliver has analyzed Kristeva's hostile reaction to Simone de Beauvoir as reflecting her ambivalence toward a powerful mother figure. See Oliver, *Reading Kristeva*, 142–43.

65. Kristeva, "Women's Time," 30.

66. Beauvoir, *The Second Sex*, 678.

67. Beauvoir, *The Second Sex*, 725.

68. Beauvoir, *The Second Sex*, introduction and 719, 729.

69. Beauvoir, *The Second Sex*, 425–528.

70. Evans, *Feminist Mandarin*, x, xi, 57, 60. Jean Leighton makes a similar charge, declaring Beauvoir a misogynist and *The Second Sex* a diatribe against the female sex. Leighton, *Simone de Beauvoir on Woman* (London: Associated University Press, 1975), ch. 1 and p. 221.

71. Toril Moi, in *Intellectual Woman*, presents a much more nuanced account of the kinds of choices and constraints Beauvoir faced as an intellectual woman in postwar France.

72. This charge is repeated by any number of Beauvoir's critics. Susan Hekman argues that "for Beauvoir, women must become like men, that is, constituting subjects, if they are to attain freedom." Hekman, "Reconstituting the Subject: Feminism, Modernism and Postmodernism," *Hypatia* 6, no. 2 (1991): 44–63, 44. (The idea of a "constituting subject" is discussed in the next chapter.) Lisa Appignanesi writes that *The Second Sex* "is imbued with the same masculine bias that created women's condition"; in it Beauvoir "attacks the mystique of femininity only to accept a masculine mystique." Appignanesi, *Simone de Beauvoir*, 96, 97. Iris Marion Young defines Beauvoir as "the exemplar of humanist feminism," a type of feminism unable to criticize male values or activities while devaluing traditionally feminine ones, and Kathy Ferguson writes that Beauvoir is too quick to identify humanness with maleness in her praise of masculine values and achievements. Young, *Throwing Like a Girl*, 74. Ferguson, *Self, Society and Womankind* (Westport, Conn.: Greenwood Press, 1980), 151. These examples are from the North American literature, but the same sort of criticism existed in France, judging by the writing of Jacques Zephir, who, in a defense of Beauvoir, asks whether hers is an "authentic feminism or unconscious misogyny" and defends her from feminists who accuse her of misogyny because of language that is "condemning (*flétrissant*) of everything feminine." Jacques

Zephir and Louise Zephir, *Le néo-féminisme de Simone de Beauvoir* (Paris: Editions Denoël/Gonthier, 1982), 162.

73. This is a brief sketch of the early Sartrean existentialist subject; it is discussed more thoroughly in chapter 3. Christine Di Stefano explores the connections between modern masculinity and this sense of autonomy in *Configurations of Masculinity* (Ithaca: Cornell University Press, 1991).

74. Genevieve Lloyd, *Man of Reason: Male and Female in Western Philosophy*, 2d ed. (London: Routledge, 1993). See my discussion in chapter 1, the section titled The Body in Political Thought.

75. Moira Gatens, *Feminism and Philosophy* and "Toward a Feminist Philosophy of the Body" in *Crossing Boundaries: Feminisms and the Critique of Knowledges*, ed. B. Caine, E. Grosz, and M. de Lepervanche (Sydney: Allen & Unwin, 1988); Elizabeth Spelman, "Woman as Body," 109–31; and Susan Suleiman, ed., *The Female Body in Western Culture* (Boston: Harvard U. Press, 1986).

76. Beauvoir, *The Second Sex*, 139–98.

77. See, for example, Elizabeth Spelman, *Inessential Woman*, 126–27; Gatens, *Feminism and Philosophy*, ch. 3, and Catherine Keller, *From a Broken Web: Separation, Sexism and Self* (Boston: Beacon, 1986), ch. 1.

78. In recent years this critical consensus has begun to break down in the light of some revaluation of *The Second Sex*. I discuss this later.

79. See, for example, Bonnelle Strickling, "Simone de Beauvoir and the Value of Immanence," *Atlantis* 13, no. 2 (1988), 36–43, 37.

80. See Margery Collins and Christine Pierce, "Holes and Slime: Sexism in Sartre's Psychoanalysis," in *Women and Philosophy: Toward a Theory of Liberation*, ed. C. Gould and M. Wartofsky (New York: Putnam, 1976), 112–27.

81. Gatens, *Feminism and Philosophy*, 2.

82. Gatens, *Feminism and Philosophy*, 3.

83. Gatens, *Feminism and Philosophy*, 5.

84. Gatens, *Feminism and Philosophy*, 6. Sonia Kruks, however, provides an alternative reading of Beauvoir's use of existentialism in *Situation and Human Existence* (London: Unwin Hyman, 1990), ch. 3. I discuss the use Beauvoir made of Sartre's existentialist ideas in chapter 3.

85. Judith Butler, "Sex and Gender in Simone de Beauvoir's 'Second Sex,'" *Yale French Studies* 72 (1986): 35–50.

86. See Judith Butler, *Gender Trouble* (New York: Routledge, 1990), 8. This is also how Sarah Heinämaa describes Butler's interpretation of Beauvoir in "What is a Woman? Butler and Beauvoir on the Foundations of the Sexual Difference," *Hypatia* 12, no. 1 (Winter 1997): 20–39, see esp. 21.

87. Butler's argument here is linked to her larger purpose to argue for an understanding of gender as performative. See *Gender Trouble*, esp. ch. 1.

88. Beauvoir, *The Second Sex*, 267.

89. This argument is developed most completely in *Hipparchia's Choice*. See also Le Doeuff, "Falling into (Ambiguous) Line," 59–66 and Heinämaa, "What is a Woman?"

90. Le Doeuff argues that Beauvoir's liberating and productive voluntarism is undermined by her turn to Sartre and Hegel to find an ontological underpinning to oppression. Accordingly, Le Doeuff dismisses Beauvoir's ontological foundation as unpersuasive. See *Hipparchia's Choice*, 117.

91. Beauvoir, *The Second Sex*, xxiii.

92. See Kathy Ferguson, *The Man Question: Visions of Subjectivity in Feminist Theory* (Berkeley: University of California Press, 1993), ch. 2; Keller, *From a Broken Web*, ch.1; Céline Léon, "Beauvoir's Woman: Eunuch or Male?" in *Feminist Interpretations*, ed. Margaret Simons, 137–59, 146; Tina Chanter, *Ethics of Eros: Irigaray's Rewriting of the Philosophers* (London: Routledge, 1995), 13, and Genevieve Lloyd, "Masters, Slaves and Others," *Radical Philosophy* 34 (1983).

93. Beauvoir, *The Second Sex*, 64.

94. Beauvoir, *The Second Sex*; O'Brien, *Politics of Reproduction*, 71. See also Tina Chanter, *Ethics of Eros*. Chanter concludes that Beauvoir's adherence to Sartrean absolute freedom caused her to misread or misuse the Hegelian drama and, in particular, kept her from making productive use of its dynamic structure. Both O'Brien and Chanter read the Hegelian key in *The Second Sex* in isolation from Beauvoir's earlier essays and to some extent in isolation from the rest of *The Second Sex*. They assume she is Sartrean and that her reading of Hegel comes through Sartre. Thus, they emphasise the first moment of the dialectic and fail to recognize Beauvoir's emphasis on "conversion" as a significant reworking of Hegel. This is discussed in detail in chapter 4.

95. Beauvoir, *The Second Sex*, 267, TA; *Deuxième sexe II*, 13.

96. See Appignanesi, *Simone de Beauvoir*, 88, and Okely, *Re-reading*, 94.

97. Catriona Mackenzie, "Simone de Beauvoir: Philosophy and/or the Female Body," in *Feminist Challenges: Social and Political Theory*, ed. Carole Pateman and Elizabeth Gross (Boston: Northeastern University, 1987), 144–56, 148.

98. Mary Lowenthal Felstiner, "Seeing The Second Sex through the Second Wave," *Feminist Studies* 6, no. 2 (1980): 247–76, 256.

99. See, for example, Beauvoir, *The Second Sex*, 21, 27, 29, 385–86, 495.

100. Beauvoir, *The Second Sex*, 386. See Plato, *Republic*, 611e and 612a. Spelman analyzes Plato's images of embodiment in "Woman as Body," 114.

101. This is a phrase coined by Spelman to refer to a cultural fear and horror of the body.

102. Sartre, *Being and Nothingness*, 607–14. See Collins and Pierce, "Holes and Slime," 112–27. Collins's and Pierce's argument that the philosophical relation between *The Second Sex* and *Being and Nothingness* is revealed through common imagery has been very influential for other feminist critics. See also Naomi Greene, "Sartre, Sexuality and *The Second Sex*," *Philosophy and Literature* 4, no. 2 (1980): 190–211.

103. Toril Moi, "Existentialism and Feminism," 88–95, 90.

104. Moi, "Existentialism and Feminism," 90.

105. Moi, "Existentialism and Feminism," 90, 93.

106. Moi, *Intellectual Woman*, 146, 177, 173.

107. Kaufmann, "Questions of Difference," 125, citing Beauvoir, *The Second Sex*, 165.

108. Kaufmann, "Questions of Difference," 126.

109. Evans, *Feminist Mandarin*, 62, 133, 134, 110.

110. Evans, *Feminist Mandarin*, 36.

111. Okely, *Re-reading*, 77.

112. Ascher, *Life of Freedom*, 110.

113. Anne Whitmarsh, *Simone de Beauvoir and the Limits of Commitment* (Cambridge: Cambridge University Press, 1981), 147. There are many other examples: Strikling writes of Beauvoir's "distaste for immanence" and "fundamental aversion to the physical except as an instrument" ("Value of Immanence," 38); Huston writes that Sartre's anguished descriptions of the vagina are equalled if not surpassed by Beauvoir's evocation of "female rut" as "the soggy palpitation of a shellfish," ("Castor and Poulou," 18).

114. Kaufmann, "Questions of Difference," 124.

115. Beauvoir, *Letters to Sartre*, trans. and ed. Quintin Hoare (New York: Little, Brown and Company, 1992), originally published as *Lettres à Sartre, 1940–1963*, ed. Sylvie Le Bon de Beauvoir (Paris: Gallimard, 1990), and *Journal de Guerre: Septembre 1939–Janvier 1941*, ed. Sylvie Le Bon de Beauvoir (Paris: Gallimard, 1990). The letters, which Beauvoir had claimed were lost, were found by her adopted daughter, Sylvie Le Bon de Beauvoir, and published in Paris in 1990. The *Journal* is different from the four-volume memoirs in that it was written at the time rather than retrospectively constructed and was edited by Le Bon de Beauvoir rather than Beauvoir herself.

116. See Margaret Simons, editor's introduction, *Feminist Interpretations*, and "Lesbian Connections: Simone de Beauvoir and Feminism," *Signs* 18, no. 1 (1992): 136–61, reprinted in *Beauvoir and the Second Sex: Feminism, Race, and the Origins of Existentialism* (Lanham, Md.: Rowman & Littlefield, 2000).

117. Kate and Edward Fullbrook have reassessed the influence of Beauvoir's novel *She Came to Stay* on the argument of Sartre's *Being and Nothingness* by comparing the dates of composition of both as given in the *Journal de Guerre* and in the letters. Fullbrook and Fullbrook, *Simone de Beauvoir and Jean-Paul Sartre: The Remaking of a Twentieth Century Legend* (Hertfordshire: Harvester Wheatsheaf, 1993). Jeffner Allen discusses how the publication of the letters has altered the Beauvoir myths, particularly the myth of the "model couple," in Allen, "A Response to a Letter from Peg Simons," in *Feminist Interpretations*, ed. Simons, 113–35.

118. A number of authors interpret *The Second Sex* as a radicalization of or a clear break with Sartre's thought circa *Being and Nothingness*. See Kruks, *Situation and Human Existence* and "Simone de Beauvoir: Teaching Sartre about Freedom," in *Sartre Alive*, ed. Ronald Aronson and Adrian van den Hoven (Detroit: Wayne State University, 1991), 285–300. See also Linda Singer, "Interpretation and Retrieval: Rereading Beauvoir," in *Hypatia Reborn*, ed. Azizah al-Hibri and Margaret Simons (Bloomington: Indiana University Press, 1990), 323–36, and Jo-Ann Pilardi, "Philosophy Becomes Autobiography: The Development of the Self in the Writings of Simone de Beauvoir," in *Writing the Politics of Difference*, ed. Hugh Silverman (Albany, N.Y.: SUNY Press, 1991), 145–64.

119. Kruks, in "Simone de Beauvoir entre Sartre et Merleau-Ponty," *Les Temps Modernes* 45, no. 520 (1989), reads Beauvoir's review of Merleau-Ponty's *Phenomenology of Perception* to argue that her view of the subject was actually closer to his than to Sartre's. Debra Bergoffen, "Out from Under: Beauvoir's Philosophy of the Erotic" and Karen Vintges, "*The Second Sex* and Philosophy," both in *Feminist Interpretations*, ed. Simons, 179–92 and 45–58, highlight the influence of Husserl's phenomenology on Beauvoir's thought.

120. Linda Zerilli, "'I Am a Woman': Female Voice and Ambiguity in 'The Second Sex,'" *Women & Politics* 11, no. 1 (1991): 93–108. See also Julie Ward, "Beauvoir's Two Senses of 'Body' in *The Second Sex*," in *Feminist Interpretations*, ed. Simons, 223–42, for a consideration of how the structure of the book reveals its critical intent.

121. Moi, in her 1994 reading of *The Second Sex*, suggests that Beauvoir's imagery remains a problem even when her work is recognized as theoretically distinct from Sartre's. Moi, *Intellectual Woman*. Linda Zerilli is the only critic I know of who is reconsidering the rhetoric and imagery in *The Second Sex*: she re-reads Beauvoir's discourse on pregnancy as a "rhetorical strategy of defamiliarization." Zerilli, "A Process without a Subject: Simone de Beauvoir and Julia Kristeva on Maternity," *Signs* 18, no. 1 (1992): 111–35. Zerilli's arguments are considered in more detail in chapter 5.

CHAPTER THREE

~

Coming of Age: Ambiguity and the Freedom of Others

The Second Sex is part of Beauvoir's larger ethical project. It is a work that is highly critical of femininity as a distortion of human potential. Less often noted by her critics, it is also a work that is highly critical of patriarchal masculinity as a distortion of human potential. To see *The Second Sex* as fundamentally an ethical work, we need to understand her point of reference. This she gives us in the beginning of *The Second Sex*—it is, she says, existentialist ethics. Typically, however, she doesn't tell us much about "existentialist ethics."[1] She had, however, developed an existentialist ethics in two postwar essays, *Pyrrhus et Cinéas* and *The Ethics of Ambiguity*.[2] Though Beauvoir doesn't explicitly direct her readers to her own earlier writings, there are good reasons to read *The Second Sex* in their light.

Beauvoir wrote *Pyrrhus et Cinéas* in the space of a few months in 1943 while living in occupied Paris. It is, not surprisingly, concerned with the problem of the effects of our actions on others and the inescapable possibility of violence in our relations to others. When it was published in 1944, one of the first essays published after the liberation of France, it was very well received.[3] *The Ethics of Ambiguity*, a longer and more thoughtfully argued essay, was composed in 1946 and published the next year. In it Beauvoir again focuses on the effects of our actions on others, but this time she develops more thoroughly the ontological foundation that will support her ethical precept that each action must take the freedom of self and others as its end.

These essays have largely been neglected both by Beauvoir's feminist critics and by most mainstream ones. *Pyrrhus et Cinéas* has not been translated in its entirety into English, a fact that both signals and has probably contributed to its neglect.[4] *The Ethics of Ambiguity* is mentioned in some critical accounts of Beauvoir but rarely analyzed in any depth. Seldom is any connection made between the ethics Beauvoir developed in these two essays and the argument of *The Second Sex*.[5] Most feminist critics focus their reading more narrowly on *The Second Sex* itself, and when they expand their consideration look either to Sartre's *Being and Nothingness* to elucidate the philosophical ideas that structure the text or to Beauvoir's novels for further discussion of women as the Other. While this is no doubt due in part to the circumstances of the feminist reception of *The Second Sex*, it is also true that these early works in some sense merit their obscurity.

The essays frustrate the reader with their limitations. They are the work of an author searching for a way to define herself in relation to Sartre's philosophy and grappling for the first time in her writing with the philosophic issues that would preoccupy her generation. Beauvoir herself made two interesting comments about her early philosophical essays. One is that *The Ethics of Ambiguity*, of all her books, is the one she later found "the most irritating."[6] She remarked to her biographer, Deirdre Bair, that *The Ethics of Ambiguity* suffered from being "neither one thing nor the other": Aiming to produce both a defense of existentialism and an ethics, Beauvoir felt she had failed at both.[7] On the other hand, she also directed Bair to look at her early philosophical essays as the works that she considered "the important starting point for any interpretation and evaluation of her *oeuvre*."[8] What are we to make of these seemingly contradictory statements? I think they can guide us to the significance of *The Ethics of Ambiguity* for our understanding of *The Second Sex* and give us some sense of what Beauvoir was aiming for with her ethics, even if she failed to achieve it in these early essays. We can take from Beauvoir's ambivalence about her early essays at least the understanding that, to her, *The Second Sex* is best understood as founded on her ethics. An ethics of ambiguity are central to the politics of "the woman question" as she presents it in *The Second Sex*.

Beauvoir's "failure" in these essays is instructive, and it provides the key for my interpretation of their relation to *The Second Sex*. Beauvoir's sense of her own failure was astute; she had, in fact, failed to produce a defense of existentialism, if by existentialism we understand Sartre's formulation in *Being and Nothingness*. She was looking for a way to found moral guidelines on Sartre's conception of humans as transcendent freedoms. Gradually through the two essays we see her grappling with the realization that in order to develop a coherent ethics, her understanding of freedom would have to change. She began, tentatively, to develop a conception of freedom not as synonymous with consciousness, but as the concrete possibilities of a situated and embodied subject: freedom as embedded in a person's physical and social existence.

It is the idea of freedom as situated that makes moral guidelines possible and meaningful. In *Being and Nothingness* Sartre had defined human being as freedom-in-situation, but since he had also argued that situation cannot determine consciousness, the end result was to deny the situation any real weight. If someone's situation does not determine their freedom, then there is little reason to work to alleviate the material conditions of those less advantaged. Indeed, there is, given Sartre's definition of freedom, no way to judge any one person's situation as more or less advantaged than another's. Beauvoir, focusing on the ways that one's situation conditions and limits the concrete expression of one's freedom, gives us reason to pay attention to the social, political, and material conditions of people's lives.

It was also when she reflected on the concrete situations of embodied subjects that Beauvoir developed the second key idea that distinguishes her thinking from Sartre's. Sartre, so Beauvoir tells us, had already defined human existence as ambiguous, because he defined humans as "that being whose being is not to be": We are always more than what we are as we project ourselves into the future.[9] For Beauvoir and Sartre alike, we are ambiguous in that we project ourselves into the future on the basis of the givens of our situation (our body, our past), but we are also ambiguous in that we experience ourselves as individual freedoms who are also immersed in the generality of the flesh, and we are ambiguous in that we experience ourselves at once as subjects and as objects for others. Ambiguity—in this complex sense—would become the keynote of Beauvoir's thought and she would develop an account of its implications for our relations with others that is quite distinct from Sartre. In what follows I argue that for Beauvoir, the lucid acceptance of ambiguity is the precondition of ethical and nonoppressive relations with others. The acceptance of human freedom as ambiguous is a moral coming of age: By fully assuming our ambiguity we will be able to resist the temptation to master and dominate others. When the acceptance of ambiguity is recognized as the sign of moral maturity in Beauvoir's ethics, a rather surprising discovery is made: Beauvoir is implicitly describing the relation to others that issues from Sartrean existentialism as an adolescent and immature response to the freedom of others.

The immediate context for these essays remains Sartrean existentialism, but in an equivocal sense. Beauvoir's ethics developed out of her reading of a number of sources; the one she cites most frequently, and directs us to, is Sartre. It would be a mistake, however, to read Beauvoir as working entirely within Sartre's philosophy, even though Beauvoir herself often represented her work in that way.[10] The circumstances in which she wrote the two essays, as she describes them in her memoirs, don't lead to the conclusion that Beauvoir was his faithful disciple. And if it is a mistake to read Beauvoir as Sartre's faithful philosophical disciple, it is also a mistake to read Beauvoir's work only in the light of Sartrean existentialism. When we concentrate exclusively on her personal and intellectual relationship with Sartre, we forget that her intellectual relationships were more various. Descartes's ghost hovers over her work, and she was influenced by Husserl's and Merleau-Ponty's phenomenological retrieval of the embodied subject as well as by Sartre's particular response to the Cartesian legacy. She developed her ideas about our relations to others by contesting not only Sartre's pessimistic analysis of the relation with the other as structured by the Look, but also Hegel's optimistic anticipation of the ultimate reconciliation of individuals in Absolute Spirit.

Beauvoir's conception of ambiguity would do justice to both the solitude and the bonds with others that characterize our condition. Her ethical coming of age is the recognition of both history and the generality of the flesh. In what follows I first situate Beauvoir in the postwar intellectual context and examine Beauvoir's retrospective account of her life in this period, considering how Beauvoir presents her own life as a model and an expression of her philosophical and ethical project, before tracing the development of her ethical thought through the two essays.

The Legacy of Descartes: Subjectivity, Dualism, and Solipsism

Beauvoir's generation has its philosophical roots in a reaction to Descartes. The problems of dualism and solipsism in his thought formed the horizon within which Beauvoir and her contemporaries—most particularly Sartre and Merleau-Ponty—thought and wrote and against which they struggled.

Descartes placed the individual subject at the center of the philosophical investigation, as its point of departure. Through a process of methodological doubt, in which every material thing, including the body, is doubted, he came to the conclusion that the one thing that cannot be doubted is consciousness, or one's existence as a thinking being.[11] The *cogito*, or the "I think," thus becomes the only reliable ground of knowledge; the "clear and distinct ideas of reason" will enable us to discover immutable laws or truths governing the material world, akin to the laws of physics.[12]

The "I" of the *cogito* is not, however, an individual with any particularity. It is instead a universal being of reason separated from its own body and thus from any particular position in space and time or any particular perspective.

It is, in this sense, unsituated and anonymous. The *cogito* is, somewhat para-doxically, an "I" stripped of all particularity, an abstract subjectivity. Descartes distinguished between the *res cogitans* and the *res extensa*, two sub-stances with different properties.[13] The mental and physical aspects of hu-man existence are of radically different substances that could exist indepen-dently; the realm of spirit is, in principle, separable from the realm of matter. With Descartes, actual embodied human subjects become simply parts of the objective world. His thought is thus profoundly dualist.[14]

In his focus on the *cogito* as the source of knowledge and thus the point of departure of philosophy, Descartes reduces the lived body to the body-as-known through science: In a sense this degrades and dismisses the lived body, which is not to be trusted, since its sense perceptions are not the source of knowledge but of confusion.[15] In his appeal to the clear and dis-tinct ideas of reason, Descartes appealed to mental perceptions rather than sensory ones. From this perspective, the body is either a source of doubt and confusion or simply a rationally designed machine, an object of knowledge for a disembodied consciousness that surveys its world. Cartesian dualism also leads to epistemological solipsism, for how is the individual subject to know another? If the self is defined as an individual cognitive capacity, then relations with others are secondary; indeed, the consciousness of the other is itself problematic. The *cogito*, or the "I think," is the ground of truth and certainty, but it can only be sure of its own existence. Others are simply objects with certain properties that exist in a particular place and time. The existence of a second consciousness is thus a problem within Cartesian thought.

In France, the beginning of the twentieth century saw a reaction against the Cartesian disembodiment of the self. Henri Bergson was perhaps the first to emphasize the importance of perception (sensory perception, rather than Descartes's mental perceptions) as our primary interaction with the world. I can't, Bergson argued, consider my own body as simply another object in the world or a lump of matter like any other. My body is not simply a thing; my body is me, because it is my mode of acting on the world and being acted on by it.[16] Gabriel Marcel, too, focused on the body in his reaction to the dan-gers of what he considered Descartes's overly scientific approach to philoso-phy. The body may be an object, mere matter, for the scientist. To the phe-nomenologist, however, the body is our way of being in the world, giving us a location, an identity, and a means of acting. When our bodies are consid-ered in this way, Marcel argues, "then I and my body cease to be treated as distinct entities: I am essentially incarnate, and my body is not a mere 'in-strument' which I use. . . . I am my body."[17]

The clearest sense of phenomenology as a reaction to Descartes, however, is in the work of Husserl, who, in his *Cartesian Meditations* also countered Descartes's degradation of the body by grounding philosophical investigation not in the subject as *cogito* but in the subject as an embodied perceiver. Husserl's discovery that the world is always experienced from a place, that is, that knowledge is always perspectival, was an attempt to overcome not only the problem of dualism but also that of Descartes's epistemological solipsism. If the world is experienced by a perceiving subject whose knowledge is perspectival, this reembodiment of the subject also opens up the intersubjective nature of the world, since a perceiving subject needs the perspective of the other to "fill out" or constitute a world.[18]

The way in which Beauvoir's generation approached the problem of the other—the problem of solipsism arising from Descartes—was influenced not only by Husserl's phenomenology but also by the French rediscovery of Hegel in the 1930s. Between 1933 and 1939, Alexandre Kojève lectured on the *Phenomenology of Spirit* in Paris, successfully reviving interest in Hegel's writings, and in 1940 Jean Hyppolite translated the *Phenomenology* into French.[19] Though Beauvoir herself probably did not attend Kojève's lectures, many of her friends did, including Merleau-Ponty and Raymond Queneau, a close friend of Beauvoir and Sartre's who later edited the lectures for publication.[20] The lectures had a profound influence on the whole generation of French intellectuals of which Beauvoir was a member.[21]

The way in which Beauvoir and her contemporaries read Hegel reveals them to be searching for a way to get beyond the problem of solipsism. Kojève's rather idiosyncratic interpretation of Hegel focuses on the *Phenomenology of Spirit* and reads the master–slave dialectic as the core of that text, marking this confrontation of consciousnesses, and the resulting confrontation with death, as the beginning of human history.[22] Hegel's master–slave dialectic describes a life and death struggle between two equals, each of whom desires recognition of his sovereign freedom from the other. The one who becomes master risks his life to affirm his freedom. While the one who becomes enslaved also risks his life in the struggle, in the end he chooses servitude over death. The slave then confirms the master's freedom through his service, but the dialectic doesn't rest with the slave's submission. The recognition granted by the slave is no longer the recognition of another free being that the master sought; the true resolution of the dialectic lies in the reciprocal recognition of both parties.[23]

On this reading the core idea of the *Phenomenology* is the intersubjective nature of the self. A consciousness can only attain self-certainty, or consciousness of himself as free, through the recognition afforded by another potentially free being. The possibility of self-understanding depends on one's access to the perspective of another, who can confirm one's freedom. Through the master–slave dialectic, Hegel provided Beauvoir's generation with a way to understand both conflict with other freedoms and our essential need for the other. He provided both an explanation of conflict and an optimistic account of conflict overcome.

Beauvoir: Between Sartre and Merleau-Ponty

The concerns of Beauvoir's generation, then, were the twin problems of the body and the other, problems bequeathed to them by Descartes. Through the influence of such thinkers as Bergson, Marcel, and Husserl,[24] Beauvoir and her contemporaries were all responding to the lasting Cartesian legacy, countering the sovereign subject of his thought with the sense of being in the world and necessarily bound up with others. Sartre, Merleau-Ponty, and Beauvoir are linked in their opposition to the perspective of the detached observer, what they called the *pensée de survol*, as a way of doing philosophy. As Sonia Kruks persuasively argues, they are all engaged in attempting to overcome the subject–object dualism by beginning with the experience of the body.[25] Their fundamental claim is that all consciousness must be manifested in a body, that is, must be embodied or situated. While situation is a broader concept than embodiment, encompassing the givens of one's past and environment, embodiment is a fundamental aspect of one's situation: Our body is in fact a necessary precondition for a past and an environment. It is our most intimate facticity. For Sartre, Merleau-Ponty, and Beauvoir alike, philosophy must begin from the body-as-lived, a more primordial, prereflective experience of the body than the cognitive understanding of the body-as-object. The body, as Beauvoir would later argue quite explicitly in *The Second Sex*, is a point of view on the world, as well as being an object in the world.

For all three thinkers, Husserl's reembodiment of the subject formed the immediate point of departure, though each took his thought in a slightly different direction. The differences between Sartre and Merleau-Ponty in this respect are clear; Beauvoir comments on them in her 1945 review of Merleau-Ponty's *Phenomenology of Perception*:

> While Sartre, in *Being and Nothingness*, emphasizes above all the opposition of the for-itself and the in-itself, the nihilating power of consciousness (*l'esprit*) in the face of being and its absolute freedom, Merleau-Ponty in contrast applies himself to describing the concrete character of the subject who is never, according to him, a pure for-itself.[26]

As Beauvoir notes, while Sartre begins from the idea of freedom-in-situation (the fact that the for-itself, as human consciousness, always exists in a body, and in a particular place and time), his main aim is to articulate the "absolute freedom" of human consciousness in relation to that situation: its power to constitute the meaning of its own situation. In contrast to Sartre's "naked" for-itself, Beauvoir describes Merleau-Ponty's embodied subject as one in which consciousness is lived through a body that immerses the subject in the world.[27] Beauvoir recognizes that the body is crucial for Merleau-Ponty; she writes that for him, consciousness is "engorged with the sensible," and the intimate relation between consciousness and the temporally/spatially lived body means that consciousness can never be absolutely free in relation to the world.[28] Merleau-Ponty's subject is, in contrast to Sartre's, a situated and conditioned freedom. While Beauvoir praises Merleau-Ponty's work in her review, she refrains from making any explicit judgment on the differences she has noted between him and Sartre.[29] We shall see that her work of the 1940s was an attempt to trace her own path between the two positions she describes them as holding. Sartre's focus on the Absolute Subject led him to emphasize separation and to interpret the relation between self and other as inevitably one of domination and hostility. Merleau-Ponty's embodied subject is thoroughly intersubjective and allows for reciprocity. Beauvoir would, in her ethical essays, try to do justice both to our existence as separate freedoms and the inescapable fact of our inherence in a situation and among others. By the time she wrote *The Second Sex*, Beauvoir had found her route between Sartre and Merleau-Ponty: In her analysis of the lived body, she would be attentive to both the dangers of domination and the possibility of generosity.

Coming of Age

In her two philosophical essays, we can see Beauvoir working out the themes that preoccupied her generation. Above all, perhaps, she is concerned in this period by the problem of the other, and this is reflected most clearly in *Pyrrhus et Cinéas*. In her first essay on ethics, Beauvoir develops her conception of freedom, pushing beyond her starting point in Sartre's thought to argue for a notion of freedom that would stress our connectedness rather than our individual being. Only once she had redefined freedom in this way, could she make freedom the basis for an ethical precept: that to will oneself free also requires that we will others free.

This development becomes clearer when we read the essays alongside Beauvoir's memoirs and letters of this period. Beauvoir's writing presents a peculiar challenge to the interpreter because she blurred the boundaries of genre—writing pieces that are both literary and essaylike—and disrupted the distinction between her personal life and her work.[30] It is in part because she made her personal experiences so public and presented them as part of her work that it is appropriate to draw on those experiences in interpreting her philosophy. Rather than reduce her philosophy to the expression of personal difficulties or personality traits, I examine one formative period in her life, and consider how she retrospectively reconstructed that period in her memoirs, to shed some light on the development of her ethics. I relate Beauvoir's philosophy not to the literal events of her life in this period, but to her commentary on them and evaluation of them. The memoirs themselves are not transparent or naive accounts of her experiences, but are very self-conscious and highly structured narratives. For Beauvoir, autobiography has a function far beyond a mere retelling of events; it functions as an integral part of her ethical project. Her memoirs are highly structured pieces that describe her moral trajectory through a retrospectively constructed life story in order to present a model moral coming-of-age story. Beauvoir presents her own coming of age as an assumption of ambiguity, in the form of her encounter with history and mortality.[31]

Beauvoir's memoir of this period, *The Prime of Life* (not written until 1960), considers the theme of having to come to terms with the existence of others. In *The Prime of Life*, this ethical imperative is presented as part of Beauvoir's own coming of age. In her retelling of her own life, Beauvoir presents a picture of ethical childhood and ethical maturity. Her life is presented as a moral lesson that parallels the developments in her writing through this period. *The Prime of Life* covers from the time Beauvoir turned twenty until the end of the Second World War, but the period I am concerned with is the first winter of the war, 1940–1941. At this time, the thirty-one-year-old Beauvoir was revising her first published novel, *l'Invitée*, which she had been working on with some difficulty since 1938. She was also living in occupied Paris.

What is most striking about the way in which Beauvoir would reconstruct the Occupation period later in her memoirs is that it is this period in which she describes herself becoming—somewhat painfully—an adult. She does not, in her memoirs, attain adult status where one might expect, when, at the age of twenty, having completed her education and met her life companion, she had literally and symbolically left her parent's house.[32] Instead, the transition to adulthood comes, in Beauvoir's own telling, over a decade later, when the pressure of world events forced Beauvoir to recognize her connection with the outside world. As Beauvoir describes it, becoming an adult required her to relinquish her illusion of sovereign freedom—an illusion that denied the perspectives of others. Tellingly, Beauvoir describes her ethical maturity as a realization that she was both a freedom embodied and a self among others.

Beauvoir's life until this point had given her a surprisingly strong sense of autonomy. She was able to believe that the events of her life were unfolding according to her will, since no major setback had occurred to give the lie to that illusion. She and Sartre were able to maintain a sense of controlling their own small world, in part because their choice of profession and lifestyle allowed them to. Beauvoir writes of Sartre and herself that in the period after the Sorbonne and before the war, they were like "two little elves"; feeling themselves to be enclosed in their own small world, and unaffected by events around them, they indulged in the illusion of their own absolute freedom. As Beauvoir writes: "At every level, we failed to face the weight of reality, we imagined ourselves to be wholly independent agents . . . no external hazard had ever compelled us to go against our own natural inclinations."[33] During this time, Beauvoir was preoccupied with the first challenge to her sense that she could order and control all the events of her life when she and Sartre entered into an intense and emotional trio with a student of Beauvoir's. For the first time, Beauvoir felt herself faced with a challenge to her own perspective on herself and found herself "looked at with alien eyes . . . transformed into an *object* that might be either idol or enemy."[34] She was forced to face a truth, she writes with some self-mockery, "which hitherto . . . [she] had been at considerable pains to avoid—that other people existed, exactly as [she] did, and with just as much *évidence* in their favour."[35] Beauvoir had finally realized that she was not "a completely autonomous, sovereign being in a world designed primarily for her benefit."[36]

This recognition of herself as an object for others is echoed, in Beauvoir's text, by her recognition of herself as embodied, when she recounts her experience of serious illness in the same year. Beauvoir writes about her illness as a recognition of mortality and as a recognition of the self as a thing in the eyes of others. She was, she writes, "stripped of her personal existence" and reduced to the generality of the body; she had abruptly become the "other people" that sickness, accidents, and misfortunes happen to.[37] Beauvoir's account of her illness is of a sudden recognition of the weight of external reality—not, as in the case of the trio, in the form of others' perspectives, but the weight of the body itself. She felt herself to be losing her individuality as she was reduced to her flesh, acutely aware of her mortality, an undifferentiated part of species life. She describes this realization as crucial in forcing her to shed her illusions of absolute freedom.[38]

But it was the war that really brought the reality of others home. The war, and the experience of living through the Nazi occupation of Paris, affected Beauvoir deeply. In her memoir Beauvoir writes that she was slowly abandoning the "quasi-solipsism and illusory autonomy"[39] she had cherished when she had graduated from the Sorbonne and begun her own life. The experience of the trio had forced her to recognize the fact of others' existence, but only in her personal relations. When the war could finally be neither avoided nor denied, the reality that she was not fully the author of her own life forced itself upon her. The war broke in upon not only her sense of autonomy, but also her defiantly enclosed world. She had been pursuing, she writes, a solipsistic project of personal happiness, one that she carried on as long as possible, despite the increasingly clear inevitability of the war. With the start of the war, "suddenly, History burst over me, and I dissolved into fragments. I woke to find myself scattered over the four quarters of the globe, linked by every nerve in me to each and every other individual."[40] As Jo-Anne Pilardi argues, for Beauvoir, History refers not to "a linear succession of events of a series of causes and effects," but to "a complexity of relationships." Beauvoir came to recognize herself as a historical being in the sense that her life, like any life, was "part of a world, a community of individuals, and a flow of activity which is not entirely in one's control."[41] Beauvoir had belatedly discovered her embodied connection to the world, in an intense and emotional way. Her philosophical and literary work of the next decade would be dedicated to working out its implications. Having ceased to regard her life as an autonomous and self-sufficient project, she had to "rediscover her links with the universe," and for this she looked to Hegel.[42]

At the beginning of the occupation of Paris, Beauvoir was reading Hegel for three hours daily at the *Bibliothèque Nationale*. As she tells Sartre in her letters to him, reading the *Phenomenology of Spirit* faithfully from two to five every afternoon, she was "rediscovering philosophy."[43] Beauvoir looked to Hegel for some consolation, some sense that the violence of the war wasn't simply futile. She found solace, in the midst of the "immense collective adventure" that was the war, in the idea she drew from Hegel that each individual destiny is a "moment of the total becoming—in which the whole past culminates and which is effectively linked to the whole future" and that individual sacrifices are thus redeemed from the perspective of universal life. She insists, in her letters to Sartre, that this perspective, which both the war and Hegel have taught her is not absurd, allows for the possibility of optimism.[44]

She would, however, soon reject the "false optimism" of the ultimate reconciliation of individual differences in Absolute knowledge promised by

Hegel's system. In her memoir she recalls a conversation with Raymond Queneau about Hegel's "end of history," when all individual differences would be reconciled. But what, Beauvoir asked, if I have a pain in my foot? We shall have pain in your foot, was the answer.[45] The example is instructive: For Beauvoir, individual pain and suffering must remain individual, intense, and to some degree incommunicable. The fact of our individual finality, and the suffering that accompanies it, cannot be redeemed as a moment of a total becoming. My own death remains a scandal for me in a way that it isn't for an observer. Because Beauvoir refuses to transcend the subjective, individual perspective toward Hegel's universalism, separation from and conflict with others always remain possibilities. Conflict is only a possibility, though, not an inevitability: As we will see, a mood of optimism and joy remains in her ethics, in contrast to the "despair and gloom" with which she charged Sartre.[46] Perhaps more importantly, the sense of human connection that the war and Hegel instilled in her remained as she developed her ethics: As she noted in her journal and in her letters to Sartre, Hegel had led her to the realization that man was embedded in a social dimension.[47]

Reading Hegel, perhaps particularly in the context of the war, revealed to her the intimate and indissoluble link between identity and alterity, or the self and the other. It revealed to her that we are not independent but rather bound up in our very being with the other. With this interdependence arises the possibility of oppression, but also the potential to overcome hostility through reciprocal recognition. We shall see that Beauvoir counters Sartre's despair and pessimism about the possibility of nonoppressive relations with Hegel's optimism and joy but that she eventually moves away from Hegel's resolution as well, in a direction that preserves the difference of the ethical other rather than incorporating and effacing difference as Hegel's reciprocal recognition does.

Beauvoir's turn to Hegel marks her first real recognition of human interdependence and her attempts to come to grips with its implications for her profoundly individualistic outlook. It took Beauvoir some time to come to grips in this way. Hegel's ultimate reconciliation of differences and restoration of individual sacrifices consoled her in the bleakest period, but she was soon disillusioned and had to work out her own response to the problem of her relation with others—a philosophical problem for her whole generation, and one with particular emotional resonance in her own case. She describes herself, in the postwar years, as abandoning her illusion that her freedom was sovereign and recognizing that her freedom was dependent on the freedom of others. She had, ethically, come of age. As she would later write, "the war had effected a decisive conversion."[48] Beauvoir's choice of the word *conver-*

sion is telling: The philosophical implications of this conversion would provide the focus for both *Pyrrhus et Cinéas* and *The Ethics of Ambiguity*.

Pyhrrus et Cinéas: Freedoms Are Interdependent

Beauvoir undertook *Pyrrhus et Cinéas* after having been asked one day in a café if she, like Sartre, was an *existentialist*, a term, she writes in *The Prime of Life*, that had recently been coined by Marcel.[49] Without being at all sure of the meaning of this new label, she began to write an essay for an anthology of existentialist writings that would "provide existentialist morals with a positive content."[50] The passage in Beauvoir's memoirs in which she describes the argument of *Pyrrhus et Cinéas* attests to Beauvoir's ambivalent relationship to Sartre's philosophy: While she declares that she initially turned down the assignment because she did not see how she could add anything to Sartre's *Being and Nothingness*, she also describes the essay as an attempt "to reconcile Sartre's ideas with views [she] had upheld against him in various lengthy discussions" about the "relationship between situation and freedom."[51] While Sartre held that freedom is a given, the very "essence of existence," Beauvoir insisted that "actual concrete possibilities vary,"[52] and that people's different situations could constrain and limit their freedom:

> I maintained that from the perspective of freedom as Sartre defined it—that is, an active transcendence of some given context rather than mere stoic resignation—not every situation was equally valid: what kind of transcendence could a woman shut up in a harem achieve? Sartre replied that even such a cloistered existence could be lived in several quite different ways.[53]

Sartre is right, of course, to claim that there are choices that can be made in even quite constraining circumstances. But Beauvoir is absolutely right—how can you call this freedom? These discussions, unresolved in 1940, haunt Beauvoir's 1943 essay.[54] Moreover, this is no minor disagreement: Sartre's conception of ontological freedom as absolute lies at the heart of his philosophical system in *Being and Nothingness*. Beauvoir's and Sartre's disagreement on the nature of freedom is also crucial to my analysis here, since it was by recognizing the inadequacy of Sartre's conception of freedom to provide the basis for an ethics that she was able to develop her own ideas.

The essay opens with a dialogue, as recounted by Plutarch, between the military adventurer Pyrrhus, King of Epirus, and Cinéas, his advisor. The two men are discussing Pyrrhus's plans to conquer the world. As Pyrrhus outlines each distinct conquest—Greece, Africa, Asia—Cinéas responds with a slightly mocking "And after that?" One conquest inevitably leads to another;

after conquering Greece, Pyrrhus will move on to Africa, to Asia, to the world. When his list has finally reached its end, Pyrrhus responds to Cinéas's insistent "and then?" with a slightly deflated "Ah, then I will rest." "Why not," replies Cinéas, "rest to begin with?"[55]

Beauvoir's essay recasts the problem. Why should we act if each separate task only leads to another to be undertaken? Doesn't the fact that each goal achieved simply brings another into being make all action futile? Why act at all? Why not, as Cinéas asks, just rest to begin with? Beauvoir's immediate answer is, following Sartre, on the level of ontology. She argues that it is simply impossible not to act, at least if inaction in any given situation is also a choice, and thus, in some sense, an act. To be human is to will, to act, and to engage in new projects: "As long as I am alive, Cinéas harasses me in vain when he says 'And afterwards? What for?' In spite of everything, the heart beats, the hand stretches out, new projects are born and push me forward."[56] "Why act?" is a pointless question since we are always inevitably acting. Moreover, actions cannot be considered futile just because the ends they aim at are not absolute. Certainly, we pose an end only to surpass it in undertaking a new project, but that doesn't make the end itself futile.

But, as I interpret the essay, Beauvoir addresses ontology only in order to get to her true concerns in the essay, which are ethical. She is not primarily interested in the inevitability of action, but in the implications of this for our relationships with others. She wants not only to convince us that action is not futile but is rather the essence of freedom, but also that recognizing this will give direction to our undertakings and give us a way to gauge the legitimacy of our projects. We must act, but we must also decide what our project should be. Voltaire's Candide tells us that we must cultivate our gardens, but what, Beauvoir asks, are the dimensions of my garden?[57] She begins to focus on what the legitimate bounds of our projects are and how we can justify one project over another. What should our relations with others and with their projects be? What do we owe others? What makes up our bond with them? We will see that as Beauvoir moves from her Sartrean starting point to consider its ethical implications, she doesn't simply reproduce Sartre's concepts of freedom or the subject but begins to move beyond them. Though she argues, following Sartre, that we are transcendent freedoms and that our freedom is individual or separate, she does not go on to conclude, as did Sartre, that our encounters with others must inevitably be hostile or indifferent.[58] Instead, as I show, she moves in a new direction, drawing out the implications of the interdependence of separated freedoms and calling for generosity in our relationships with others.

Pyhrrus et Cinéas is at first, however, an attempt to define an existential ethics and thus Beauvoir begins with the Sartrean understanding of the self as a transcendent freedom. Freedom, for Sartre, is transcendence, or the negation of a given tradition, a given world. If freedom is simply this power to nihilate what is, then consciousness is, in a sense, nothingness, in contrast to the plenitude of things.

If consciousness is nothing in itself, it is consciousness of something, always referring to an object standing beyond it.[59] Sartre uses the phenomenological principle of intentionality to argue that there is a radical separation between consciousness and its object, or between consciousness and the world. Consciousness itself is nothing, and exists only in a relation or as an opening to things that have being. Thus Sartre's ontology begins with the distinction between two modes of being, *being-for-itself*, or conscious being, and *being-in-itself*, or nonconscious being. Conscious being, or being-for-itself, is the uncaused upsurge of freedom in the world, radically distinct from the realm of things governed by laws of causality, or being-in-itself. Nothing from "outside" it, nothing from the realm of being-in-itself can cause consciousness to come into being; consciousness is, literally, nothing. It is an active nothingness or negativity; the power to put things into question and to transcend them: "The For-itself, in fact, is nothing but the pure nihilation of the In-itself."[60] In this sense, Sartre, and following him, Beauvoir, argues that individuals, the incarnation of conscious being, are always a reflection on themselves, always "at a distance"—judging, perceiving, choosing—from what they are.

This conception of the for-itself as a nihilating freedom means that what we are is always inseparable from what we think of ourselves as being and what we make of ourselves through our actions. Though Sartre recognizes that there are many things that are true of us despite what we may think of them (such as our sex, race, or nationality), these aspects of our facticity, the givens of our situation, can never determine how we respond to them. Nothing determines how the free consciousness exists in its situation. My freedom lies in how I think about or assume my situation and how I freely constitute its meaning. Sartre's clearest example of this is that of the climber facing the crag of rock: This huge rock is an obstacle to the one who aims to move it; to the person whose project is to climb the rock and admire the landscape, the rock is an aid. The climber constitutes the meaning of the rock as something to be climbed.[61]

Beauvoir follows Sartre in arguing that we cannot but be free and express this freedom: to deny it is bad faith, and to recognize it is authenticity. We are inevitably choosing and acting, projecting ourselves into the world as a freedom, or as a project. She stresses, however, the way our original freedom or spontaneity involves us in the world and expresses our relation to the world, to the future and to others. As a freedom, I project myself toward others through and as a project: "I am not first a thing, but a spontaneity which desires, which loves, which wants, and which acts."[62] A refusal to be involved with others is impossible. Beauvoir writes that to try to evade the continual transcendence of the self toward the world is futile; we are inevitably engaged in a project, in choosing, and thus our being presupposes some involvement with the world: Man, Beauvoir writes, "is constituitively oriented toward things other than himself."[63] And to be engaged in the world means to be involved with others:

> It is because my subjectivity is not inertia, a withdrawing into itself, a separation, but on the contrary a movement toward the other, that the indifference between the other and myself is abolished and I can call the other mine; the bond that unites me to the other I alone can create; I create it by the fact that I am not first a thing, but a projecting of myself towards the other, a transcendence.[64]

However, my projects and the projects of others will sometimes be in conflict. Individual freedoms are neither unified nor inevitably opposed, but they are separate.[65] Beauvoir argues that we cannot find preexisting grounds for solidarity with others. Again her argument here follows Sartre's. She considers and finds lacking various arguments for a priori solidarity: a transcendent God, a belief in Humanity, in devotion to a cause or a particular other. Solidarity must be won; it is not given, but neither is it impossible: "It is in projecting himself into the world that a man situates himself in situating other men around him."[66]

Sartre's argument assumes that since we are individual freedoms, and our projects are separate, our relation to the other is inevitably hostile. In Being and Nothingness, the other is first revealed to me as an object of my consciousness, as a being-in-itself. However, when the other looks at me, Sartre argues, I become aware of that other as a center of subjectivity, a consciousness, that is, as a being-for-itself. I also become aware that in the gaze of this other I am transformed into an object, a being for the other, part of a situation constituted by this foreign consciousness.[67] The other, as a freedom, a transcendent being, objectifies me and threatens me, threatens to transcend my transcendence. Since as a transcendent consciousness I constitute the meaning of my own situation, the existence of another center of subjectivity, another constituting consciousness, can only be a threat. Sartre plays out the conflict of consciousnesses, in which each consciousness desires the death of the other, as he has drawn it from Hegel.[68] For Sartre, however, the relation to others structured by the look has no resolution. According to his conception of the self as an absolute freedom, a constituting subject, there is no possibility of bonds with others, or rather, the only bonds possible are those of hatred, subjugation, and dominance.[69]

Beauvoir also recognizes the dual nature of our existence in the world, the fact that we exist for the other as an object and for ourselves as subject:

> We have seen that man is present in the world in two ways. He is an object, a given which is surpassed by other transcendences; and he is himself a transcendence which thrusts itself toward the future.[70]

However, at this point, Beauvoir does not go on to make Sartre's argument about the hostility of freedoms, instead developing her own argument about the interdependence of freedoms and our need for free recognition of our project by others. She doesn't contest Sartre's argument directly, but quietly sidesteps it by shifting her consideration of freedom from ontological freedom, or the original upsurge of consciousness in the world, to freedom as it is expressed in concrete projects. We are, paradoxically, both radically separate freedoms and in need of others to recognize our freedom and justify our actions:

> Only the other can create a need for that which we give him; every appeal, every demand comes from his freedom; for the object I have created to appear as a good, the other must make it his own: thus I am justified in having created it.[71]

Human freedoms are thus separate, but they are also interdependent. My freedom, or project, is meaningless unless it is recognized and taken up by another. Beauvoir makes this argument by making a connection between my project and a future. My project loses meaning, becomes swallowed by contingency, if it has no future. To have a future, it must be taken up by others and used as a starting point for their own free projects:

> And thus my situation in the face of the other: men are free and I am thrown into the world among these strange freedoms. I need them, for once I have surpassed my own goals, my acts will fall back upon themselves inert and useless if they are not carried forward by new projects toward a new future.[72]

My project becomes futile not, she argues, in the face of my inevitable death, but in the possibility of the end of the world.[73] That is, in a depopulated world I would be paralyzed by the futility of all my actions. I need another freedom to recognize my project and in taking it up, give it a future. I need someone to respond to my appeal and thus become my ally. I cannot compel this recognition or demand it; for free recognition of my own project to come into being, there must be other freedoms with the capacity to make my attainments the point of departure for their own projects. Indeed, I need a multiplicity of freedoms to take up my project and give it a future and thus a meaning, a multiplicity of people before me who can respond to my appeal, who can "accompany my transcendence," people whose liberty isn't consumed in fighting sickness, ignorance, and misery.[74]

This is, for Beauvoir, why willing my own freedom (choosing to undertake concrete projects on the basis of the original upsurge of my being) also implies that I must will others free. The interdependence of freedoms and the connection between freedom and an open future can give us guidance in undertaking our projects. I have a basis for ethics in gauging the effects of my actions on others' situations: My acts either increase or decrease their possibility of free action and choice. And of course the converse is also true: The acts of others help to structure the situation that I live out, and I need others to create a situation in which I can act freely in the world. Beauvoir argues that all situations are not equal from the point of view of freedom: Some, whose liberty is "consumed" in a fight for survival, cannot either make or respond to an appeal. My project should be to ensure that others have the possibility of freedom, so that they can respond to the appeal of my freedom and thus become my allies.

It would seem that this ethic is not a very far-reaching one. Why, if I have some allies who are able to accompany my transcendence, should I concern myself with all or even any others? Beauvoir addresses this in her discussion of violence. She argues that we should not resort to violence lightly, for if I use violence against one man, he will no longer be my peer, and I need others to be my peers.[75] If I do violence to all men, I depopulate the world, but even if I oppress only one man, "in him all humanity appears as pure thing."[76] That is, violence and oppression—the refusal to will others free by creating the conditions they need to make their freedom effective—either actively practiced or simply tolerated, lessens us all.[77]

The distinction Beauvoir makes here between those whose liberty is consumed and those who, because of their material situation, can "accompany my transcendence" and give me the free recognition that I require is not one that could be made from within Sartre's vision of absolute freedom in *Being and Nothingness*, and it signals the distance that Beauvoir has traveled from her Sartrean starting point. For according to Sartre, there is no situation in which one could say that liberty had been consumed: Because the free consciousness constitutes the meaning of its situation, all situations—or material conditions—are equal from the point of view of freedom. This is because for Sartre freedom does not refer to the success of our projects in the world but simply to our capacity to sustain an active project: to live out a situation in a number of different ways. As Beauvoir shifts her focus to the ways in which freedom must be made concrete in the world and is embodied, she is also forced to recognize that situation—one's body, one's past, the material conditions of one's life—must condition freedom.[78]

This was a recognition that would be crucial for *The Second Sex*, with its condemnation of the many ways in which women's freedom has been consumed and women have been denied an open future. In *Pyrrhus et Cinéas*, however, its implications are not fully explored. Beauvoir falls back on a Cartesian and Sartrean distinction between power and freedom that fits only uneasily with this suggestion that freedom can be consumed.[79] We can, Beauvoir states, only touch the outside of another's freedom, their capacity to undertake concrete projects in the world, when we withhold opportunities from them, imprison them or harm them. We can lessen their power, but not touch the freedom (and here she refers to ontological freedom) that is their original and spontaneous upsurge toward the world. In a sense, then, her analysis is not fully developed here. In *The Ethics of Ambiguity*, and later in *The Second Sex*, the idea of freedom consumed will be developed into a more nuanced conception of the dynamics of mystification.[80]

Beauvoir develops her argument to show that existentialism does provide grounds for choosing one course of action over another. What I want to highlight about her analysis, however, is that her sense of the self is quite distinct from Sartre's: Rather than our relation with the other being dominated by the Look, and inevitably a relation of hostility, we are open to the other, because we need the other to recognize and take up our projects. We need others to give us a future by responding to the appeal of our freedom. And conversely we are vulnerable to the other, to a refusal of recognition, and a closing of the future. The self is interdependent rather than independent.[81] This sense of our fundamental interdependence would be enriched and deepened in *The Ethics of Ambiguity*.

The Ethics of Ambiguity: Freedom and Conversion

By the time Beauvoir wrote *The Ethics of Ambiguity*, she publicly identified herself more clearly as an existentialist, and specifically as a Sartrean one. The essay was to be a defense of some of Sartre's ideas that she felt were being misunderstood and distorted in France and would provide the ethics that Sartre had promised in the last few pages of *Being and Nothingness*.[82] Beauvoir wrote to combat the popular charge that existentialism as a philosophy provided a license to do anything and that its conception of freedom could provide no moral code of conduct.[83] As she wrote in her memoirs, "in my opinion it was possible to base a morality on *Being and Nothingness*, if one converted the vain desire to be into an assumption of existence."[84] She wrote, then, specifically to show that the ontology Sartre had developed in *Being and Nothingness* could be the ground of an ethics. The development of this ethics, however, would take her further from her starting point in Sartrean thought than she had traveled in *Pyrrhus et Cinéas*. The key concepts in that development are the ambiguity of the human condition and the need to assume that ambiguity through the conversion of the desire to be into a desire to reveal being.

In one respect, *The Ethics of Ambiguity* simply pushes the argument of *Pyrrhus et Cinéas* further. In it, Beauvoir develops more fully the conception of freedom as "concrete possibility" with which Sartre had disagreed, arguing that freedoms are interdependent. Our freedom is both dependent on the freedom of others and vulnerable to the actions of others. This interdependence of freedom, she writes, "explains why oppression is possible, and why it is hateful."[85] In making this analysis, Beauvoir again shifts her ground from the ontological to the political, in order to make an ethics possible. Indeed, Beauvoir moved away from her starting point in Sartre's thought precisely because of the demands of an ethics. The analysis of oppression that Beauvoir provides in *The Ethics of Ambiguity* is not one that would have been possible to make had Beauvoir remained strictly within the terms of Sartre's philosophy. Her failure to do so was more fruitful than her success might have been, for in quietly moving away from Sartre's ontology, Beauvoir was able to lay the foundation for her thinking in *The Second Sex*.

But in another respect the argument of *The Ethics of Ambiguity* shifts decisively away from her earlier work in *Pyrrhus et Cinéas*. She argues that the possibility of ethical relations with others will require a conversion, and she pursues the implications of this conversion for our relations with others.[86] She also develops the idea of ambiguity, now not only the sense of being at once an individual freedom and an object in the worlds of others—the problem she was focused on in *Pyrrhus et Cinéas*—but also the ambiguity of being both freedom, or consciousness, and flesh: a body-subject. When she begins to consider the implications of this ambiguity and to consider what it would mean to assume and live out this ambiguity, she is led to a most un-Sartrean conclusion, and her thought takes a direction that alters our understanding of the free project, revealing both its drive to mastery and its ultimate limits and failure. Indeed, she is led to consider the absolute subject as an immature response to the freedom of others and to question the project's orientation to the future, to time, and to progress as implicated in the drive to mastery.

Ambiguity

The ethics that Beauvoir developed in *The Ethics of Ambiguity* and that provides the structure for *The Second Sex* centers on the idea of ambiguity. Ambiguity refers to two contradictory aspects of the human experience that have equal weight. Beauvoir describes the ambiguity of our condition in a number of ways, but fundamentally it is the ambiguity of being and becoming: We are transcendent freedoms who live this transcendence in a situation. We project ourselves into the future but always on the basis of the givens of our situation: our body, our past. Assuming our ambiguity is a matter of assuming ourselves as both transcendent and immanent at once. We are, Beauvoir writes, both a consciousness, an internality, and a thing; both a freedom and a body that is born to die. This is the ambiguity of our condition as embodied freedoms or embodied subjects. Beauvoir writes (citing Montaigne) that the "tragic ambivalence" or ambiguity of human existence is that "the continuous work of our life is to build death."[87] The tragic aspect of the ambiguity of existence stems not from the fact of our death itself but from our awareness of it: Awareness of death implies an awareness of our own material existence as bodies. "Man knows and thinks this tragic ambivalence which the animal and the plant merely undergo."[88] We feel ourselves to be infinite freedoms, but are also aware of the limitations and frailties of our bodies and their inevitable end. Humans are thus in a peculiar position among living creatures: able to escape from our condition without being free of it. As consciousness we experience an escape from the brute reality of the world, but we are still a part of the world: "he asserts himself as a pure internality against which no external power can take hold, and he also experiences himself as a thing crushed by the dark weight of other things."[89]

This quote illustrates the point at which the first aspect of ambiguity connects to the second.[90] We experience ambiguity not only as a consciousness embodied, but also as an individual freedom at the heart of a collectivity. As such, we experience ourselves as both a unique subject and an object-for-others. We know ourselves, as individual freedoms, to be the "end to which all action should be subordinated," and recognize at the same time that the "exigencies of action force [us] to treat each other as instruments or obstacles, as means."[91] The more widespread our mastery of the world becomes, the more we "find [ourselves] crushed by uncontrollable forces,"[92] and the more we find this mastery, and the harmony it promises, undermined.

Ambiguity for Beauvoir is complex: it characterizes our relation to the world, others, our bodies, and time. Beauvoir argues that philosophy has always reflected the difficulty the human subject has in accepting this ambiguity. Philosophies, she claims—dualist, idealist, materialist—have tried to "reduce mind to matter or to absorb matter into mind."[93] Denial of ambiguity can take a number of forms: "denying death, either by integrating it with life or by promising man immortality" or denying life, "considering it as a veil of illusion beneath which is hidden the truth of Nirvana,"[94] "making oneself pure inwardness or pure externality, escaping from the sensible world or by being engulfed in it, by yielding to eternity or enclosing oneself in the pure moment."[95]

The main thrust of Beauvoir's argument in *The Ethics of Ambiguity* is that assuming, or accepting, ontological ambiguity is the basis of ethical action. Her ethical imperative is that we assume our fundamental ambiguity: "To attain his truth, man must not attempt to dispel the ambiguity of his being, but on the contrary, accept the task of realizing it."[96] She distinguishes her injunction that we "affirm the irreducible character of ambiguity"[97] from Hegel's attempt to reconcile all of the aspects of man's condition in the manifestation of Spirit in the world. In this sense she sides against Hegel's optimism, describing it as one of a number of "reasonable metaphysics [and] consoling ethics" that "choose to leave in the shadow certain troubling aspects of a too complex situation" and in the end "only accentuate the disorder from which we suffer."[98] Beauvoir argues that existentialism is the only philosophy to account for this irreducible ambiguity, since it conceives of man as "the being whose being is not to be, that subjectivity which realizes itself only as a presence in the world."[99] As embodied, we are a unique perspective on the world, but we are also an object among others.

The Desire to Be

Sartre had, of course, already defined the human situation as ambiguous in *Being and Nothingness*. Because we are freedom-in-situation, there are objective and contingent facts in our situation that we cannot change. On the other hand, he had also argued that this facticity does not condition freedom at all.[100] We cannot help but act, make free choices, and thereby make ourselves. As we make ourselves we aim at goals and create ourselves as if we were giving ourselves an essence, making of ourselves a definable object. Nevertheless, we remain a subject, freely choosing. In choosing ourselves, we are in a sense aspiring to be God: We aim to be a being with an essence, a necessary being, but still entirely free and creative; both the source and ground of our values. Man tries to make himself a synthesis of the for-itself and in-itself, to make himself a God, and inevitably fails to be. Beauvoir, following Sartre, describes this impossible task as a "useless passion," since man has no means of becoming the being that he is not.[101]

This desire to be (*désir d'être*) that is man's passion does not, Beauvoir writes, imply unhappiness, but it is inevitably a failure. It is also the source of our bad faith, or capacity to lie to ourselves in hiding our freedom from ourselves. Sartre wrote that the desire to be—the result of our anxiety in the face of our freedom—could be overcome by a conversion, but he did not go on to explore or enlarge on this idea. In Beauvoir's work, however, conversion is a key term that threads through her memoirs, essays, and *The Second Sex*, marking the moment of ethical maturity or moral "coming of age."

Conversion and Coming of Age

In *The Ethics of Ambiguity*, the idea of conversion is embedded in Beauvoir's account of moral coming of age, as it is in her memoirs, but this time presented in a more abstract form.[102] She presents an abstract and idealized picture of childhood and adolescence, using it not as an empirical description but as a heuristic model to argue that our desire to be isn't the inevitable result of our ontology, as it is for Sartre, but is the result of a nostalgia for childhood, and that a moral conversion is made possible by the opportunities opened to us in adolescence.

The Desire to Be and Nostalgia for Childhood

Beauvoir argues that the freedom of children is hidden from them. In existentialist terms, they live in a serious world in which they experience themselves as having being in the eyes of others.[103] Their parents' gaze, their parents' reactions, and the world set up around them hides their freedom and allows them to delight in their being. Thus, the situation of childhood satisfies and fulfills the desire to be. Children exist in the eyes of others, who guarantee their sense of identity, and the values that spring up around them seem to be simply and objectively there. These values seem to have their origins outside, in the world of the adults; they come down as rules from God:

> The child's situation is characterized by his finding himself cast into a universe which he has not helped to establish, which has been fashioned without him, and which appears to him as an absolute to which he can only submit. In his eyes, human inventions, words, customs and values are given facts, as inevitable as the sky and the trees.[104]

Though the limitations of the child's world can be experienced in frustration, they are the condition of his eventual realization of his freedom. The child is able to experience his subjectivity through play. Within the given limits of the serious world, the child feels himself happily irresponsible: He pursues his goals without feeling the weight of his freedom, only its joy, because the domain open to his subjectivity is insignificant and limited.[105] The child knows the joys, but not the risks, implied by human freedom: "Even when the joy of existing is strongest, when the child abandons himself to it, he feels himself protected against the risk of existence by the ceiling which human generations have built over his head."[106] He can do as he likes: Since it is only play, he can't make a dent in the serene order of this world that existed before him.[107] The limits set by adults to the child's actions prepare him for the time at which he can challenge the givens of the adult world and feel the efficacy of his actions in the world.[108] As a child, however, this free play of subjectivity within the security of a bounded and given world is a particularly privileged situation. Whatever the frustrations and difficulties of the child's situation, in this sense, Beauvoir argues, childhood is "metaphysically privileged."[109] Whether the world the child experiences is oppressive or benign, he will still experience it as a given.

This is an idealized and romantic portrayal of childhood, in two senses. Certainly, Beauvoir fails to take many of the factors that shape childhood, such as class or gender, into account. She would later recognize her failure to ground her analysis in a more complex account of material conditions as a limitation in her essay.[110] This is a limitation she would address in *The Second Sex*, with its much richer account of the material differences in individuals' situations and its claim that the childhood experiences of many girls don't, in fact, constitute an apprenticeship for freedom, but rather prepare them for a constrained and limited future. In another sense, though, Beauvoir's portrayal of childhood is romantic in that many children, even materially privileged ones, may not experience themselves as secure within a given and bounded world. Beauvoir may be underestimating the extent to which children's imaginative lives are fraught with insecurities and anxieties. Rather than experiencing meaning as secured by their parents, many children imagine themselves responsible for events that are clearly beyond their control.[111] Of course, even if they feel themselves responsible for the world in their imaginative lives, children's lives are constrained in many ways, and Beauvoir is right to claim that adolescence marks the beginning of a wider sphere of concrete freedom for most people.

The Promise of Adolescence

Beauvoir presents adolescence as the moment when freedom is fully revealed: the moment at which the adolescent is first aware of the cracks appearing in the serious world of the adults and he sees that the world around him is made up of human significations. Through the revelation that the values of the adult world are not cast in stone, but are the result of human actions, he begins to sense his own power to disclose the meaning of a situation through his projects.[112] He begins, as Beauvoir writes, to sense that he can make a dent in the world. His own capacity for initiation seems to carry real weight for the first time.

Adolescence is also, importantly, the time at which he begins to exist in time in a different way from when he was a child. The child lives in a world not only circumscribed by the givens of the adult world, but also limited in time. The child lives in the midst of the present moment: "no moral question presents itself to the child as long as he is still incapable of recognizing himself in the past or seeing himself in the future."[113] The adolescent becomes aware of the world as a field of possibilities that appeal to him to choose and becomes aware for the first time that his choices project him into the world and into the future, just as his life is being revealed to him as opening onto a future. The adolescent enters into what Kristeva describes as historical time.[114]

The collapse of the serious world at adolescence is both a deliverance and an abandonment, and it provokes, Beauvoir writes, both joy and confusion.[115] In the serious world the child has the joy of irresponsibility but also the frustration of not being able to make a mark on the world; the child also feels himself to be vaguely menaced by all the things he can't control: "although he was irresponsible, the child also felt himself defenceless before obscure powers which directed the course of things."[116] Adolescence can thus be experienced as a liberation. But of course the collapse of the serious will also provoke anxiety because of the responsibility for the self that is implied in freedom. The adolescent finds himself "cast into a world which is no longer ready-made, which has to be made; he is abandoned, unjustified, the prey of a freedom that is no longer chained up in anything."[117]

In The Ethics of Ambiguity Beauvoir doesn't explore the ways in which different childhood and adolescent experiences would condition adult choices, but her analysis does suggest that our reaction to freedom will depend to some extent on our situation and personal history.[118] Our reaction to the anxieties freedom provokes will depend on what we experience in our childhood and what adolescence opens to us. This new departure in her thought is essential for her analysis in The Second Sex. Childhood is in a sense a preparation for freedom, and adolescence will present us with both anxiety and joy—whether we succumb to one or experience the other will depend on what avenues and what concrete possibilities are opened to us by others at the moment when our freedom is revealed to us and we are first aware of living in time oriented to the future. However, the promise of adolescence is not held out to everyone.

Bad Faith and Mystification

Some people never experience the liberation of feeling their own subjective power to remake the world and are not permitted to see the cracks in the serious world. These are people who in a sense never experience adolescence, because their situation does not offer them the possibilities that adolescence affords. Those who haven't experienced the promise of adolescence—the experience of their own freedom and subjectivity disclosing meanings in the world—experience their situation as a natural condition rather than as a human construct. Beauvoir cites the example of slaves and "women in many civilizations," and "women who have not had in their work an apprenticeship in freedom" as people who can be said to be mystified rather than in bad faith.[119] Beauvoir ascribes this to ignorance and error, and economic and social circumstances, in a word, to situation: "the less economic and social circumstances allow an individual to act upon the world, the more this world appears to him as given."[120]

Keeping someone from the experience of their freedom can be described as keeping them in a child's world, barring them from access to the future: "there are beings whose life slips by in an infantile world because, having been kept in a state of servitude and ignorance, they have no means of breaking the ceiling which is stretched over their heads."[121] There are some situations, she writes, "where the future is radically blocked off,"[122] situations so limited that any positive action is impossible.

People in the oppressive situations Beauvoir is here describing cannot necessarily be judged as being in bad faith.[123] Here we arrive at Beauvoir's clearest divergence from Sartre and one of the most evident ways in which her analysis in The Ethics of Ambiguity provides a foundation for her more developed account of oppression in The Second Sex. Not all those who live in a serious world—who are unaware of their own freedom—can be accused of bad faith. We have to remember the situation of the child. The freedom of the child is hidden from him, and the child delights in the fulfillment of his desire to be because he experiences the values of the adult world as givens that confer on him an identity. The child lives in a serious world but cannot be accused of bad faith because the child has never had access to his freedom: He experiences this situation as a natural condition, and in a sense it is because it is based on his physiological development. But others who are kept from the experience of their freedom, and are forced by their situation to live in a serious world, also cannot be accused of bad faith, and their experience of their situation as natural, their mystification, cannot be justified in any way.

The Possibility of Conversion

One response to the sense of abandonment adolescence provokes is a powerful nostalgia for the certainties of childhood, and Beauvoir argues that as adults, our flight from our own freedom can be understood as this nostalgia getting the better of us. As she cites Descartes: All our unhappiness is the result of our having once been children.[124] The anxiety that freedom provokes in us, Beauvoir suggests, is assuaged by a retreat into a nostalgia for the security of being that we experienced in childhood.[125] Because as children we delighted in our being, as adults we are led to flee the anxieties of freedom for the illusion of being able to recapture the certainty of childhood. The crucial connection is that in childhood, the joy of existing (the irresponsible freedom of the child) coincided with the fulfillment of the desire to be: "the misfortune that comes to man as a result of the fact that he was a child is that his freedom was first concealed from him and that all his life he will be nostalgic for the time when he did not know its exigencies."[126] But there is no going back to childhood; as adults, Beauvoir insists, we will only regain our joy in existing by accepting the failure of our desire to be.

It is this acceptance of the failure of our desire to be that Beauvoir calls a conversion.[127] The desire to be, she writes, is not our only desire. It is contested by the desire to reveal being:

> There is an original type of attachment to being which is not the relationship "wanting to be," but rather "wanting to disclose being." Now, here there is not failure but rather success. . . . It is not granted to him to exist without tending toward this being which he will never be. But it is possible for him to want this tension even with the failure that it involves.[128]

Conversion, then, is an act of assuming the failure of the desire to be. These two moments of our consciousness (of our intentionality, our relation with the world) cannot be separated: It is only through the failure of our desire to be, the failure to regain childhood certainty, that we can experience the joy of revelation.[129] Beauvoir insists that in assuming this failure we will find joy[130]: the joy of generously recognizing intersubjective meanings in the world. It is through our failure to master others or external reality in projecting ourselves toward the world, and in our acceptance of our failure to impose our own meaning on the world to the exclusion of others, that we are able to delight in the disclosure of a world rich with intersubjective meanings—a world revealed to us through multiple freedoms—and recognize that our responsibility to others is to widen the sphere of freedom.

Our interdependence is thus linked to disclosure, since we communicate with each other through the meanings we disclose. The bond with others that it implies "does not immediately reveal itself to everybody."[131] In fact, she writes, the young man first experiencing his subjectivity often perceives only that his freedom is limited by the freedom of others. He wants to be All.[132] The free subjectivity of others—their capacity to constitute meaning—threatens his sense of himself as the sole source of meaning in the world:

> Often the young man perceives only that aspect of his relationship to others whereby others appear as enemies. . . . He sees in every other man, and particularly in those whose existence is asserted with most brilliance, a limit, a condemnation of himself.[133]

Beauvoir associates this immature, adolescent response to the freedom of others with the first moment of Hegel's master–slave dialectic. She might, of course, also have noted its parallel with Sartre's constituting consciousness. Each consciousness desires the death of the other. However, Beauvoir writes, this desire and hatred of the other is naive, and it "immediately struggles against itself"[134] since my freedom also requires the freedom of others:

> By taking the world from me, others also give it to me. . . . To will that there be being is also to will that there be men by and for whom the world is endowed with human significations. One can reveal the world only on a basis revealed by other men.[135]

This is to realize that our freedom depends on a human world, a human past, and a history constructed by other freedoms.[136] The first moment of Hegel's dialectic (and thus also Sartre's constituting consciousness) is linked with a rebellious rejection of the freedom of the other as it is embodied in this past. Beauvoir stresses that subjectivity is linked to the recognition of human meanings already invested in the world.

If we assume the failure of the desire to be, we find that in projecting ourselves into the world and failing to be we have instead revealed being—we have revealed the existence of human meanings in the world and have thus revealed the world as a human world.[137] In the desire to be, fueled by anxiety, we find the inevitable failure of attempts to regain our childhood certainty, but in the desire to reveal being we find delight and joy, and we find our bond with others. The movement from the first moment of intentionality to the second is the basis for an ethics that recognizes the interdependence of freedom and the freedom of the other. It is, as Beauvoir portrays it, the act of growing up, forgoing our nostalgia for the certainties of youth and accepting the tensions and ambiguities inherent in human freedom. It is an ethical coming of age.

Our projecting ourselves into the world is always a way of aiming at being, a being that is never attained, and in this Beauvoir's thinking is identical to Sartre's. There will always remain a possibility of hostility in our relations with others. The difference is that, for Beauvoir, assuming this failure opens us to a new way of existing with others. Another way of saying this is that if our projects always aim to control or master an aspect of external reality, they also always contain an element of failure.

Beauvoir writes that we must accept the ambiguity of being at once free to invest the world with meaning and dependent on others to give meaning to our acts, to carry on or to contest the meaning of our projects. This is the significance of being at once an individual freedom and immersed in a shared world of meanings. We must, Beauvoir writes, be aware of the "risks and the inevitable element of failure involved in any engagement with the world."[138] It is this sense of freedom to initiate without remaining sovereign[139] that led Beauvoir, in *Pyrrhus et Cinéas*, to describe our projection into the world as a risk:

> We depend upon the freedom of the other: he may forget us, misrecognise us, use us for ends which are not our own. . . . What the other creates starting with me will belong to him and not to me. I can act only by assuming the risks of this future; they are the inverse of my finitude and in assuming my finitude I am free.[140]

The anxiety that fuels the desire to be is the familiar existential "angst" we experience in the face of our many possibilities, which is mentioned by Kierkegaard, Heidegger, and Sartre in turn. But Beauvoir's account of our existential reaction to freedom differs from Sartre's in one crucial respect. In Sartre's account, anxiety in the face of our freedom, the desire to be, and the response of bad faith are the almost inevitable result of our ontology; Beauvoir's account suggests in contrast that the bad faith of nostalgia is only one possible reaction to the exigencies of our freedom, and an immature reaction at that. We can succumb to our nostalgia, fleeing from our freedom in a number of ways, or we can face our freedom—that is, assume our failure to be and recognize this failure as a source of joy (the joy of the revelation of being). Whereas, in childhood, joy and delight in our subjectivity had been aligned with the fulfillment of our desire to be and had involved no risk, in adult life the joy of freedom will be realized only if the failure of the desire to be—and the real risks of freedom—are assumed.

The Desire to Be and Others

Mastery

Our response to the freedom we first experience in adolescence, Beauvoir insists, always involves others. If we do succumb to our nostalgia, there are a number of forms that this can take, and much of *The Ethics of Ambiguity* is an outline of various types—the serious man, the adventurer, the passionate man—each of whom serve as an example of a different expression of the bad faith of the desire to be.[141] In each case, Beauvoir is concerned to show us two things: how the desire to be is always a failure, and how our response to our freedom has an ethical dimension, as it always involves us in relations with others.

All these modes of living the desire to be seek to deny freedom by becoming a thing or possessing a thing. The desire to be, it turns out, is implicated in oppressive relations: the serious man and the passionate man, elevating the object of value or desire to the status of an absolute end, treat others as instruments and means to their ends. They sacrifice others for the cause; they seek to possess the other as a thing. Beauvoir reveals that the serious man, the passionate man, and the adventurer are all, in their own ways, implicated in tyranny: their *désir d'être* leads them to treat others not as individual freedoms but as objects. The desire to be is implicated in attempts to master others and the world, to deny and disavow our bond with others and our need for others' freedom. It is, she says, a way of being that avoids the risks involved in being a freedom among freedoms.[142] Oppression is revealed as a result of our denial that our freedom is linked to and dependent on the freedom of others. It is an attempt to maintain the illusions of absolute independence (in relation to others and to the world) and sovereign freedom.

The attitude of the serious is the most common reaction, according to Beauvoir, because it is the most clear route back to the childhood situation; it is the choice to live in an infantile world.[143] The serious man denies his own freedom in favor of a cause or value which he accepts as a given. He hides from himself the subjective origins of his values. The serious man subordinates his own freedom to the cause, but Beauvoir is perhaps even more concerned to reveal the ways in which he thereby also denies the freedom of others: he is as willing to subordinate other freedoms as he is his own to a cause which he insists is paramount. In this sense he is close to a tyrant, and his *désir d'être* manifests itself as a desire to master the external world.[144]

If the serious man stands accused of what might be called the bad faith of immanence (denying his own freedom and thus also that of others), the adventurer is an example of the bad faith of transcendence.[145] The adventurer asserts the value of his own transcendence but at the cost of denying the freedom of others. He freely throws himself into his projects without, in the manner of the serious man, setting up his goal as absolute. At the subjective moment, Beauvoir argues, this is a perfect expression of freedom, and if existentialism were only concerned with this moment of individual freedom, "it would have to regard the adventurer as its perfect hero."[146] Indeed, Beauvoir in her memoirs describes Sartre as an adventurer in this sense when she recounts their relations to others before the war.[147] But by the time she wrote *The Ethics of Ambiguity*, it had become clear to her that this conception of freedom was implicated in oppression. The adventurer's expression of freedom is satisfying only at its subjective moment: The adventurer is a man who thinks that he can assert his own existence without taking into account that of others.[148] Nothing prevents the adventurer from sacrificing others and treating them as instruments, and in this case the adventurer's assertion of his own freedom is also very close to tyranny.[149]

Tyranny and the Body

As Beauvoir investigates it further in *The Ethics of Ambiguity*, the tyranny that denies the freedom of others and reduces them to immanence does so by limiting what their bodies can express, in effect making their bodies express only immanence. Tyranny works by enclosing people in the immanence of their facticity, and their most intimate facticity is the body. Though both *Pyrrhus et Cinéas* and *The Ethics of Ambiguity* are centrally concerned with the relation of situation to freedom, Beauvoir doesn't provide an explicit analysis of the relation of the body to freedom or to subjectivity in her ethical essays. It is clear that for Beauvoir our embodiment is a fundamental aspect of our situation. As the ambiguity of consciousness and facticity, we are embodied subjects immersed in a situation. In other terms, the ambiguity of freedom and flesh is an aspect of the ambiguity that characterizes the human situation. The body, she writes, isn't "a brute fact. It expresses our relationship to the world" without, however, determining our behavior.[150] The body incarnates our ambiguity: It expresses concretely the ambiguity of transcendence and immanence. We can't then, from Beauvoir's comments on the body (limited as they are in these essays), identify the body unambiguously with immanence. What tyranny aims to do, however, is to impose such an identity on the body of the oppressed, to enclose the oppressed in the facticity (or givens) of the body and cut them off from the body as intentional: "the body" as expressive of their relation to the world and as their means of relation to the world; "aims to" because it is significant for Beauvoir that tyranny is always in some sense a failure.

The tyrant, in treating the other as a thing, must "enclose a man in the immanence of his facticity" and try to forget that he is also a "movement toward the future."[151] Tyranny encloses the oppressed within what Beauvoir, and following her, Kristeva, identifies as cyclical time: time experienced as pure repetition, an "absurd vegetation."[152] Clearly tyranny works by imposing a situation on the oppressed that is extremely limiting: The oppressed is "reduced to pure facticity, congealed in his immanence, cut off from his future [and] deprived of his transcendence and of the world which that transcendence discloses."[153] This involves not only a denial of the ambiguity of the oppressed as a freedom embodied, but also that of the tyrant. The tyrant is an Absolute Subject: He asserts himself as a transcendence and projects pure immanence onto others: "Of the ambiguous condition which is that of all men, he retains for himself only the aspect of transcendence . . . for the others, the contingent and unjustified aspect of immanence."[154] Here Beauvoir makes explicit what she had only suggested in her analysis of that "perfect existentialist hero," the adventurer. It is only because the tyrant, or the adventurer, reduces others to immanence that he can experience himself as a pure transcendence, an Absolute Subject.

The violence of tyranny is of course committed on others' bodies. However, it is not just this obvious fact that Beauvoir stresses in her discussion of oppression. Tyranny is maintained not simply by committing violence against the bodies of humans, but by reducing humans to their bodies-as-immanent.[155] Oppression changes the lived meaning of the embodied existence of the oppressed. Rather than reflecting the ambiguity of an individual freedom concretely embodied, the bodies of the oppressed come to represent only animal flesh. Writing of the horrors of Buchenwald and Dachau, Beauvoir suggests that such atrocities can only be sustained by such a deliberate denial of the ambiguity of existence, and that this denial marks the body itself. Ground down by illness, pain, and hunger, the prisoners in a sense became their bodies, but not their bodies infused with individual or even human meanings. The prisoners were reduced to their bodies as flesh, becoming "an animal horde . . . whose very revolts were only the convulsions of beasts."[156] The Nazi tyranny created a situation so limiting that even revolt lost its human meaning of resistance to oppression and became only the instinctive convulsions of cattle being led to the slaughter.[157] At the same time that the flesh can express only generality, it also encloses us in solitude: No human communication is possible. Beauvoir's point here is not that the Jewish prisoners at Buchenwald literally became less than human, but that some situations are so limiting that almost no expression of transcendence is possible, and that since this frustration is lived concretely by the oppressed, the body of the oppressed loses its potential to express transcendence and is lived as flesh. Even the prisoner himself is led in this situation, Beauvoir insists, to see himself and his comrades as abject flesh.

Beauvoir's rather extreme claim about the dehumanizing effect of the Nazi concentration camps (a claim made, it should be remembered, in the immediate aftermath of the Second World War), is undermined somewhat by what we now know of the communal survival strategies of those victimized by the Nazis. However, her account of the effect of tyranny as a reduction to the body-as-flesh is supported by Primo Levi, who writes that the radical blocking off of the future that the concentration camp enacted effectively "confined prisoners to the present moment like animals."[158]

Tyranny succeeds to the extent that it can make of those it oppresses, be they Jews, natives, or blacks, into abject bodies.[159] Oppressive regimes are always strengthened to the extent that they can render the oppressed abject. As abject, the oppressed are reduced to bodies that can express only the generality of the flesh and not human individuality. And the more miserable the oppressed, the more contemptible to the oppressor. It is only a short distance from the abject bodies of skeletal concentration camp victims to the body truly reduced to an object: the corpse. Our horror at Nazi atrocities is transmuted into indifference, Beauvoir argues, by the photographs of endless corpses: "that decomposed flesh, that animal flesh, seems so essentially doomed to decay that one can no longer even regret that it has fulfilled its destiny."[160] It takes great commitment to remain capable of perceiving humans through these "humiliated bodies."[161]

In another sense, however, Beauvoir's analysis also suggests how much effort it takes to maintain this denial of ambiguity and the other's freedom—and thus how precarious is oppression that rests on the illusion of the oppressor as pure transcendence and the oppressed as the embodiment of immanence. The Nazi regime required all the ideology and dehumanizing technology of the concentration camp to turn Jews into others who were only abject flesh. The colonial French in Algeria can create abject natives "ravaged with disease and famine,"[162] but the lie, Beauvoir insists, will always be given to the oppressors' ruse by the signs of transcendence in the body itself. A child laughing and playing in the midst of a desolate Algerian village undermines the colonists' insistence that the natives "are all animals," because the child is then transmuted from suffering flesh into a "living affirmation of human transcendence . . . an eager hand held out to the world . . . a hope, a project."[163] The denial of ambiguity that allows the tyrant to assert himself as pure transcendence seems only precariously maintained.

The Desire to Disclose and Others: Generosity

Beauvoir's analysis of oppression thus reveals not only its implicit connection with the body, but also the sense in which it must be seen as a failure. Attempting to impose our own meanings on the world to the exclusion of others will always fail. Accepting this failure allows us to hear other voices and allows us to accept our dependence on others and on the meanings they bring to the world. It is through this failure that we realize that our freedoms are interdependent and we can see that our project must involve setting others free. In this regard Beauvoir's most interesting example of an "existential attitude" is that of passion.

The passionate man is, in *The Ethics of Ambiguity*, another figure caught up in the snares of bad faith. He expresses his subjectivity by disclosing a thing or a person as the object of his passion. But passion, Beauvoir argues, becomes maniacal when it sets up the object of passion as an absolute. Then the passionate man desires to be, to attain being through possession of the desired object. Again the failure of the passionate man comes from a stubborn refusal to accept his dependence on others. His drive for mastery and control of the other through possession most clearly reveals his failure: "Having involved his whole life with an external object who can escape him, he tragically feels his dependence. Even if it does not definitely disappear, the object never gives itself."[164] Possession of another freedom is never possible.[165]

However, Beauvoir writes, a conversion can begin within passion itself.[166] To renounce this impossible desire to possess, appropriate, and identify oneself with the object of desire means to desire the disclosure of being, recognizing that one cannot possess or be it: It is to disclose being in its strangeness and foreignness: "it is only as something strange, forbidden, as something free, that the other is revealed as an other."[167] Beauvoir describes the relationship to the other that such a desire opens up: the generous passion—as distinct from the maniacal passion that vainly tries to possess the freedom of the other—recognizes the freedom of this other, loving him "in his otherness and in that freedom by which he escapes."[168] Mlle. de Lespinasse is a figure in *The Ethics of Ambiguity* who is an example of this truly ethical relation to the other. She serves as an example of the ambiguity of a freedom that assumes its dependence on the freedom of the other. Her love of the other is an amorous passion and at the same time a generous, nonpossessive love that confirms the other's independence and wills the other's freedom. This is a freedom that is frightening and, Beauvoir insists, involves risks.[169]

For Beauvoir, generously recognizing the freedom of others means recognizing them in their singularity and difference—in that by which they escape our control. Writing critically again of Hegel, Beauvoir notes that his moment of reciprocal recognition is really a recognition of the other as substantially identical with the self. The other is recognized in his "universal truth" but his individuality is in this way denied.[170] Beauvoir argues instead that what needs to be affirmed is the irreducible individual reality of our projects[171]: "individuals must recognise themselves in their differences."[172]

But what does Beauvoir mean by generosity? Beauvoir had already mentioned the possibility of generosity in *Pyrrhus et Cinéas*. The difference between most acts and those undertaken in a generous spirit, she writes, is that generosity doesn't demand anything of the other (i.e., of the recipient of the generous act) but that the free action be recognized as such. This seems to be a relation to the other distinct even from needing the other to be an ally for my project. The generous person doesn't ask that the other take up her project, but asks only to be recognized as a freedom. Generosity is being able to accept the other as an other and as a subject in his or her otherness and difference.

> In lucid recognition, consenting, we must be able to maintain, face to face these two freedoms which seem to exclude each other: that of the other and mine; I must seize myself as at once object and as a freedom, I must recognise my situation as founded by the other even in affirming my being through the situation.[173]

Thus not only do we need others as allies who will take up our projects and stop them from becoming futile and thus open a future for us, but we need to act/approach the other with generosity: "A lucid generosity should guide our acts. We assume our own choices, we pose as our ends the situations which will be for others new points of departure."[174] This means, for Beauvoir, to recognize the other as other and subject/freedom simultaneously, and likewise to give up the illusion of absolute subjectivity in recognizing myself as at once object and freedom.

Conclusion

So what has Beauvoir accomplished through these essays? She has revealed that bad faith is expressed either as a denial of our transcendence or a denial of our immanence. It manifests itself in attempts to master and dominate others, and in the most extreme sense, in attempts to reduce others to their bodies-as-flesh. For Beauvoir, the relation between embodiment and relations of domination would become clearer as she analyzed the relations between women and men in *The Second Sex*.

Beauvoir's analysis suggests that her understanding of the project has shifted from its Sartrean starting point. The act of projecting ourselves into the world has become, in her account, rather complex. Our project aims to control some aspect of external reality, and this is why it is important to have concrete possibilities rather than an empty revolt. Our aim is to make a mark on the world. Our projects intersect with others: They take up and continue other projects but they also contest others and there will always be the possibility of violence implied in our individuality, separation, and freedom. But we undermine our own freedom if we see control and mastery as the essence of our freedom projecting itself into the world, because to do so is to deny the freedom of others. So the ethical imperative demanded by the ambiguity of our condition is to project ourselves into the world to shape it and mark it with our meanings while joyously assuming our inevitable failure to master it or have it fully under our control.

By stressing ambiguity and the need to accept it, Beauvoir challenges the Sartrean idea of the project and its connotations of mastery, by confronting the desire for mastery with the desire for disclosure. Rather than experiencing anxiety in the face of our freedom, Beauvoir insists, we can experience the joy of existing and disclosing human meaning in the world. Beauvoir's insistence on the joy of existence rather than only anguish of freedom distinguishes her from Sartre and allows for that moment at the end of *The Second Sex* that is not only a moment of risk—risking bodily abandon in the gift of self—but also a moment of joy and pleasure in existence. Beauvoir hasn't yet very directly confronted the Look with another model of relation to the other,[175] but she does suggest something intriguing that is wholly absent from *Being and Nothingness*: the possibility of generosity in our relations with others.

So far, in her ethical essays there isn't any explicit connection between her analysis of the project as mastery/recognition of the failure of mastery and the hints at embodied subjectivity. And there still seems to be a distinction embedded in her work, if not between freedom and the body per se, then between freedom and flesh (the body-as-flesh). That is, so far the ways in which the body undermines mastery (in its suffering and neediness) all seem to be negative. There is very little sense that the body experienced as flesh can be free or joyous.[176]

In *Pyrrhus et Cinéas* the analysis of generosity is not integrated into the analysis of the project and our need for allies to respond to the appeal that we make. I want to suggest that Beauvoir was searching here for something, a way of relating to the other that her analysis so far would not quite support. But if tyranny is the denial of bodily ambiguity, then generosity can be conceived of as generous acceptance of the ambiguity of embodiment, and the real risks of freedom can be conceived of as the risks of assuming this ambiguity. This is what I show in my analysis of *The Second Sex*.

Notes

1. Simone de Beauvoir, *The Second Sex*, trans. and ed. H. M. Parshley (New York: Vintage, 1989), xxxiv. *Being and Nothingness* ends with Sartre's refusal to propose even the rudiments of an ethics and his promise that in a future work he would explore the possibility of a coherent ethics. Sartre, *Being and Nothingness*, 625–88. Later, in 1947–1948, he returned to the question of ethics in his *Cahiers pour une morale*, but this work remained unfinished and unpublished until after his death. Sartre, *Cahiers pour une morale* (Paris: Gallimard, 1983).

2. Joseph Mahon, in *Existentialism, Feminism and Simone de Beauvoir* (New York: St. Martin's Press, 1997), supports my contention that Beauvoir made an original contribution to existentialism in the form of existentialist ethics and that we should see the seeds of *The Second Sex* in her postwar ethical essays. See Mahon, ix.

3. See Beauvoir, *Force of Circumstance*, trans. Richard Howard (London: Penguin, 1964), 21. Beauvoir attributes the success of her essay not to its own merits but to the general euphoria of the liberation and the fact that Parisians had been starved of new writing for four years.

4. Jay Miskowiec has translated selections from the essay into English, which are printed under the confusing title of "Selections from *Towards a Morals of Ambiguity, According to Pyrrhus and Cinéas*." This title should simply be "Selections from *Pyrrhus and Cinéas*"; it is a mistranslation of the title used for the French reprint of both of Beauvoir's ethical essays: *Pour une Morale de l'Ambiguïté suivi de Pyrrhus et Cinéas*. I will be using my own translations throughout. The essay does not seem to have influenced French feminist evaluations of Beauvoir any more than it has English-language ones; I have not found any reference to it in French-language commentary on Beauvoir.

5. Some notable exceptions are Sonia Kruks, Jo-Ann Pilardi, and Debra Bergoffen, who consider both essays in their accounts of Beauvoir's intellectual development, noting the continuity between the argument in the essays and her argument in *The Second Sex*. Toril Moi also notes the significance of *The Ethics of Ambiguity* for our understanding of *The Second Sex*, though in a more critical fashion. Kruks, *Situation and Human Existence: Freedom, Subjectivity and Society* (London: Unwin Hyman, 1990), 85–99; Pilardi, *Simone de Beauvoir Writing the Self* (London: Greenwood Press,

1999); Bergoffen, *The Philosophy of Simone de Beauvoir: Gendered Phenomenologies, Erotic Generosities* (New York: State University of New York Press, 1997), ch. 3; Moi, *Intellectual Woman*, 148–50. Nancy Bauer makes the same observation about critics' failure to consider the links between the essays and *The Second Sex*. See Nancy Bauer, *Simone De Beauvoir, Philosophy and Feminism* (New York: Columbia University Press, 2001), 265, fn. 28.

6. Beauvoir, *Force of Circumstance*, 75. Toril Moi provides an interesting analysis of the effects of Beauvoir's editorial comments on her own work in her *Intellectual Woman*.

7. Bair, *Simone de Beauvoir, A Biography* (New York: Summit Books, 1990), 321 (citing a personal conversation with Beauvoir late in her life).

8. Beauvoir specifically mentioned *Pyrrhus et Cinéas, The Ethics of Ambiguity*, and the collection *Privilèges*, containing the essay *Must We Burn Sade*, as important. Bair, *Simone de Beauvoir*, 269. Bair cites Beauvoir's response in the context of her discussion of Beauvoir's professed lack of philosophic originality and independence. Bair finds it puzzling that Beauvoir would both proclaim her fidelity to Sartre's philosophy and point readers toward her philosophical essays. She writes: "It is curious that [Beauvoir] dismissed her intellect and ability as a philosopher but thought that any key to understanding her creative life must begin with her few and brief philosophical writings." Bair did not take this puzzle into account in her short commentaries on Beauvoir's essays; in the few pages devoted to *Pyrrhus et Cinéas* and *The Ethics of Ambiguity*, she presents a Beauvoir with a "steadfast determination to remain faithful to Sartre's precepts." See Bair, *Simone de Beauvoir*, 639ff, 271.

9. Beauvoir, *Ethics of Ambiguity*, 9–10.

10. I am referring here to Sartre's early thought, circa *Being and Nothingness* (published in 1943), not his later work written and published after *The Second Sex*. There are a number of different accounts of the relationship between this later work and Beauvoir's philosophical essays, some arguing that it is more accurate to see Beauvoir's work as influencing Sartre's subsequent writings than vice versa. See Sonia Kruks, "Simone de Beauvoir: Teaching Sartre about Freedom," in *Sartre Alive*, ed. Ronald Aronson and Adrian van den Hoven (Detroit: Wayne State University, 1991), 285–300, and Kate Fullbrook and Edward Fullbrook, *Simone de Beauvoir and Jean-Paul Sartre: The Remaking of a Twentieth Century Legend* (Hertfordshire, U.K.: Harvester Wheatsheaf, 1993).

11. René Descartes, *Meditations on First Philosophy with Selections from the Objections and Replies*, trans. John Cottingham (Cambridge: Cambridge University Press, 1986), first and second meditations, 17–23.

12. Descartes, *Meditations*, fifth meditation, 47–9.

13. Descartes, *Meditations*, sixth meditation, 54.

14. Though some would argue that we should distinguish between the views held by Descartes in the primary texts and the conception of Cartesian dualism that has developed in the secondary literature (see Amelie Oksenberg Rorty, "Descartes on Thinking with the Body," in *The Cambridge Companion to Descartes*, ed. John Cottingham (Cambridge: Cambridge University Press, 1992) and see chapter 1, note 9.

It is perhaps more this latter that Sartre, Merleau-Ponty, and Beauvoir were responding to.

15. See Descartes, *Meditations*, sixth meditation, 56–57. See also Bergoffen's argument in *Philosophy of Simone de Beauvoir*, 13.

16. Bergson, *Matter and Memory*, 133, cited in Eric Matthews, *Twentieth Century French Philosophy* (Oxford: Oxford University Press, 1996), 28.

17. Gabriel Marcel, *Metaphysical Journal*, cited in Matthews, *Twentieth Century French Philosophy*, 50. See also Kruks, *Situation and Human Existence*, 31–35.

18. Bergoffen, *Philosophy of Simone de Beauvoir*, 15.

19. It was Hyppolite's translation that Beauvoir read. Kojève lectured in Paris from 1933 to 1939, publishing a translation and commentary on chapter IV A of the *Phenomenology* (the master–slave dialectic) in 1939; however, his lectures were only fully collected and published in France posthumously in 1947. Alexandre Kojève, *Introduction à la lecture de Hegel; leçons sur La phénoménologie de l'espirit professées de 1933 à 1939 à l'École des hautes-études*, réunies et pub. par Raymond Queneau (Paris: Gallimard, 1947); Alexandre Kojève, *Introduction to the Reading of Hegel*, trans. James H. Nichols Jr., ed. Allan Bloom (New York: Basic Books, 1969).

20. There is no evidence that either Beauvoir or Sartre attended these lectures. Beauvoir doesn't mention attending Kojève's lectures in her memoirs of the period, and from one who was a compulsive diarist, the omission would be a surprising one had she attended them. In *Force of Circumstance* she recalls a discussion she had with Queneau about Hegel's "end of history"; she notes that it was a common subject of discussion at the time. Beauvoir, *Force of Circumstance*, 43. See later in this chapter.

21. For an account of the introduction of Hegel into France in the 1930s and 1940s, see Mark Poster, *Existential Marxism in Postwar France: From Sartre to Althusser* (Princeton, N.J.: Princeton University Press, 1975), 3–32. See also Vincent Descombes, *Modern French Philosophy* (Cambridge: Cambridge University Press, 1980).

22. Reading Hegel through Marx, Kojève lends political and historical significance to this dialectic, stressing the way in which the unfolding of history is driven by the slave's transcendence of his slavery through labor. This interpretation, making the dialectic more concrete, also made it more accessible to a generation that was just discovering Marx's early manuscripts. For an account of this confluence of influences in France in the 1930s, see Jean Hyppolite, *Studies on Marx and Hegel*, trans. John O'Neill (London: Basic Books, 1969), v–x; Jean Hyppolite, *Études sur Marx et Hegel* (Paris: Marcel Rivière et cie., 1955).

23. See Hegel, *Phenomenology of Spirit*, trans. A. V. Miller (London: Oxford University Press, 1977), sect. 178–96, pp.111–19. I use masculine pronouns to denote both master and slave in Hegel's text, since one of the effects of Beauvoir's appropriation is to reveal the ways in which Hegel's account cannot be presumed to be sex-neutral. I analyze Beauvoir's use of Hegel's master–slave dialectic in greater depth in the next chapter.

24. Husserl is the influence most cited by them, but Kruks makes a persuasive case for the continuity of thought between Marcel and the three younger thinkers, Sartre,

Merleau-Ponty, and Beauvoir. She argues that Sartre and Beauvoir probably down-played the influence of Marcel on their thought because of their disagreement with his Catholicism and the mystical aspects of his thinking. Though Beauvoir probably never read his work directly, Heidegger was also clearly an important source for Sartre. Kruks notes that some of Heidegger's insights were very close to those Beauvoir and Sartre had already gained from Marcel. Kruks, *Situation and Human Existence*, 32–33.

25. Kruks, *Situation and Human Existence*. This is the foundational claim of Kruks's book; she argues that they did so with varying degrees of success.

26. Beauvoir, "La phénoménologie de la perception de Maurice Merleau-Ponty," *Les Temps Modernes* 2 (1945): 363–67, 366, my translation.

27. Beauvoir, "La Phénoménologie," 366.

28. Beauvoir, "La Phénoménologie," 367, citing Merleau-Ponty.

29. In her 1955 essay "Merleau-Ponty and Pseudo-Sartreanism," Beauvoir did make such a judgment, arguing that Merleau-Ponty, who had criticized Sartre as a philosopher of the Absolute Subject, had in fact created a pseudo-Sartre and that Sartre's true position was that of situated rather than pure freedom. It is striking, however, that Beauvoir's pseudo-Sartre of 1955 is almost identical to the Sartre she describes in 1945. See Bergoffen, *Philosophy of Simone de Beauvoir*, 16–22, and Kruks, "Teaching Sartre about Freedom," in *Feminist Interpretations*, ed. Simons, 88, for interpretations of Beauvoir's turnaround.

30. As I have noted in chapter 2. This is also an explicit principle of Sartre's writing.

31. Karen Vintges and Jo-Ann Pilardi also argue that Beauvoir's memoirs should be read as philosophical writing and as part of Beauvoir's ethical practice. Pilardi argues that in the memoirs, Beauvoir presents her philosophical conception of the self within her own life story, implicitly contrasting the existential self derived from Sartre with a new conception of gendered selfhood she had developed in *The Second Sex*. Jo-Ann Pilardi, *Simone de Beauvoir Writing the Self: Philosophy Becomes Autobiography* (London: Greenwood Press, 1999). I focus here not on selfhood, but on how Beauvoir presents her ethical demand for conversion by using her own life story as a model. Vintges's argument goes further than Pilardi's: she claims that Beauvoir's "autobiographical work emerges as the core of her oeuvre" because it both enacts and presents her ethics as an "art of living," consciously constructing "an individual identity and way of life." Vintges, *Philosophy as Passion: The Thinking of Simone de Beauvoir*, trans. Anne Lavelle (Bloomington: Indiana University Press, 1996), 81. On Vintges's reading, Beauvoir's life and work are thoroughly intertwined: she lived her philosophy and philosophized her life. Vintges, *Philosophy as Passion*, 8–9.

32. These events are detailed at the end of Beauvoir's first volume of memoirs, *Memoirs of a Dutiful Daughter*.

33. Beauvoir, *The Prime of Life*, trans. Peter Green (London: Penguin, 1965), 362.

34. Beauvoir, *Prime of Life*, 260, emphasis in original. This relationship sparked a series of events that Beauvoir would fictionalize in *l'Invitée*, translated as *She Came to Stay*. *L'Invitee* (Paris: Gallimard, 1970); *She Came to Stay*, trans. Yvonne Moyse and Roger Senhouse (London: Fontana, 1984).

35. Beauvoir, *Prime of Life*, 259, emphasis in original.

36. Beauvoir, *Prime of Life*, 259. Robert Cottrell criticizes this as an "embarrassingly naive realization for a thirty-one year old woman," but Beauvoir's self-mocking tone is intended to convey as much. Cottrell, *Simone de Beauvoir* (New York: Unger, 1975), 55. This ironic tone and self-deprecating commentary on her younger self is a prominent feature of Beauvoir's memoirs. See Pilardi, *Writing the Self*, 49–52.

37. Beauvoir, *Prime of Life*, 292. Beauvoir also presented a fictionalized version of this event in *She Came to Stay*.

38. As well as detailing her acute awareness of her embodiment in the experience of illness, Beauvoir's memoirs are studded with passages describing her awareness of her mortality, and the effects of ageing on her body and sense of self. As I suggest later (see chapter 4), in some respects the experience of illness and ageing can be seen as parallel to the experience of the erotic in that they undermine the illusion of absolute freedom and thus give us access to our fundamental ambiguity.

39. Beauvoir, *Prime of Life*, 369.

40. Beauvoir, *Prime of Life*, 369. See also 599–600.

41. Pilardi, *Writing the Self*, 118.

42. Beauvoir, *Prime of Life*, 370.

43. Beauvoir, *Letters to Sartre*, 312, 324 (letters of July 11, 1940, and July 13, 1940). Sartre was in a German prisoner of war camp during this period. Deirdre Bair writes rather dismissively that Beauvoir was reading Hegel simply to keep up with Sartre's developing philosophy. Whether this was Beauvoir's original intent or not, the chronology of the letters shows that she was reading Hegel quite independently of Sartre (his letters from prison were not reaching her at this point) and her many comments comparing Sartre's thought with Hegel's and offering to instruct Sartre in Hegel suggest rather that she may have been introducing him to Hegel's thought (Sartre had just begun *Being and Nothingness*). She studied Hegel again, with Sartre this time, in 1947 while she was drafting *The Second Sex*. Bair, *Simone de Beauvoir*, 233, 357. Beauvoir, *Letters to Sartre*, trans. and ed. Quintin Hoare (New York: Little, Brown and Company, 1992), originally published as *Lettres à Sartre, 1940–1963*, ed. Sylvie Le Bon de Beauvoir (Paris: Gallimard, 1990): 336, 345, 368 (letters of July 19, Oct. 29, 1940, and Jan. 22, 1941), and *Journal de Guerre: Septembre 1939–Janvier 1941*, ed. Sylvie Le Bon de Beauvoir (Paris: Gallimard, 1990), 339–63.

44. Beauvoir, *Letters to Sartre*, 315, 335 (letters of July 11 and 19, 1940).

45. Beauvoir, *Force of Circumstance*, 43.

46. Beauvoir, *Letters to Sartre*, 336 (letter of July 19, 1940). Beauvoir actually began reading Hegel in the summer 1940 and found some consolation in his thought, but she was disillusioned by January 1941, a date she repeatedly cites as a turning point in her memoirs.

47. Beauvoir, *Journal de Guerre*, 361; *Letters to Sartre*, 366, 369 (letters of Jan. 8 and 23, 1941).

48. Beauvoir, *Force of Circumstance*, 12.

49. Beauvoir, *Prime of Life*, 547–49.

50. Beauvoir, *Prime of Life*, 549.

51. Beauvoir, *Prime of Life*, 548–549, 434. Beauvoir describes these conversations as having taken place in 1940, during one of Sartre's leaves from the front. Sartre was writing *Being and Nothingness* at the time. Beauvoir had read and edited it extensively in manuscript form by the time she wrote *Pyrrhus et Cinéas*.

52. Beauvoir, *Prime of Life*, 549.

53. Beauvoir, *Prime of Life*, 434.

54. Beauvoir reports that, having held her position for a long time, in the end she made only a "token submission" to Sartre. Beauvoir, *Prime of Life*, 434.

55. Beauvoir, *Pyhrrus et Cinéas*, 233–34. All quotations from the text are my translation.

56. Beauvoir, *Pyhrrus et Cinéas*, 235

57. Beauvoir, *Pyhrrus et Cinéas*, 236.

58. See later in chapter.

59. Sartre, *Being and Nothingness*, lii–liii. Beauvoir composed *Pyrrhus et Cinéas* in 1943, the same year that *Being and Nothingness* was published. Beauvoir was familiar with Sartre's arguments in that text when she wrote her essay, and so I feel it is justifiable to cite it here. See my note 51.

60. Sartre, *Being and Nothingness*, 617.

61. Sartre, *Being and Nothingness*, 562.

62. Beauvoir, *Pyrrhus et Cinéas*, 245.

63. Beauvoir, *Pyrrhus et Cinéas*, 256.

64. Beauvoir, *Pyrrhus et Cinéas*, 245.

65. Beauvoir, *Pyrrhus et Cinéas*, 282.

66. Beauvoir, *Pyrrhus et Cinéas*, 282.

67. Sartre, *Being and Nothingness*, 351.

68. See Sartre, *Being and Nothingness*, 235–44.

69. See Sartre, *Being and Nothingness*, "Concrete Relations with Others," 361–430.

70. Beauvoir, *Pyrrhus et Cinéas*, 291.

71. Beauvoir, *Pyrrhus et Cinéas*, 338.

72. Beauvoir, *Pyrrhus et Cinéas*, 355.

73. Beauvoir, *Pyrrhus et Cinéas*, 338.

74. Beauvoir, *Pyrrhus et Cinéas*, 358, 359, 361. The term Beauvoir uses to describe those who can respond to my appeal is *mes pairs*, which translates as *my peers*, as in the phrase "a jury of my peers." I interpret this to refer not to equality of condition, strictly speaking, but in a more general sense to people whose situation gives them a capacity to act in the world that is roughly similar to mine.

75. Beauvoir, *Pyrrhus et Cinéas*, 362.

76. Beauvoir, *Pyrrhus et Cinéas*, 362.

77. Robert Stone argues that Beauvoir's argument about our need for allies can be extended to include all individuals, though admittedly Beauvoir herself doesn't make

a convincing case that I need *all* others as my peers. Stone, "Simone de Beauvoir and the Existential Basis of Socialism," *Social Text* 17 (1987): 123–33.

78. Though Beauvoir never explicitly distinguishes her position from Sartre's in *Pyrrhus et Cinéas*, elsewhere she is explicitly critical of the conception of freedom (and its implications for our relations with others) that he held at the time of writing *Being and Nothingness*. In her memoirs Beauvoir describes Sartre's contention that all situations are equivalent from the point of view of freedom as "very close to stoicism," and a "little deception" that he practiced on himself. In her account, it was a little deception that he could no longer maintain once he had been through the experience of the war. (*Being and Nothingness* was published in 1943, but composed primarily during the "phony war" of 1939–1940.) Beauvoir, *Force of Circumstance*, 13.

79. Beauvoir, *Pyrrhus et Cinéas*, 327. See Kruks for a criticism of this distinction. Kruks, *Situation and Human Existence*, ch. 3.

80. Beauvoir uses the term *mystification* to describe those whose situations are so constricting that they are experienced as natural and immutable. I argue later that the concept of mystification undermines Beauvoir's clear distinction here between power and freedom.

81. Pilardi argues that in the essays Beauvoir outlined a conception of existential selfhood drawn from Sartre and in *The Second Sex* presents a new conception of self: the gendered self. I have argued in contrast that already in the ethical essays Beauvoir's conception of selfhood had diverged substantially from Sartre's. Pilardi, *Writing the Self*.

82. See note 1. Sartre never wrote this ethics, though an incomplete outline of an ethics can be found in his *Cahiers pour une morale*, written in 1947–1948 but abandoned as a failure. Kruks argues that the *Cahiers* was a failure precisely because Sartre had not yet abandoned his conception of man as an "absolute subject." Kruks, "Teaching Sartre about Freedom," 91–92. Sartre's essay *Existentialism and Humanism*, trans. Philip Mairet (London: Methuen and Co., 1948), first published in French in 1946, did, however, make ethical claims that Beauvior would defend in the *Ethics of Ambiguity*.

83. Beauvoir, *Force of Circumstance*, 76.

84. Beauvoir, *Force of Circumstance*, 75.

85. Beauvoir, *Ethics of Ambiguity*, 82.

86. Beauvoir, *Ethics of Ambiguity*, 13. Here my interpretation of Beauvoir's ethics differs significantly from that of Kristana Arp, who reads Beauvoir's ethics as an exististial ethics of liberation. She interprets Beauvoir's concept of conversion as central to her ethics, but, because she does not read *The Second Sex* as part of Beauvoir's ethical project, she does not see embodiment as central to conversion. Arp, *The Bonds of Freedom: Simone de Beauvoir's Existentialist Ethics* (Chicago: Open Court, 2001). See my argument later and in chapter 5.

87. Beauvoir, *Ethics of Ambiguity*, 7. Beauvoir uses these two terms—*ambiguity* and *ambivalence*—synonymously here, though elsewhere in *The Ethics of Ambiguity* she uses the term *ambiguity* consistently. Ambivalence, however, seems apt, since she is suggesting both our human condition (ambiguity) and our reaction to it (ambivalence).

88. Beauvoir, *Ethics of Ambiguity*, 7.

89. Beauvoir, *Ethics of Ambiguity*, 7.

90. In *The Ethics of Ambiguity*, Beauvoir simply aligns the sense of ourselves as infinitely free yet surrounded by a collectivity with her characterization of ambiguity as freedom and flesh. She doesn't analyze the relation of these two aspects of ambiguity beyond suggesting to us that they are closely linked.

91. Beauvoir, *Ethics of Ambiguity*, 9.

92. Beauvoir, *Ethics of Ambiguity*, 9.

93. Beauvoir, *Ethics of Ambiguity*, 9.

94. Beauvoir, *Ethics of Ambiguity*, 8.

95. Beauvoir, *Ethics of Ambiguity*, 8.

96. Beauvoir, *Ethics of Ambiguity*, 13.

97. Beauvoir, *Ethics of Ambiguity*, 9.

98. Beauvoir, *Ethics of Ambiguity*, 8.

99. Beauvoir, *Ethics of Ambiguity*, 10.

100. In this sense, Sartre's conception of ambiguity is not really of two aspects of the human condition with equal weight. In ascribing to his thought a fundamental ambiguity, Beauvoir is being somewhat disingenuous, since for Sartre consciousness and facticity can't be said to be of equal weight: consciousness constitutes the meaning of its situation, and the freedom that is consciousness is indestructible. For Beauvoir, too, our ontological freedom, or our potential freedom, is also indestructible, but her emphasis on the need to make our freedom concrete in the world gives the situation far more weight than it has for Sartre.

101. Beauvoir, *Ethics of Ambiguity*, 11.

102. Conversion is also presented as a moral coming of age in Beauvoir's appropriation of Hegel in *The Second Sex*. I discuss this in chapter 4.

103. Beauvoir, *Ethics of Ambiguity*, 35.

104. Beauvoir, *Ethics of Ambiguity*, 35. In this essay, Beauvoir follows the convention of her time and the French language in using the masculine pronoun to indicate both males and humans in general. I follow her usage in this section, except where her text indicates females specifically. I do so because, as will become clear, in many respects the idealized portrait of childhood and adolescence she presents is only characteristic of boys.

105. Beauvoir, *Ethics of Ambiguity*, 35.

106. Beauvoir, *Ethics of Ambiguity*, 36.

107. Beauvoir, *Ethics of Ambiguity*, 37.

108. Beauvoir, *Ethics of Ambiguity*, 141.

109. Beauvoir, *Ethics of Ambiguity*, 36.

110. See Beauvoir, *Force of Circumstance*, 75–77.

111. I am indebted to Jennifer Nedelsky and Sara Ruddick for insisting that I attend to the imaginative experiences of children.

112. Beauvoir, *Ethics of Ambiguity*, 39.

113. Beauvoir, *Ethics of Ambiguity*, 27.

114. Kristeva, *Women's Time*, 17.

115. Beauvoir, *Ethics of Ambiguity*, 39.

116. Beauvoir, *Ethics of Ambiguity*, 39.

117. Beauvoir, *Ethics of Ambiguity*, 39.

118. Beauvoir, *Ethics of Ambiguity*, 39, 40. Monika Langer argues that Beauvoir's analysis in *The Ethics of Ambiguity* is impoverished because she doesn't take account of the different childhood experiences that boys and girls are likely to have. It is true that this kind of analysis is missing from *The Ethics of Ambiguity*, in which Beauvoir seldom grounds her ethical claims in sociological description. However, the differences between the childhood experiences of boys and girls will be part of her analysis in *The Second Sex* (see next chapter). Monika Langer, "A Philosophical Retrieval of Simone de Beauvoir's *Pour une morale de l'ambiguïté*," *Philosophy Today* 38 (Summer 1994): 181–90.

119. Beauvoir, *Ethics of Ambiguity*, 37, 47–48, 85.

120. Beauvoir, *Ethics of Ambiguity*, 48.

121. Beauvoir, *Ethics of Ambiguity*, 37.

122. Beauvoir, *Ethics of Ambiguity*, 32.

123. Beauvoir, *Ethics of Ambiguity*, 38.

124. Beauvoir, *Ethics of Ambiguity*, 35.

125. We might, if we recognize childhood as a time of anxieties rather than security, want to think about this nostalgia as being a longing for an ideal childhood that was never actually experienced. I think the nostalgia would be as strong.

126. Beauvoir, *Ethics of Ambiguity*, 40.

127. Beauvoir, *Ethics of Ambiguity*, 13.

128. Beauvoir, *Ethics of Ambiguity*, 12, 13.

129. I am indebted to Debra Bergoffen for her exploration of the implications of these two distinct intentional moments in Beauvoir's thought. See Bergoffen, *Simone de Beauvoir*, 78–82. See also Fullbrook and Fullbrook, *Simone de Beauvoir, A Critical Introduction* (Cambridge: Polity, 1998), 72–74.

130. Beauvoir, *The Ethics of Ambiguity*, 135.

131. Beauvoir, *The Ethics of Ambiguity*, 70.

132. Beauvoir, *The Ethics of Ambiguity*. Here Beauvoir is citing Georges Bataille, *The Inner Experience*, trans. Leslie Anne Boldt (Albany: State University of New York Press, 1988).

133. Beauvoir, *Ethics of Ambiguity*, 70.

134. Beauvoir, *The Ethics of Ambiguity*, 71.

135. Beauvoir, *The Ethics of Ambiguity*, 71.

136. Beauvoir, *The Ethics of Ambiguity*, 92, 133. See also Bergoffen, *Simone de Beauvoir*, 86.

137. Of course, Beauvoir's analysis of mystification (see the section titled Bad Faith and Mystification) shows that she is aware that not all potential human meanings are revealed in the world, or, in other words, that inequalities of social and political power mean that some meanings or discourses are dominant and others are

silenced or distorted. This, again, will become central to Beauvoir's more developed analysis of oppression in *The Second Sex*.

138. Beauvoir, *Ethics of Ambiguity*, 67.

139. Beauvoir's description of the ambiguity of the human condition and its relation to freedom bears, it seems to me, some relation to what Hannah Arendt describes as the nature of action and its relation to freedom and sovereignty. Arendt writes, in *The Human Condition*, that action reveals freedom and sovereignty to be incompatible, since action is unpredictable. Once we have acted in the world we cannot remain master of our acts or sovereign over them. Alone, we can only initiate. Arendt, *The Human Condition* (Chicago: University of Chicago Press, 1958), 190, 233–34, 244–45.

140. Beauvoir, *Pyrrus et Cinéas*, 365.

141. I am again following Beauvoir's usage in using the word *man* to designate these types. Most women, as Beauvoir has already noted, constrained by the limitations of their situations to live in a childlike world, are not granted the possibilities of adolescence and thus do not have the opportunity, as it were, to exhibit these moral failings.

142. Beauvoir, *The Ethics of Ambiguity*, 44.

143. Beauvoir, *The Ethics of Ambiguity*, 46–47.

144. Beauvoir, *The Ethics of Ambiguity*, 49, 51.

145. I have borrowed these terms, the *bad faith of immanence* and the *bad faith of transcendence*, from Fullbrook and Fullbrook, *Simone de Beauvoir*, 67–70.

146. Beauvoir, *The Ethics of Ambiguity*, 59.

147. Beauvoir, *Force of Circumstance*, 13.

148. Beauvoir, *The Ethics of Ambiguity*, 61.

149. Beauvoir, *The Ethics of Ambiguity*, 61.

150. Beauvoir, *The Ethics of Ambiguity*, 41.

151. Beauvoir, *The Ethics of Ambiguity*, 102.

152. Beauvoir, *The Ethics of Ambiguity*, 83. Kristeva characterizes time in this way in "Women's Time," 16.

153. Beauvoir, *The Ethics of Ambiguity*, 100.

154. Beauvoir, *The Ethics of Ambiguity*.

155. A striking parallel with Beauvoir's analysis here can be seen in Elaine Scarry's analysis of the effects of torture. Elaine Scarry, *The Body in Pain: The Making and Unmaking of the World* (New York: Oxford University Press, 1985).

156. Beauvoir, *The Ethics of Ambiguity*, 101, TA.

157. Primo Levi, *The Drowned and the Saved* (New York: Random House, 1989), 75. Jean Amery, another camp survivor, has compared torture to rape, in that both reduce the victim to his or her body-as-flesh, undermining their being-in-the-world. Amery, "Torture," in *Art from the Ashes: A Holocaust Anthology*, ed. Lawrence Langer (New York: Oxford University Press, 1995), 126.

158. Beauvoir, *The Ethics of Ambiguity*, 101.

159. Beauvoir, *The Ethics of Ambiguity*, 102–3.

160. Beauvoir, *The Ethics of Ambiguity*, 101.

161. Beauvoir, *The Ethics of Ambiguity*, 101.

162. Beauvoir, *The Ethics of Ambiguity*, 102.

163. Beauvoir, *The Ethics of Ambiguity*, 102.

164. Beauvoir, *The Ethics of Ambiguity*, 65.

165. In this sense, Beauvoir's analysis of passion is parallel to Sartre's analysis of love (*Being and Nothingness*, 490–91). However, in Beauvoir's view passion can open up the possibilities of a generous relation with the other, something not possible in Sartre's thought.

166. Beauvoir, *The Ethics of Ambiguity*, 66.

167. Beauvoir, *The Ethics of Ambiguity*, 67.

168. Beauvoir, *The Ethics of Ambiguity*, 67.

169. Beauvoir, *The Ethics of Ambiguity*, 67.

170. Beauvoir, *The Ethics of Ambiguity*, 104.

171. Beauvoir, *The Ethics of Ambiguity*, 106.

172. Beauvoir, *The Ethics of Ambiguity*, 108.

173. Beauvoir, *Pyrrhus et Cinéas*, 324.

174. Beauvoir, *Pyrrhus et Cinéas*, 325.

175. That will be more fully drawn out in *The Second Sex*; see chapter 4.

176. Only in the example of the festival—and possibly in the example of the generous passion—do we get a sense of communication with others through flesh rather than the flesh as that which encloses us in solitude. Beauvoir, *The Ethics of Ambiguity*, 125.

CHAPTER FOUR

~

The Second Sex:
Ambiguity and the Body

Beauvoir's criticism of patriarchy's denial of full subjectivity to women, of women's Otherness, is also a criticism of patriarchal masculine subjectivity itself, of the way patriarchal definitions impoverish the lived and embodied experience of both women and men by limiting the body's possibilities and what the body can express. To see this, we need to read *The Second Sex* as an integral part of Beauvoir's ethical project and as a text that follows on and develops the thought of her earlier ethical essays.

Some critics have argued that Beauvoir, in *The Second Sex*, holds to a masculine conception of subjectivity as transcendence that denies the body and suggests that the female body is a barrier to freedom. This interpretation is often based on a contentious passage in *The Second Sex* that describes the origin of and key to women's oppression in early nomadic societies in terms of Hegel's master–slave dialectic.[1] For Beauvoir, women's oppression seems to have its foundation in women's bondage to reproduction, since, as she writes, "it is not in giving life but in risking life" that humanity distinguishes itself from the animal, and women were biologically destined to give life and not to risk their lives in the nomadic horde.[2]

However, this passage may give us the key to Beauvoir's analysis of subjectivity in a different sense. If we consider the continuities between Beauvoir's ethical essays and her analysis of the structure of oppression in *The Second Sex*, and specifically the concepts of ambiguity and conversion that thread through both texts, we can and should read these passages in a different light. Just as in the ethical essays we see Beauvoir jumping off from her starting point in Sartre and developing the ideas of ambiguity and conversion considerably, in *The Second Sex* we see her appropriating Hegel for her own purposes. She reads the master–slave story in terms of her framework of bad faith, the desire to be, and conversion. The effect is startling: Beauvoir removes the dialectic from the historical grounding given it by Hegel. She describes patriarchy as a stage of the dialectic stuck in time, and she reworks and changes the notion of risk that founds human subjectivity. Rather than the risk of life in the context of a violent struggle to the death that marks Hegel's account, the risk that founds subjectivity is transmuted by Beauvoir into the risk of asserting oneself as a freedom while assuming one's ambiguity. The nomadic scene describes a time in which women didn't have the opportunity to risk, and *The Second Sex* as a whole argues that patriarchy is to be condemned for creating a feminine situation that continues to bar women from risk—in essence, for illegitimately excluding them from the struggle for recognition. But as I read *The Second Sex*, it also argues that in the context of patriarchy men also avoid the real risks of human subjectivity, because patriarchy provides a situation in which they can maintain the bad faith of their *désir d'être*, and the illusion of pure transcendence, and avoid assuming the ambiguity of their condition.

As Beauvoir tells it, patriarchy maintains this illusion by assigning different aspects of the human condition to women and to men, both symbolically and concretely. That is, women both symbolize immanence and are constrained economically and socially from transcendence, while men are able to maintain the illusion of pure transcendence. Further, this gendered division gains its strength from its being rooted in the body: Patriarchy creates, out of the sexually differentiated but ambiguous body, the masculine body as transcendent and the feminine immanent body, a kind of mythical body that mystifies and naturalizes oppression. It is clear that it is women's lived experience that is most limited and constrained by this social transformation of the female body into flesh, but it is also true that men do not live their bodies authentically within patriarchy.

If the structure of the Subject–Other dynamic is maintained by the denial of ambiguity, and true human subjectivity is not the dream of pure transcendence and the *désir d'être* but is realized through a conversion that recognizes the freedom of the other and the otherness of the self, then the meaning of risk changes dramatically. The risk that founds subjectivity will not be just the risk of self-assertion, but must also be the risk of taking otherness into the self, of offering oneself to the other in generosity, and this will be a bodily risk taking, an assumption of the self as freedom and flesh at once. In *The Second Sex*, this bodily risk taking is made manifest in the erotic encounter, in which each partner risks the self in a generous abandon to the other that opens each to otherness within.

Beauvoir's Critique of the Masculine Subject

Subject and Other

If we read *The Second Sex* in isolation from Beauvoir's other writings, and particularly if we fail to attend to her quiet divergence, through her ethical essays, from Sartre's arguments in *Being and Nothingness*, it is easy to misread her account of women's oppression as stemming directly from Sartre's idea of freedom as transcendence, in which freedom is ontological, absolute, and individually self-constituted. Additionally, it is easy to assume that Beauvoir accepts Sartre's reading of Hegel's master–slave dialectic as revealing our inevitable hostility to the freedom of others.[3] At the beginning of *The Second Sex*, Beauvoir identifies subjectivity with transcendence and transcendence with the free project. Her analysis of women's oppression is famous, stated early in the text. Woman is man's Other: "She is defined and differentiated with reference to man and not he with reference to her; she is the incidental, the inessential as opposed to the essential. He is the Subject, he is the Absolute—she is the Other."[4]

But what does it mean to be made Other? Beauvoir says that her perspective is that of existentialist ethics,[5] a perspective from which liberty, or freedom, becomes the core value. From this perspective, to be a subject is to be freely engaged in projects that serve as a mode of transcendence. It is important to remember here that Beauvoir has significantly changed the meaning of freedom by moving from the level of ontology to the social level of analysis. For Sartre, all humans are inevitably transcendent, and their situation cannot condition this ontological freedom, though it may limit the modes of transcendence that are possible. For Beauvoir, though all humans are free ontologically, this freedom can be denied or frustrated. People can be denied access to an open future and can be denied the ability to undertake the concrete projects that make their freedom real, effectively negating their ontological freedom.[6] A human existence is only justified, Beauvoir argues, by a continual expansion into an open future. For a woman to be made Other means that the future—her freedom, her subjectivity—is closed to her, because she is kept from the engagement in freely chosen projects that marks a fully human existence.[7] Thus Beauvoir writes, in perhaps the most important passage of the book:

> What particularly signalizes the situation of woman is that she—a free and autonomous being like all human creatures—nevertheless finds herself living in

a world where men compel her to assume the status of the Other. They propose to stabilize her as object and to doom her to immanence since her transcendence is to be overshadowed and forever transcended by another ego which is essential and sovereign. The drama of woman lies in this conflict between the fundamental aspirations of every subject—who always regards the self as essential—and the compulsions of a situation in which she is the inessential.[8]

Here Beauvoir seems to assume that one only attains a sense of self by defining oneself against an Other. That is, at least at first in *The Second Sex*, Beauvoir links the "fundamental aspirations" of humans—to assert themselves as subject—with the social and political phenomenon of oppression. In Beauvoir's analysis, the oppression of women seems to be the direct and necessary outcome of the human drive to self-assertion. In *The Second Sex*, the drive to become subject seems (at first) necessarily taken at another's expense.

At the beginning of *The Second Sex*, Beauvoir presents the alterity of women as just one example of a larger phenomenon. The category of the Other precedes the division of male and female: "otherness is a fundamental category of human thought"[9]; "the category of the *Other* is as primordial as consciousness itself."[10] Beauvoir argues that creating an Other is essential to the formation of identity, and particularly group identity. The subject relies on an Other and can only pose itself in opposition to another. No group "ever sets itself up as the One without at once setting up the Other over against itself." Communities can only constitute themselves by defining themselves against what they are not, by creating an Other that is "vaguely hostile." Anyone can become Other in the eyes of the group solidifying its identity: a stranger in a village or a foreigner in a country.[11]

At this point Beauvoir first makes reference to Hegel to explain the phenomenon of Otherness. Following Hegel, she writes, "we find in consciousness itself a fundamental hostility toward every other consciousness."[12] Should we take her at her word? If we do, the implications are troubling: If a fundamental hostility is inevitable, a self can only define itself by creating an Other and is founded on separation and the attempt to master others. Some critics argue that this model of subjectivity or selfhood is necessarily tied to domination of and violence toward others.[13]

It soon becomes clear, however, that oppression is only one possible outcome of the human aspiration toward subjectivity. Otherness does not necessarily result in domination in Beauvoir's analysis. If the villager views the stranger as an Other, to the outsider the villager is also Other or strange. The "other consciousness sets up a reciprocal claim" to be the one.[14] Interaction between groups, whether overtly hostile or not, tends to make the relative nature of otherness evident. Oppressed peoples have claimed their subject status, and have said "we," claimed a group identity, in the face of hostility; Beauvoir cites colonized peoples and American blacks as examples of peoples who have contested their definition as Other by claiming subject status for themselves. These groups, Beauvoir argues, have forced the oppressor to recognize the reciprocity of otherness.[15] Our ontological aims (to posit ourselves by creating an Other) will always create the possibility of oppression and exploitation, but oppression is not the necessary outcome of those aims.

Thus there is a clear difference between the Other, who makes no claim to sovereign subject status, and otherness, which has to do with whether the relations are characterized by reciprocity. Between the other that is also the same and the absolute Other, Beauvoir argues, "the mistake has come from a confusion of two forms of alterity or otherness, which are mutually exclusive in point of fact"[16]; "to say that woman was the *Other* is to say that there did not exist between the sexes a reciprocal relation . . . she was no fellow creature in men's eyes . . . for the male it is always another male who is the fellow being, the other who is also the same, with whom reciprocal relations are established."[17]

The important question then is why women became the Absolute Other—that is, the nonreciprocal other—and why they have not insisted on the recognition of their subjectivity. The Otherness of women, Beauvoir writes, is of a different nature, and more intractable, than that of other groups.[18] Other oppressed groups have been subjugated at some specific point in time, such as a conquest, or have been subjugated through a historical development (such as the proletariat). These groups have the memory of a time before to draw upon in contesting their status of Other. In the case of women, however, there has been no historical event or social change. The oppression of women is not something that can be said to have occurred; it "lacks the contingent or incidental nature of historical facts,"[19] and therefore seems like a natural condition that defies change. A second difference is that women don't form a group in the way that others do—they don't stand together in opposition to men, sharing a common history or sharing common interests: "the bond that unites her to her oppressor is not comparable to any other. The division of the sexes is a biological fact, not an event in human history."[20] Women are bound up in an intimate *Mitsein* with men, and the extermination of the oppressor is unthinkable.[21] For both these reasons the subordination of women is unique and more intractable than that of other groups. We are led to believe in its naturalness and we are more likely to find both parties complicit in it.[22]

Beauvoir turns to Hegel's master–slave dialectic to capture this sense of reciprocal need and complicity. But let us also respond to her cue that the subordination of women is one that is intimately tied up with women's *Mit-sein* with men and that it has to do with cultural responses to the biological fact of sexual difference.

Masters and Slaves, Men and Women: Hegel Rewritten

Beauvoir turns to Hegel to understand and explain the masculine "ontological pretensions" that make of women the Other.[23] She looks to Hegel both to find the origin of women's subordination in historical contingencies and to explain its enduring ontological foundation in masculine bad faith. Though Beauvoir cites Hegel's fundamental hostility,[24] her analysis offers hope that it will be overcome. She suggests that hostility is only one possible reaction to the presence of free others; there will always remain the possibility of conversion and reciprocal recognition.

Hegel presents some difficulties to a writer intending to use his thought for feminist purposes. Beauvoir was well aware that Hegel did not include women as subjects who could take part in the struggle for recognition.[25] Though Hegel never explicitly addresses the way in which women relate to the master–slave dialectic, women for Hegel live out an ahistorical existence in the private sphere, excluded from the work and struggle that drives history.[26] Many feminist critics have located the difficulty with Beauvoir's use of Hegel's dialectic in her attempt to apply it to women without following through the application with any consistency.[27] That is, if men are to women as masters are to slaves, then why don't women in Beauvoir's analysis learn of their freedom through their labor in the way that slaves do for Hegel in the second phase of the dialectic?

But Beauvoir doesn't precisely apply the dialectic to the relation between men and women. It would be more accurate to say that she appropriates it. By this I mean that Beauvoir doesn't simply use the master–slave dialectic as an analogy of the relations between men and women, in which masters are to slaves as men are to women. Rather, she transforms the dialectic by changing the meaning of risk that drives it. From Beauvoir's perspective the great crime of patriarchy is that in it the dialectic that Hegel describes between Master and Slave, which is eventually resolved in their reciprocal recognition, is stuck at its first stage, in which the master appears to have won the fight for recognition but paradoxically has also lost, since the recognition he compels from the slave is worthless. At this first stage, the master's illusion of pure freedom is sustained by the slave's submission.

The story of the master and slave enters Hegel's *Phenomenology* at the point at which consciousness, in its drive toward understanding, discovers itself as self-consciousness. The master and slave episode marks the shift from the life of sense-certainty, or animal life, to self-consciousness, a truly human life. It marks the beginning of human freedom. The precondition of this unfolding is the confrontation of one self-consciousness by another equal and potentially free self-consciousness. Self-consciousness experiences itself as essential; what is other to it is inessential.[28] The desire of self-consciousness is to use, consume, and destroy the objects of its desire. A struggle ensues, then, when a self-consciousness encounters another identical to itself, for the other is both an object for self-consciousness and also another self-consciousness.[29] Each self-consciousness desires recognition from the other, since alone it can have only "subjective certainty" of itself, and from the other it can gain "objective confirmation" of its freedom. Each desires to be recognized as the only subject.

Freedom also requires risk: In the struggle between the two self-consciousnesses, both risk their lives. The struggle becomes a matter of life and death when one of the antagonists values the recognition of his freedom above his life itself. Indeed, he must risk his life to gain freedom because it is only through this risk that he reveals his essence as not simply contained in its immediate form, or "submerg[ed] in the expanse of life."[30] He who values freedom risks his life to enslave the other, who, valuing his own life above the recognition of himself as a freedom, voluntarily chooses servitude over death. The slave is the one who, in the face of death, accepts bondage in return for his life. This begins the dialectic of the master and slave, who represent for Hegel "two opposed shapes of consciousness."

The master, the "independent consciousness whose essential nature is to be for itself" demands and receives recognition as a free subject from the slave, the "dependent consciousness whose essential nature is simply to live or to be for another."[31] The slave, having in effect declared himself dependent on material things,[32] becomes like a thing himself. In this confrontation the master has displayed, according to Alexandre Kojève, the truly human desire, that for the recognition of his superiority, while the slave has acted from a simple animal or biological desire to avoid death.[33] In this sense, the master has transcended and displayed his superiority over biological life. Because he can force the slave to work for him, the master no longer has to make any effort to satisfy his natural desires; the master "dominates nature and lives in it as master."[34]

Hegel's story, at this point, is not resolved. The master has not gained the recognition he sought because recognition can only come from a free subject. The recognition he compels from the slave is worthless since this recognition has come from one enslaved and thing-like, not from one he can himself recognize as a free subject. The slave, deprived of his potential for freedom, cannot serve the purpose of recognizing the master's freedom. Kojève's interpretation of this struggle stresses the irony implicit in the result: "The Master . . . is not what he wanted to be in starting the fight: a man recognized by another man." The master has won the struggle but paradoxically has also lost, since "if man can be satisfied only by recognition, the man who behaves as a Master will never be satisfied."[35]

Beauvoir's first use of the dialectic, to describe early nomadic societies, parallels this first stage of Hegel's dialectic. In Beauvoir's telling, men in these societies prove their detachment from the claims of life not in a struggle with another consciousness who also aims to assert himself as subject, but by risking their lives by hunting animals. This is not, then, a fight for recognition in the sense that it is for Hegel.[36] Indeed, what men seem to achieve through hunting is a confirmation of their own agency and creative powers; they learn to create tools for their own use and in so doing, humanize brute need. Beauvoir finds the key to women's subordination in the physical weakness and frequent pregnancies that excluded women from the hunt. Beauvoir writes infamously that "it is not in giving life, but in risking life" that man asserts himself as subject, and that woman was doomed because she was excluded from the warlike forays of the men.[37] Beauvoir's appeal to Hegel here is clear in that she equates subjectivity with the risk of death: Becoming a subject requires risk.

But it is also here, when applying Hegel's dialectic to early nomads, and later, to early agricultural societies, that Beauvoir argues that some aspects of Hegel's story apply better to men and women than they do to actual masters and slaves. In a sense, women are more slavish than slaves. Unlike Hegel's slave, women, Beauvoir claims, have never risked their lives, even if only to choose servitude over death.[38] The crucial difference between the early nomadic woman and the slave is that the nomadic woman is in a situation in which she cannot exercise any individual choice and does not have the opportunity to assert her individuality by risking her life. But we must be clear about the point that Beauvoir is making in her analysis of nomadic life: Women were not "doomed" by any action of men but by the constraints of the available technology and level of societal development. In the early nomadic horde, women lived out a situation in which their individual lives were subordinated to the species; their reproductive activities, in this context in which they could exercise no choice, cannot be understood as a risk that would found subjectivity. Reproduction in nomadic times certainly involved danger, but Beauvoir makes a distinction between danger undergone and risk consciously chosen. Women could neither choose freely to undertake reproduction nor refuse to.

Beauvoir also adds that reproduction could not be experienced as a creative undertaking or a project among the primitive nomads, since, with no store in posterity and property, living a subsistence life, more mouths to feed could only be felt as a burden and not as a value. Even when a more settled way of life enabled people to value their children, women's reproductive role wasn't seen as a creative one.[39] The reproductive process was still perceived as a magical process, not one under the control of human power or choice. Woman's role in reproduction led to her assimilation to nature itself and made her the symbolic repository of all its frightening and awe-inspiring powers. Thus women commanded some respect, and men were held, in their fear and awe, in a kind of dependence that gave the relations between men and women more of the reciprocity—or at least a kind of mutual dependence—that Hegel saw in the relation between master and slave. But it is important to note that the powers accorded to women weren't individual creative powers that would attest to their subject status, but a kind of magical emanation of the powers of the universe channeled through them. In this sense the analysis Beauvoir is making isn't contradictory: Women's involvement in reproduction can't be seen (because of the constraints of the technology and knowledge of early nomadic societies) as allowing for their agency—whether they were valued as reproducers or not, it was not their agency or power that was recognized, but the obscure and frightening powers of nature of which women were simply a conduit. In the context of early nomadic life, then, reproduction couldn't be undertaken in any way that would humanize it: It remained, for the women involved in it, an animal destiny.[40]

In Hegel's telling, the master–slave dialectic does not end with the master's hollow victory. Just as the master, who appeared to win, has not really won, the slave, who appeared to lose the fight, has not really lost. The story is resolved by the slave, who actualizes freedom through his labor. He learns that life—and the material conditions of life—are an essential part of what it is to be human and an essential aspect of freedom. The master's desire, at the end of the confrontation, is still the "pure negating of the object." The slave, however, through work, or what Hegel calls "desire held in check, fleetingness staved off,"[41] becomes aware that he exists essentially in his own right and not just in his relation to the master.[42] He sees his own independence in the independence of the object that he shapes and forms.[43] It is the slave who in the end, through his forced work for the master, masters his own instincts and by transforming nature through this work succeeds in dominating nature and his own "animal" nature.[44] The objects that he shapes and forms also shape and form us as humans. The labor of the slave and the slave's attempts to overcome his slavery are what, in the end, will drive history.

For Beauvoir, men and women never take this second step, and this is where the differences between Hegel and Beauvoir become telling. One difference is that the risk that men take, for Beauvoir, is not simply the risk of life in the struggle with another, but more generally the risk of asserting themselves as free, the risk of creating something new in the world. In Beauvoir's story, men learn, in a certain sense, the lessons of the slave. In contrast, women have not had the opportunity to risk, and they also don't have, in their work, an apprenticeship in freedom. They are kept from the kind of activities that would teach them about their creative powers and their freedom.[45] Beauvoir's early nomadic society thus represents only one moment of Hegel's dialectic. The relations of man and woman are like the relations of the master and slave but stuck in time: The dialectic never continues, and the relation is congealed. Men and women are stuck in a relation that is maintained through illusion, one about which neither party reaches clarity or lucidity.[46] By having the story end here, Beauvoir highlights the partial, illusory nature of the master's original assertion of a freedom that is free of the claims of life and necessity. As Beauvoir has already alerted us in *The Ethics of Ambiguity*, this is an immature or adolescent response to the "problem" of free others in the world, since it casts the Other as one who will steal our freedom.[47]

This point becomes clear when Beauvoir uses the master–slave dialectic for a second time, not this time to describe the historical stage of the nomads, but to describe the masculine "ontological pretensions" that underlie patriarchy.[48] Here, Beauvoir stresses the ways in which the relations between men and women differ from Hegel's master–slave dialectic. The salient fact about woman as Other is that she allows men to escape "that implacable dialectic of master and slave which has its source in the reciprocity between free beings."[49] Woman as Other is a way for man to escape the movement of the dialectic, not a way to enter into it. This is because men have constructed, upon the foundation of women's original exclusion from risk, a situation in which women continue to be barred from risking and testing themselves in the world. Women have been kept in a childlike situation and denied the promise of adolescence. Because they have been defined as Other, women have collectively been denied the chance to experience their own subjective powers in the world and have been constrained by institutions and customs that configure them as the eternal child.

In this second use of Hegel's dialectic Beauvoir echoes her analysis in *The Ethics of Ambiguity* when she writes of the necessity of a conversion in order to recognize and accept the ambiguity of our human condition.[50] Conversion will resolve the master–slave dialectic, though at the price of a "constant tension." The recognition that we seek and require from other freedoms engages us in a constant tension: We must constantly renounce the desire to be in order to desire that there be being, to desire the revelation of being in the world.[51] She demands that we recognize the other as also a source of meanings in the world and as a freedom who can confirm our freedom. I have already argued that for Beauvoir, the conversion should be seen as a coming of age, a transition from adolescence to adulthood. Thus, in her analysis of the relation between men and women, Beauvoir suggests that we have collectively not come of age: Women have not been granted the promises of adolescence, and men have had the illusions of adolescence sustained for them.

As long as patriarchy survives, men have an easy way out of this tension by making women into Woman, the Other who can embody immanence for them. As Other, Woman allows man to evade the risks and difficulties of reciprocity. Woman as Other allows him to avoid this difficult conversion and to gratify his *désir d'être*, allows him to play at being God—a freedom also endowed with being—since she appears to him not as another equal freedom who appeals to him for recognition, but as a consciousness who can somehow also be possessed as a being.[52] Through Woman, man can confirm his sense of freedom without the difficulties and dangers of a reciprocal relationship. He can avoid the real risks of engagement with an other who is also a subject, because she appears to be a magical combination: an object that is not mute nature, and a free subject that is docile; since it seems that he can possess her as an object, he has a connection to life without having to assume its ambiguities within himself. Men can posit Woman as bound to necessity and maintain the illusion of pure freedom detached from the claims of life.[53]

This last point is the one most essential for my reading of *The Second Sex* and the one that is made most obliquely in her text. If Woman as Other allows man to evade the risks of reciprocity, then these risks must be seen in a new light, as not only the risks involved in self-assertion, but also the risks of assuming one's ambiguity as immanent and transcendent at once. Beauvoir suggests that Woman as Other allows man to evade a sort of risk that doesn't arise in Hegel: that of assuming fully the ambiguity of his existence. This will mean not just recognizing the other as a freedom who can confirm his freedom, but also recognizing the self as other, as connected to life, and as enmeshed in the species.

Masters, Slaves, and Bodies

It is here that another connection between Hegel's master–slave dialectic and Beauvoir's account becomes apparent. Beauvoir's analogy between Hegel's master and slave and the relation of men and women suggests the connection between the master's project, his aim of mastering the other, and his attempt to disassociate from the body, as it evokes the flesh. The Hegelian story is of the place of desire in the construction of subjectivity, but it reveals, as well, the significance of corporeality in this construction—an aspect of this story that is not often enough noted. The master's desire projects embodiment, as necessity, onto the slave: The slave is all body, the master, disembodied desire. In Judith Butler's phrase, the master is "the denial of embodiment and the embodiment of denial."[54] The slave is forced to recognize and accept mortality (or rather, the coincidence of mortality and human freedom) while the master lives with the precariously maintained illusion of absolute freedom (freedom as pure consciousness). The illusion that marks patriarchy, the illusion that a congealed master–slave relation is maintaining, is that men, as Absolute Subject, are free of the body and necessity, and that women, as Other, are only their bodies, their bodies exist as a constraining, restrictive identity, as a destiny, as a nature. Butler calls this the "masculine disembodiment and feminine enslavement to the body" that marks modern political thought.[55]

For Beauvoir, however, it is not precisely that men maintain the illusion that they are disembodied, which is surely a difficult illusion to maintain. Rather, men live their bodies in a particular mode: Their bodies are perceived as and experienced by them as instruments that express their will and enable them to fulfill their projects, as tools that are under their control. Beauvoir's point is not that bodies don't have these qualities, but that we can only maintain the illusion that this is all our bodies are by projecting their other aspects onto the Other. That is, what is projected is precisely those aspects of the body that would undermine this sense of ourselves as in control of body-instruments or body-machines. This is the body-as-flesh, uncontrollable and mortal, enmeshed in species-life, and prey to its hormones and reproductive cycle, in which the individual is simply an expendable and mortal part. Woman is identified with the body-as-flesh, and thus women are forced to experience their bodies as constraining identities: They are forced to *be* these constrained bodies. Woman is enclosed in the body as facticity and cut off from the body as intentional, expressive of a relation to the world, while Man is associated with consciousness, with the project. Thus men experience themselves as *having* bodies that are their instruments, are expressive of their individuality, and are responsive to their will. Neither way of experiencing the body can be said to be a real acceptance of human embodiment, or a lucid recognition of ourselves as body-subjects. In addition, this division imposes cruel limitations on women: It is the equivalent of living in a child's world, having to be identified with their bodies as natural objects.

While Beauvoir certainly accepts Hegel's claim that subjectivity or self-certainty requires risk, she doesn't always identify, as he does, that risk with the risk of death, or with the attempt to master another freedom. In Beauvoir's telling, the meaning of risk expands and changes considerably. Among the early nomads, risk is identified with the struggle with a wild animal, the risk of death involved in the hunt. Among the nomads, then, becoming a subject is a matter of asserting oneself against the species in the only way available: by risking one's life to assert and create values beyond life or mere survival. However, by the end of *The Second Sex* Beauvoir has implicitly rewritten the meaning of risk: There is indeed risk in self-assertion, in challenging the given, creating something new and opening oneself to the other for recognition, but there is also risk involved in accepting the ambiguity of our embodied condition, in risking self-abandon in generous bodily communication with the other. This is what I explore in the next two sections.

The Body and Ambiguity

From Beauvoir's existentialist perspective, humans are transcendent freedoms who express their freedom through activity that creates meaning and challenges the given. Humans are distinct from animals in that we can't be considered simply as a species or defined as a fixed given; humans are a becoming. However, we live out this transcendence as incarnated subjects—our bodies have a double aspect as objects in the world and as our perspective on the world. They are objects for others and also the objective possibilities and limits of our activity in the world. The body has objective characteristics, or facticity, but the meaning of those characteristics is not inherent in them; rather, they acquire significance within society. The body is an essential aspect of our situation in the world; we are situated freedoms.

Because we are incarnated and situated freedoms, our transcendence has an ambiguous character: The correlative of our individual assertion and expression of freedom is our immersion in a species and in a collective or society. When seen in this perspective, transcendence can be seen as a relationship to both time and the species. Transcendence, as creation, is an expansion into an indefinitely open future, but the correlative of this, and the condition of its possibility, is rootedness in a history and a past, being in the grip of time. Transcendence is an expression of individual creativity and freedom, but again, the correlative of this is the individual's immersion in a species (implying individual limitation, mortality, and immersion in the cycles of the species), and a society (implying interdependence and immersion in historical time). This is all to say that transcendence has as its correlative immanence, or that as incarnated freedoms, transcendence and immanence are the two irreducible aspects of our human condition.

What emerges in the chapters in The Second Sex on biology and mythology is an account of our existential drama—the same drama that Beauvoir described more dispassionately in The Ethics of Ambiguity—the tension and ambiguity of being at once an infinite freedom or spirit in a finite body, experiencing both the linear time of projection into the future and the cyclical time of the species, both asserting individual will and subordinated to species "destiny." She describes men and women both as transcendent freedoms who don't blindly submit to a biological destiny but must take up an attitude toward, or in other words, assume, their embodiment. As we see in our examination of Beauvoir's account of the myths that sustain patriarchy, its great lie is to deny this ambiguity. By defining women as the Other, men are able, however precariously, to experience themselves as purely transcendent freedoms while evading the risks of real reciprocity with others.

To see this we have to be very clear about how the idea of ambiguity informs her writing, and, particularly, the analysis of oppression in The Second Sex. Ambiguity functions on two levels for Beauvoir. In one sense she uses the word to refer to the existentialist claim that the meaning of human life is never fixed or defined by nature but always remains open. In this use of the term she is essentially following Sartre. She also uses the term, however, to refer to certain truths of the human condition that are inherently contradictory and are experienced by humans as an enduring tension: our sense of ourselves as infinitely free and at the same time as limited, as beings of flesh destined to die, and our essential solitude and our essential bond with others. In characterizing existence as ambiguous in this second sense, describing its condition as contradictory rather than just its meaning as open, Beauvoir diverges from Sartre and moreover argues for the recognition and acceptance of ambiguity as the condition of ethical relationships with others.

Biology

In The Second Sex Beauvoir associates the fundamental ambiguity of the human condition more clearly with the body than she had in her ethical essays. Beauvoir shows us that the structure of Absolute Subject/Inessential Other is written into the bodies of men and women. Patriarchy takes the givens of the body, which have no inherent meaning in themselves, and constructs the feminine immanent body and the masculine transcendent body. In its examination of patriarchal myths and the lived experience of women, The Second Sex charts the transformation of the female body into flesh.

As human subjects, Beauvoir argues, the body plays a central role in our existence. It is only as embodied that we can affirm our transcendence: "the body is our grasp on the world,"[56] it is "the radiation of a subjectivity, the instrument that makes possible the comprehension of the world."[57] However, it is also as embodied that the human subject can be reduced to immanence: My body in illness or extreme pain may effectively reduce me to living in the present moment.[58] If I am apprehended by the other as an object, my body in effect becomes an object that alienates me from myself.[59] The body is, then, most fundamentally the incarnation of our ambiguity as human subjects: It is as body that we are both freedom and flesh. Our freedom is made real only through concrete projects that engage the body[60]; and conversely, it is because we are embodied that we are vulnerable to the flesh itself and to the power of others to reduce us to flesh. The lived body reveals our ambiguity to us.

In *The Second Sex*, in contrast to the essays, Beauvoir recognizes that bodies are sexed, and in the first chapter she aims to analyze the importance of biological differences between the sexes. Since our body is our grasp on the world, biological differences will mean that we grasp the world in different ways. Bodily differences will give rise to differences in experience: "the body being the instrument of our grasp on the world, the world is bound to seem a very different thing when apprehended in one way or another."[61] The differences she takes to be important in this respect are that women's bodily being is more involved in reproduction than are men's, and that women have on the whole less muscular strength than men.[62] Is she, in attending to the biological differences between women and men, arguing that biology is the ground of women's oppression? Some of her comments about the "enslavement" of women to the species have been interpreted in this way by feminist critics.[63] But Beauvoir is not presenting anything as simple as a biologically determinist or reductionist argument.

Beauvoir does argue that male bodies have a biological advantage compared with female ones. The individual female organism is involved in the life of the species in a way that is of no physiological benefit to it as an individual organism and that may even be a danger to it.[64] But her use of the word *advantage* should not be misunderstood. A biological advantage has no meaning other than from a purely physiological point of view, and she also writes, as if in the next breath, that the body is never experienced as physiological. Indeed, this marks the failure of the biologist's understanding of the body and its human meaning: The biologist studies the body as an object rather than as a situation. The givens of the body must be understood in the light of a broader situation.[65]

Beauvoir thus begins with the analysis of women's biology in order to reveal the limits of an analysis that seeks to explain causally the oppression or subordination of women, or that even seeks to define women, based on this understanding of the body as an object. She refuses to say that women's involvement in reproduction or physical strength have any inherent meaning: Sexual differences are made meaningful in a complex human situation. However, because the existent is a body, the givens of the body are both the ground of and a real constraint and limitation on our freedom. And because women and men are embodied differently, these differences will express themselves in different lived situations. These differences, though, gain significance only as part of a larger social, psychological, and economic situation, and in the light of our ontological aims (that is, as part of the total existential situation that Beauvoir is aiming to analyze). Physical strength, for example, may be significant in early nomadic hunter-gatherer societies, but many of the advantages of physical strength are nullified by the bronze-age tool. Biological differences cannot, in any case, be experienced on a purely physiological level, since they are always lived out in situation.

This moves us immediately from the considerations of biological givens to the question of how biology is taken up and made meaningful in a human (existential) context. That is, it can't be said that biology is a cause of subordination, but the question of what humanity has made of sexual (biological and anatomical) differences is fundamental to the situation women will live out. As Beauvoir writes, it is not the body as a biological object that the subject lives, but the body as subject to taboos and to laws, a body that "reflects the desires and fears that express [our] ontological attitude."[66]

Mythology

These desires and fears are reflected in the myths that sustain patriarchy. These myths, as Beauvoir presents them, show that to be made Other is to be made the repository of all that is difficult and frightening in our embodied condition: Men project onto women those aspects of themselves that they would deny. It is the feminine as flesh that is, above all, reflected in masculine myths. Men associate mortality, frailty, indeed fleshiness in all its limiting aspects, with the Mother, and thus with women. In the various myths, the Mother as Earth, as Death, as Nature, as limitation itself is the Other that supports the masculine Absolute Subject. This Other is, then, the cultural representation and construction of the feminine body-as-flesh, and the cost of the masculine assertion of freedom and autonomy—conceived as freedom from limitation—is this close association and denigration of Woman and body-as-flesh.[67]

One of the forms in which this is played out is in the association of women with Nature. Nature inspires tremendous ambivalence in man—it signifies both his subjection to the species and the "realm that he subjugates to his will."[68] Man exploits nature but is also immersed in it, an immersion that, Beauvoir writes, is experienced as an imprisonment. Men of course know on some level that they are subject to nature like any animal and know that their freedom is necessarily dependent on this animal life.[69] But the ambiguity of our relation to nature is not easy to accept. Humans are of nature but not of it as other animals are; we are animals who are aware both of our consciousness and of our mortality, animals who "know and think the tragic ambiguity that other animals merely undergo."[70]

Patriarchal myths allow man to deny this fundamental ontological ambiguity of his condition. Just as the Subject-Other relation allows men to avoid the risks of reciprocity with a free other, the patriarchal myths allow man to evade the ambiguous truth of his embodied being. The myths separate an ambiguous unity into two unmixable aspects: "Since the coming of the patriarchate," Beauvoir writes, "life has worn in his eyes a double aspect: it is consciousness, will, transcendence, it is the spirit; and it is matter, passivity, immanence, it is the flesh."[71] Patriarchal myths, by associating matter, passivity, and immanence with women, allow men to disassociate themselves from these troubling aspects of their human condition, and yet give them some connection with the life that surrounds them, in the form of women who can be possessed, controlled, and domesticated. Woman as Nature— both wildly uncontrolled and tamed—is the site upon which men play out their ambivalence.

The strongest mythological connection is Woman as Mother, who connects man to the cycles of life and death and signifies the limitations of man as carnal: "In all civilizations and still in our own day woman inspires man with horror: it is the horror of his own carnal contingence, which he projects upon her."[72] Man's "curse is to be fallen from a bright and ordered heaven into the chaotic shadows of his mother's womb . . . he would be inevitable, like a pure Idea, like the One, the All, the absolute Spirit; and he finds himself shut up in a body of limited powers, in a place and time he never chose."[73] She is the reminder of his own fleshiness: "the contingency of all flesh is his own to suffer . . . she also dooms him to death. This quivering jelly which is elaborated in the womb (the womb, secret and sealed like the tomb) evokes too clearly the soft viscosity of carrion for him not to turn shuddering away."[74]

> This is woman's first lie . . . life itself . . . which . . . is always infested by age and death . . . infirm, homely, old, woman is horrifying. She is said to be withered,

faded, as might be said of a plant. To be sure, in man, too, decrepitude is terri-
fying; but normally man does not experience other men as flesh; he has only an
abstract unity with these separate and strange bodies. It is upon woman's
body—this body which is destined for him—that man really encounters the de-
terioration of the flesh. . . . The old woman, the homely woman, are not merely
objects without allure—they arouse hatred mingled with fear. In them reappears
the disquieting figure of the Mother . . .[75]

Thus what man cherishes and detests first of all in woman—loved one or
mother—is the fixed image of his animal destiny; it is the life that is necessary
to his existence but that condemns him to the finite and to death. From the
day of his birth man begins to die: this is the truth incarnated in the Mother.
In procreation he speaks for the species against himself: he learns this in his
wife's embrace . . . although he endeavours to distinguish mother and wife he
gets from both a witness to one thing only: his mortal state.[76]

Autonomy thus depends on separation from the mother and maternal
flesh. The male child's relation to the mother is one in which his autonomy
seems to be threatened by her symbolization of immanence and his dependence on her: "the quicker and more decisively the child realizes himself as
subject, the more the fleshly bond, opposing his autonomy, is going to become harassing to him."[77] The mother "reminds him of his own birth, an
event that he repudiates with all his strength."[78] "Man feels horror at having
been engendered; he would fain deny his animal ties; through the fact of his
birth murderous Nature has a hold upon him."[79] Beauvoir interprets rituals
to do with the placenta in the light of these fears—the placenta is the sign
of the dependency of the fetus on the mother; when it is ritually destroyed
"the individual is able to tear himself from the living magma and become an
autonomous being."[80] In this sense the woman as mother, since she symbolizes man's connection to larger cycles of birth, decay, and death, undermines
his sense of independence and separation, and this is why he must assert his
difference from her.

The masculine Absolute Subject, then, stands revealed as fantasy of omnipotence based on a denial and repudiation of the mother (and its mirror
image: the sanctification of the domesticated mother). Casting the Mother
as dangerous, uncontrollable nature and also as nature transformed and domesticated allows men a fantasy of omnipotence and invulnerability that
ushers in a conception of the subject as independent, autonomous, and
bounded: self-contained, self-controlled, and self-constituted. Beauvoir's
analysis reveals the Absolute Subject as a masculine illusion, a subject ob-
sessively and defensively concerned with shoring up his boundaries against
the engulfing, death-dealing mother of infantile fantasy.[81]

Men's fears and desires are also projected onto woman as an erotic partner: In this case the fear is of fecundity and its ties to life and death, but there
is also a desire in man to possess and tame these powers through the possession and domestication of woman.[82] The fascination with virginity in patriarchal societies is, Beauvoir argues, connected to this always impossible
dream of possession. The dream of possession always ends in frustration, in
part because woman survives the embraces of man and "becomes again a
stranger to him . . . new, intact, ready to be possessed by a new lover in as
ephemeral a manner."[83] But worse than this, in the attempt to possess the
other and control the powers with which she is charged, man finds himself
made into flesh:

> She makes her lover in truth her prey. Only a body can touch another body;
> the male masters the flesh he longs for only in becoming flesh himself . . . his
> mistress, in the vertigoes of pleasure, encloses him again in the opaque clay of
> that dark matrix which the mother fabricated for her son and from which he
> desires to escape.[84]

The legends of women as seductresses (the Sirens, Circe) have at their
root this sense of the dangers of desire. They articulate the sense of desire as
a passive, magic force that emanates from the other and enthrals and en-
slaves the consciousness. The man captivated by the charms of the seductress
"no longer has will-power, enterprise, future; he is no longer a citizen but
mere flesh enslaved to its desires,"[85] "with her, man senses most definitely the
passivity of his own flesh."[86]

Lived Experience

Beauvoir's depiction of women's lived experience is a picture of biology lived
out in the context of the male power and the patriarchal myths outlined earlier. Here we encounter the discourse of "horror" and Beauvoir's intensely
evocative language on female embodiment. As I have argued, this language
of horror has often been understood as revealing Beauvoir's own horror of the
female body.[87] Rather than trying to locate the source of Beauvoir's imagery
in her psyche, I highlight Beauvoir's curiously intense language in order to
consider its effect in her text. As I read it, the imagery functions to drama-
tize the tensions and frustrations of the feminine position as Other. In her descriptions of the girl's development, puberty, and sexual initiation, Beauvoir
depicts most concretely the frustrations of being "a free and autonomous being . . . compell[ed] to assume the status of the Other."[88] Beauvoir's language
of horror, I suggest, dramatizes women's lived experience as the embodiment

of masculine fantasy. I don't mean to claim, of course, that women (actual women in their concrete multiplicity) actually become Woman, the figure of masculine fantasy. What I do want to make clear, however, is Beauvoir's insistence on the extent to which patriarchal mythology shapes and constrains women's lived experience of their bodies. And I want to take seriously her claim that to know oneself to be a free being, yet experience oneself as flesh, in a culture that denigrates and devalues the flesh, could be an experience of horror.

Beauvoir writes that the little girl first lives her body as the radiation of her subjectivity: "In girls as in boys the body is first of all the radiation of a subjectivity, the instrument that makes possible the comprehension of the world."[89] However, everything in a young girl's upbringing discourages her from experiencing her body in this way: She is kept from experiencing the power of her body and its strength in games, adventures, and in violent confrontation.[90] She is trained in passivity. Her body seems to her mysterious and threatening; Beauvoir writes that she has "threatening insides."[91] But she truly becomes aware of herself as flesh at puberty, in the gaze of others. In contrast to Sartre, for whom the gaze, abstracted from its social context, is powerful and turns one into the other, it is the gaze in the social context of patriarchal power and mythology that turns the girl's reproductive possibilities into a destiny and the girl into an embodiment of Woman. Beauvoir explicitly links the moment of becoming flesh with the girl's first experience of the male gaze. At puberty, Beauvoir writes, the female child's body is "becoming the body of a woman and is being made flesh."[92] The physiological changes in her body that mark puberty—the growth of her breasts, of hair—are horrifying because in them "she senses a finality which tears her away from herself . . . she divines a dependence which dooms her to man, children, and to death."[93] Beauvoir links this moment of puberty with the girl's first awareness that her body is an object for others: "this body, which the girl has identified with herself, she now apprehends as flesh. It becomes an object that others look at and see."[94] Her body is no longer her own, no longer simply the expression or radiation of her subjectivity, because it has somehow been taken from her:

> The young girl feels that her body escapes her. It is no longer the straightforward expression of her individuality, it becomes alien to her, and at the same moment, she is taken as a thing by others. On the street men follow her with their eyes . . . she is afraid of becoming flesh and afraid of showing her flesh.[95]

The girl's experience of herself as flesh is physiology lived in the context of male power. With puberty, her insides really become threatening.[96] But Beauvoir insists that this is not simply a physiological phenomenon. Rather, the physiological changes gain their significance in a particular context—the socially created destiny that is lowering upon her.[97]

This becomes clear in Beauvoir's account of the lived experience of sexuality. Beauvoir's images and descriptions of women in the throes of desire as like mollusks and bogs, engulfing stickiness, seem to identify women with immanence. Indeed Beauvoir's metaphors go so far as to suggest that women become somewhat less than human in the sexual embrace, that women become something akin to lower-order animals, plants, even earth itself. What are we to make of her contention that "feminine sex desire is the soft throbbing of a mollusc"?[98] One infamous passage runs thus:

> Woman lies in wait like the carnivorous plant, the bog in which insects and children are swallowed up; she is suction, absorption, humus; she is pitch and glue, a motionless appeal, insinuating and viscous: thus, at least, she silently feels herself to be.[99]

Not only do women become like plants, they seem to lose themselves, become strangers to themselves: As Beauvoir writes, they do not recognize themselves in their desires, that is, as desiring beings. They become alien to themselves. Women lose their subjectivity in the sexual embrace or in the throes of desire. In direct contrast to the sex organ of a man, Beauvoir writes, which is as "simple and neat as a finger,"[100] exhibited innocently and proudly, the feminine sex organ:

> is mysterious to the woman herself, concealed, tormented, mucous, and humid, it bleeds every month, it is often sullied with bodily fluids, it has a secret and perilous life of its own. Woman does not recognise herself in it, and this explains in large part why she does not recognise its desires as hers.[101]

Women's bodies, in desire or sexual arousal, are mysteries, strangers, to women themselves. Again, in contrast to men, who remain self-possessed in their desire (*désir*), women "suffer or undergo a true alienation." A man is often afraid of the woman in his embrace, "so absent from herself she seems, prey to her turmoil,"[102] she is "more profoundly alienated than is man" because of her diffuse rather than localized bodily pleasure: "she is desire and sexual excitement (*désir et trouble*) in her whole body."[103]

When these horrifying descriptions of female sexuality are contrasted with what seems to be an idealized description of the male sexual experience—the sex organ, simple and neat as a finger—the male seems to be the incarnation of the active, transcendent consciousness, projecting into the world. In

Beauvoir's prose, men's penises project outward and upward: they are not troubling, unwieldy, or fleshy but are literally tools, just as responsive to the demands of consciousness as are their hands. It seems that Beauvoir has accepted and reproduced a sexist idealization of the desiring male and a disgust with female sexuality.[104]

However, Beauvoir is describing sexuality in conditions of inequality and as structured by patriarchal mythology. Her description of women as bogs comes in the context of an account of what women's sexuality has come to mean, socially, for them, in a situation of imposed femininity where they have internalized shame about their sexuality: "Woman is thoroughly indoctrinated with collective representations that give masculine desire (*rut*) a glorious character and make a shameful abdication of feminine sexual excitement (*trouble*)."[105] In this situation, desire is surely not a simple thing for them: split as they are by the demands of patriarchal femininity, an Other for the male, both subject for themselves and made into object.[106] It is scarcely surprising that sexuality as experienced by women in these conditions would undermine their selfhood: The woman who loses herself in the sexual embrace hardly had a self to begin with.[107]

Indeed, the male as the principle of activity, projecting himself outward and upward, "simple and neat as a finger" may be an idealized description of the male sexual experience, but it is certainly not Beauvoir's ideal. In fact, it is a description of sexuality in bad faith: that is, a description of the sexual body as men mythologize it, in a situation of inequality, and in the mode of denial. For what is revealed in this image of projection, action, "simple and neat," is a male illusion of invulnerability and autonomy. What this image describes is man's desire, even in the sexual embrace, to divorce himself from the flesh, to maintain the illusion of mastery and autonomy. Terry Keefe argues that in *The Second Sex*, if women are prone to one kind of bad faith, desire to or complicity with falling into immanence, men are prone to another, to the equation of subjectivity with pure transcendence or disembodied consciousness.[108] As Beauvoir writes:

> Masculine pride hides from men all that is equivocal in the drama of eroticism. They lie to themselves spontaneously, whereas women, who are more easily humiliated, more vulnerable, are more lucid; they manage to pull the wool over their own eyes only by means of a more cunning bad faith.[109]

Women, Beauvoir writes, have more difficulty than men do with the conflict that the erotic encounter presents. The erotic experience discloses to men and women both the ambiguity of their condition as freedom and flesh;

woman, already cast in patriarchy as cultural incarnation of the flesh, as Other, has difficulty assuming herself as a subject. In another sense, however, this position makes it more likely that a woman will be able to live out her eroticism authentically:

> The very difficulty of her position protects her against the traps into which the male readily falls; he is an easy dupe of the deceptive privileges accorded him by his aggressive role and the lonely pleasure of the orgasm; he hesitates to see himself fully as flesh. Woman lives her love in a more genuine fashion.[110]

Thus what Beauvoir depicts is a structure of oppression maintained by bad faith, mythology, and illusion. However, she also suggests that the body can only be lived out in this illusory way with some difficulty. Just as in her account of the myths of women as erotic object, Beauvoir stresses that the masculine dream of remaining pure freedom in the erotic embrace is undermined because one becomes transmuted into flesh through desire, in her account of the lived body, the male illusion of invulnerability is precarious precisely because of the body: The body always undermines the masculine sense of self as pure transcendence or pure freedom. The penis, however much idealized as a simple tool or instrument, persists in revealing itself also as flesh, not always responsive to individual will.[111] This is a curious parallel of the way in which Beauvoir suggests that the body undermines the illusions that sustain oppression in *The Ethics of Ambiguity*. There, the smile and eyes of a child, a hand reaching out, reveal the transcendence in immanence.[112] In *The Second Sex*, Beauvoir reveals the Absolute Subject to be fragile in a peculiar way: It requires all the force of myth and social power to sustain it, because it is inevitably undermined by the lived experience of the body.

Modes of Subjectivity: The Temptations of Mastery and the Possibility of Generosity

Risking: Subjectivity as Transcendence

Beauvoir's point about the conception of selfhood outlined earlier—that is, defensive masculine selfhood, the Absolute Subject, the self as pure transcendence—is twofold: first that it is, precisely, an illusion (the precariousness of which is always revealed by the body itself), and, second, that the illusion is sustained only at the cost of the oppression and domination of those designated as Other. What is the solution? To the extent that Beauvoir is focused on disrupting the cultural association of women with passive flesh, she advocates transcendence for women. She argues that women must have full access to concrete projects in the world. Part of the requirement for this is that women not be held to traditional feminine pursuits that don't enter onto a broader project and thus don't give women access to the public political world. She also explicitly argues that economic independence for women is a necessary precondition for their liberation. As she writes, "only independent work of her own can assure woman's genuine independence."[113] This also implies the end of institutions like traditional marriage, which maintain female dependence.[114]

But does this mean that as women become subjects, someone else will become the Other? Many of Beauvoir's feminist critics, as I have pointed out, argue that this is indeed the distressing outcome of her work.[115] Does the project, and transcendence as a model of subjectivity, imply violence or hostility toward the other whose own subjectivity must be disavowed? Certainly, Beauvoir's analysis does suggest that the attempt to master others will always remain a possibility. In *The Ethics of Ambiguity* Beauvoir took violence to be an inescapable possibility. My project may conflict with another's, and in bringing my own meanings to the world I may contest the meanings of others, even when building on the world which they have helped to shape.[116]

But, on the other hand, even when writing of the early nomads, Beauvoir doesn't unambiguously identify the risk that founds subjectivity (the risk of death that for Hegel announces our difference from other animals) with attempts to master the other who seems to threaten our freedom or whose free project contests ours. There, men were able to prove their freedom from the claims of the species in the cooperative hunt rather than in a struggle to the death with another consciousness.[117] She also suggests another sense of risk: risking the body against the given world in activities such as sport or mountain climbing, for example.[118] She does insist that part of subjectivity is being able to experience one's body as expressive of one's will, as responsive to one's desires. She argues that it is crucial for women to develop, and be able to use, the bodily capacity to mark the world with their meanings.[119] As she writes, "not to have confidence in one's body is to lose confidence in oneself . . . every subject regards [his] body as [his] objective expression."[120] She doesn't clearly distinguish here between transcendence and subjectivity: To experience oneself as a free subject, one must at least have the concrete opportunities to see the ways in which one can mark, change, or transform the world through one's actions, and to do this one must be able to experience the body as an instrument (or, better, to experience it as the instrumentality that one is, as an expression of one's will). Women must fundamentally have access to world making and to their own "adolescence." Here Beauvoir is pointing to the risks of asserting oneself as free in the face of others: the risk of putting oneself and one's work out in the world to be accepted, judged, and possibly rejected; the risk of appealing for recognition as a freedom and having one's appeal either taken up or contested. Thus for Beauvoir, experiencing my body as the radiation of my subjectivity and experiencing it as an instrument that challenges, dares, and transforms the given through activity or violence, are usually one and the same.[121]

In this sense Beauvoir doesn't directly answer Hegel or Sartre. She argues that it is crucial that women have concrete possibilities to exercise their transcendence and that there will always be the temptation to try to master the other whose project contests mine and whose freedom seems to confront and undermine mine. But this is only one possible reaction, and it is one that, in The Ethics of Ambiguity, Beauvoir suggests is immature or adolescent, and one that, in my analysis of The Second Sex, I have argued underlies the structure of patriarchy. She also gestures, in her development of the idea of conversion, toward another possibility: If we instead acknowledge the debt we owe to the other, the ways in which our freedoms are interdependent, the reciprocity of otherness, we won't be led into the attempt to master others in order to found our own subjectivity.

Generosity: The Erotic as Risk and Gift of Self

There are some suggestions in The Second Sex itself that projection into the future, and making a mark on the world, is not Beauvoir's only model of subjectivity. In a short analysis of women's role in social life and in salons, she suggests that subjectivity can be lived not by projection out into the future, but by the generous creation of a space for communication: She mentions the "gracious gifts" and the "pure generosity" involved in creating the space for celebration. The woman who creates such a space, such a moment, is "a gratuitous source of joy."[122] Beauvoir is attentive to the way in which women's situation of dependence may yield this generosity: "Her dependence forbids detachment, but from the well of her imposed self-sacrifice she sometimes draws up real generosity. She forgets herself in favour of her husband, her lover, her child; she ceases to think of herself, she is pure gift, pure offering."[123] Of course Beauvoir is aware that there are dangers in emphasizing this mode of subjectivity in a context in which women have always been expected to be self-sacrificing. The gift of self in the context of inequality and dependence can be a trap for both the one who gives it and for the receiver; it can be a frustrated attempt to justify oneself through devotion to another, a tyrannical gift.[124]

Beauvoir's scattered mentions of generosity, as another potential mode of subjectivity that is open to the other, is finally connected clearly to a way of living the body in her discussion of eroticism. With a "reciprocal generosity of body and soul,"[125] she suggests, we can assume our situation, and come to recognize the reciprocity of otherness: that each subject is, for the other, also an other, and that we all harbor otherness within. The erotic encounter is a moment that reveals our ambiguity to us:

> The erotic experience is one that most poignantly discloses to human beings the ambiguity of their condition; in it they experience themselves as flesh and as spirit, as the other and as subject.[126]

This vision of the possibilities of the erotic—though only briefly sketched—is the moment that most clearly fulfills the promise of Beauvoir's ethics of ambiguity. The erotic experience, lived in equality and authentically, is as much an acceptance of the body-self, of the strangeness within, as a recognition of the other. Here the two are connected: Recognition of the other requires the understanding that we are ourselves other for the other, that otherness is reciprocal. It means ceasing to project the abject parts of the self onto the other; taking this "otherness," or "strangeness" within the self.[127] Beauvoir describes eroticism as the theater for the tension between the self and other that she has already alerted us to is really an inability to accept certain aspects of the self:

> In those [erotic] combats where they think they confront one another, it is really against the self that each one struggles, projecting onto the partner those aspects of their own self that they repudiate; instead of living the ambiguity of their condition, each tries to make the other bear the abjection and tries to reserve the honour for the self. If, however, both assumed it [the ambiguity] with a lucid modesty, correlative of an authentic pride, they would recognise each other as equals (*semblables*) and live out the erotic drama in amity.[128]

Beauvoir's use of the term *recognise* here is telling—she is describing the reciprocal recognition that is the resolution of the master–slave or Subject–Other dynamic. "In a form concrete and carnal, the reciprocal recognition of self and other is accomplished in the most acute consciousness of the other and of the self."[129] We no longer see the other as hostile and as a threat to our freedom: "the dimension of the *other* remains, but the fact is that alterity no longer has a hostile character."[130]

There are crucial differences between Beauvoir's account of this conversion, or reciprocal recognition, and Hegel's. As Beauvoir noted in *The Ethics of Ambiguity*, according to Hegel I recognize the other as like myself.[131] For Beauvoir, what is central to the erotic encounter is that it is a space that allows differences to be:[132]

It is the awareness of the union of bodies in their separateness which gives the sexual act its moving characteristics; it is all the more overwhelming as the two beings who together passionately deny and affirm their boundaries are similar and yet different. This difference, which too often isolates them, becomes the source of their wonder when they meet.[133]

In this relation of reciprocity the dissimilarity of male and female eroticism— localized male *désir* in contrast to feminine *trouble* throughout the body—will be resolved, not in the direction of sameness, but of differences unmoored from the Subject–Other dynamic.

The erotic encounter thus most clearly makes concrete the new model of subjectivity Beauvoir's ethics promises. If Hegel's model of subjectivity (as Beauvoir reads him, freezing his dialectic in time) is the master and slave's duel to the death, echoed in *The Second Sex* by the murderous hunting forays of the nomads, and Sartre's model of subjectivity in *Being and Nothingness* is the inevitable hostility of the Look, by the end of *The Second Sex* Beauvoir has developed a new model: the erotic encounter. The erotic encounter can be seen as a sort of bodily risk taking that echoes and contrasts with Hegel's model of the risk that founds subjectivity. Here risk is connected to generosity and our bond with the other rather than with the assertion of self. Here risk is not associated with asserting oneself as a freedom, with challenging the given with one's capacity to initiate and remake the given world, but with the generous gift of self, the abandon of self to and with the other.[134] Here, true subjectivity, and an ethical relation with the other, requires not the self-assertion of the project, but a bodily generosity. The risk that founds subjectivity has, by the end of *The Second Sex*, been transmuted from the risk of death that originated in Hegel into the risk of assuming ambiguity by offering oneself as flesh and freedom, risking being made into object through one's gift of self to the other. Beauvoir describes the erotic encounter as the moment where both partners risk bodily abandon, recognizing themselves as at once consciousness and body (a freedom and a plaything of hormones), or subject and other, or "freedom" and species being (mortal):

As a matter of fact, man, like woman, is a flesh, thus a passivity, the plaything of his hormones and of the species, the uneasy prey of his desire. And she, like him, in the midst of the carnal fever, is a consenting, a voluntary gift, an activity; they live, each in their own manner, the strange ambiguity of existence made body. . . . In both sexes is played out the same drama of the flesh and the spirit, of finitude and transcendence; both are gnawed away by time and laid in wait for by death, they have the same essential need for the other and can gain from their freedom the same glory.[135]

In this account of the erotic we can see that the flesh has possibilities for Beauvoir beyond its disavowal in patriarchal societies. Throughout *The Second Sex* Beauvoir has been concerned to describe the frustrations and limitations inherent in the feminine situation—the way in which the feminine transformation into flesh imposes unbearable limitations on women (just as in *The Ethics of Ambiguity* the transformation into flesh makes one something like an animal or a corpse). However, here the flesh connotes not so much limitation as the possibility of a mode of risk, subjectivity, and communication with the other. We don't fully overcome our separateness as existents, but for a moment we are aware of a "union of bodies in their separateness."[136] We suspend for a moment our relentless projection into the future and live existence in its immediacy: "there is in eroticism a revolt of the instant against time, of the individual against the universal."[137] As Beauvoir writes in *The Ethics of Ambiguity*, in eroticism there is "an immediate communication with the other."[138]

In *The Second Sex* Beauvoir only gestures toward this vision of the possibilities of the erotic in a few passages. However, in her later essay "Must We Burn Sade?" she returns to the theme of the erotic and the transformation into flesh, and it is even clearer that the meaning of flesh has shifted. As Beauvoir presents him, the Marquis de Sade is a figure who is unable to see that his freedom depends on the freedom of the other. He lives out his eroticism as an Absolute Subject. His sadistic cruelty in sexuality is, as Beauvoir reads it, an attempt to compensate for his lack of emotional empathy, a kind of "autism" that made him unable to be genuinely aware of the reality of the other person.[139] Sade was both unable to forget himself or to connect with the other either in life or in his erotic encounters. In his erotic encounters he remains self-possessed: "There is an experience which he seems never to have known: that of emotional intoxication (*trouble*). Never in his stories does sensual pleasure appear as self-forgetfulness, swooning, or abandon."[140]

In "Must We Burn Sade?" Beauvoir argues that the state of emotional intoxication (*trouble*) "allows one to grasp existence in one's self and in the other as both subjectivity and passivity." This is what Beauvoir describes as "the transformation of the body into flesh."[141] Through such erotic abandon "the two partners merge in [an] ambiguous unity; each one is freed of his own presence and achieves immediate communication with the other."[142] Sade's cruelty is interpreted by Beauvoir as an attempt to compensate for both his separateness from others, his inability to reach them, and his own inability to escape his consciousness by becoming flesh. Instead of becoming flesh through "the vertigo of the other made flesh," Sade "remains confined within the solitude of his consciousness."[143] His "deliberate tyranny" is a failed attempt to recognize his own state in the passivity of the other.[144] Sade exemplifies the "tension of a will bent on fulfilling the flesh without losing itself in it."[145]

Conclusion

In *The Second Sex* Beauvoir is clear that there will always remain the possibility of struggle between the sexes. As soon as women are free, there is the possibility that they will enter into a struggle for recognition on Hegelian lines, equating violence with the risk that founds subjectivity.[146] And Beauvoir certainly does want women to experience their transcendence and welcomes the chance for women to experience their bodies as expressive of their will, for example, in concrete projects and in sport. But she also holds out, in the erotic embrace, the possibility of a conversion. Her analysis suggests that we can forgo the temptations of mastery in accepting our embodied subjectivity as ambiguously immanent and transcendent at once. The erotic moment stops us from forgetting that while we are transcendence and spirit, we are also flesh. The passage on the erotic moment is an opening in her text to a model of subjectivity that fully does justice to her analysis of the dynamics of oppression.

Undermining the cultural conflation of woman with the flesh is only part of Beauvoir's broader aim in *The Second Sex*, which is to criticize the masculine Absolute Subject and reveal the illusion on which it rests. The fantasy of pure transcendence must be seen as a form of bad faith, a flight from true human freedom with its limitations and neediness. If this is seen as Beauvoir's larger project, then her pointing out the ways in which women are not at one with the flesh removes a crucial prop from the masculine subject.[147] The outcome of this attempt to sever a too-easy conflation of women with the flesh isn't to deny the flesh itself, but is to underscore the extent to which we all, always, embody an uneasy tension of freedom and flesh, men as well as women.

I explore the possibility of developing an account of subjectivity as the ambiguity of immanence and transcendence by looking in the next chapter at Beauvoir's account of subjectivity in pregnancy and maternity. It is her evocation of this bodily experience that grapples with the most difficult questions her analysis raises—immanence and transcendence, the embodied subject—and while it doesn't fully resolve them, it points toward the idea of subjectivity as simultaneous immanence and transcendence that her work promises. In her account of free maternity, to experience the body as the radiation of my subjectivity is to experience it *at once* as instrument and flesh; indeed the dichotomy of active instrument and passive flesh breaks down in the consenting or free gift of self.

Notes

1. See, for example, Mary O'Brien, *The Politics of Reproduction* (London: Routledge & Kegan Paul, 1981), and Kathy Ferguson, *The Man Question: Visions of Subjectivity in Feminist Theory* (Berkeley: University of California Press, 1993). See also my discussion in chapter 2, the section titled The Body as a Philosophical Problem.

2. Simone de Beauvoir, *The Second Sex*, trans. and ed. H. M. Parshley (New York: Vintage, 1989), 64.

3. Jean-Paul Sartre, *Being and Nothingness*, trans. Hazel Barnes (New York: Philosophical Library, 1956), 235–44.

4. Beauvoir, *The Second Sex*, xxii.

5. Beauvoir, *The Second Sex*, xxxiv.

6. See my discussion in chapter 3.

7. Beauvoir, *The Second Sex*, xxxv.

8. Beauvoir, *The Second Sex*, xxxv.

9. Beauvoir, *The Second Sex*, xxiii.

10. Beauvoir, *The Second Sex*, xxii.

11. Beauvoir, *The Second Sex*, xxiii.

12. Beauvoir, *The Second Sex*, xxiii.

13. Le Doeuff argues that Beauvoir's use of this model of subjectivity is *The Second Sex*'s great weakness. She suggests that to make use of *The Second Sex* we should disregard its unpersuasive ontological foundation—a foundation that she argues is neither compelling nor politically useful, for if women succeed on this model in becoming subjects, they will replicate the oppression by defining themselves against a new Other. Le Doeuff, *Hipparchia's Choice: An Essay Concerning Women, Philosophy, etc.* (Oxford: Blackwell, 1991). Catherine Keller, for one, has suggested that this Other will be other women. Keller, *From a Broken Web: Separation, Sexism and Self* (Boston: Beacon, 1986), ch. 1. See also Ferguson, *The Man Question*.

14. Beauvoir, *The Second Sex*, xxiii.

15. Beauvoir, *The Second Sex*, xxv.

16. Beauvoir, *The Second Sex*, 71.

17. Beauvoir, *The Second Sex*, 70, emphasis in original.

18. Beauvoir, *The Second Sex*, xxiv.

19. Beauvoir, *The Second Sex*, xxiv.

20. Beauvoir, *The Second Sex*, xxv.

21. Beauvoir, *The Second Sex*, xxv. Note that Beauvoir's use of the term *Mitsein* here is different from Heidegger's. In his terms, men and women would not be in a genuine *Mitsein*, since this "being with" presumes two equal subjects.

22. Beauvoir, *The Second Sex*, 58.

23. Beauvoir, *The Second Sex*, 139.

24. Beauvoir, *The Second Sex*, xxiii.

25. Beauvoir, *The Second Sex*, 247.

26. See, for example, Hegel, *Philosophy of Right*, trans. T. M. Knox (London: Oxford University Press, 1967), sect. 166. For feminist critiques of Hegel's position on women, see Genevieve Lloyd, *Man of Reason: Male and Female in Western Philosophy*, 2d ed. (London: Routledge, 1993) and "Selfhood, War and Masculinity," in *Feminist Challenges: Social and Political Theory*, ed. Carole Pateman and Elisabeth Gross (Boston: Northeastern University Press, 1986), 63–76; Patricia Mills, *Woman, Nature and Psyche* (New Haven: Yale University Press, 1987); and Seyla Benhabib, "On Hegel, Women and Irony," in *Situating the Self: Gender, Community and Postmodernism in Contemporary Ethics* (New York: Routledge, 1992), 242–59.

27. See, for example, O'Brien, *The Politics of Reproduction*; Mills, *Woman, Nature and Psyche*; Jaggar and McBride, "'Reproduction' as Male Ideology," in *Hypatia Reborn*, ed. Azizah al-Hibri and Margaret Simons (Bloomington: Indiana University Press, 1990), 249–69.

28. Hegel, *Phenomenology*, sect. 186.

29. Hegel, *Phenomenology*, sect. 186.

30. Hegel, *Phenomenology*, sect. 187.

31. Hegel, *Phenomenology*, sect. 189.

32. As Kojève writes: "the slave binds himself completely to the things on which he depends." Kojève, *Introduction to the Reading of Hegel*, trans. James H. Nichols Jr. and ed. Allan Bloom (New York: Basic Books, 1969), 17. See also Hegel, *Phenomenology*, sect. 190.

33. Kojève, *Introduction to Hegel*, 40, 42.

34. Kojève, *Introduction to Hegel*, 46. The influence of Kojève on Beauvoir is most clearly seen in these passages, in the emphasis placed on the difference between human and animal life.

35. Kojève, *Introduction to Hegel*, 19–20. Hegel, *Phenomenology*, sect. 192.

36. Beauvoir, *The Second Sex*, 63. Though, as Tina Chanter notes, in Beauvoir's version the men gain prestige in the eyes of others in the horde by partaking in the hunt and risking their lives, and in that sense could be said to gain recognition from the group, even if not in individual struggle with another. Chanter, *Ethics of Eros: Irigaray's Rewriting of the Philosophers* (London: Routledge, 1995), 61.

37. Beauvoir, *The Second Sex*, 64.

38. Beauvoir, *The Second Sex*, 64.

39. Beauvoir, *The Second Sex*, 67–69, 78; and see also Keller's analysis of early agricultural societies in *From a Broken Web*, 27.

40. There are certainly some questionable aspects to this part of Beauvoir's analysis, and it is, as anthropology or history, quite flawed. For example, the masculine activities that she takes as indicators of transcendence, of risking and challenging the given and creating anew, of individual assertion, are hunting and fishing—activities that it could easily be argued are as much the result of necessity as is reproduction. See Kathryn Pauly Morgan, "Romantic Love, Altruism and Self-Respect: An Analysis of Simone de Beauvoir," *Hypatia* 1, no. 1 (1986): 117–48; esp. 120–23. I elaborate on the significance of pregnancy in the next chapter.

41. Hegel, *Phenomenology*, sect. 195.

42. Hegel, *Phenomenology*, sect. 196.

43. Hegel, *Phenomenology*, sect. 195.

44. Kojève, *Introduction to Hegel*, 49.

45. Beauvoir's analysis of housework makes this explicit. Domestic work, she writes, "provides no escape from immanence and little affirmation of individuality. . . . Few tasks are more like the torture of Sisyphus than housework, with its endless repetition: the clean becomes soiled, the soiled is made clean, over and over, day after day." Beauvoir, *The Second Sex*, 451.

46. Note that here my reading contrasts most with Tina Chanter's. She argues that Beauvoir misreads Hegel by not taking his dialectic seriously: She doesn't recognize the transformation the slave undergoes in her application of the Hegelian framework to men and women. Chanter argues in *Ethics of Eros*, 66, 72, that this is because Beauvoir was working with a Sartrean conception of absolute freedom. If freedom is a given, then the encounter with the other in the Hegelian dialectic (as it is applied to men and women) doesn't change the subject, doesn't create a free subject. But as I have argued in chapter 3, Beauvoir isn't working with a conception of absolute freedom. She develops a concept of freedom as interdependent. She argues that the individual's freedom presupposes the social relation, and the individual's capacity to act ethically depends on her recognition of her dependence on the other's freedom. Beauvoir in this sense does write about a transformation—but it is not, as it is for the slave, one achieved through labor. Beauvoir's term in *The Second Sex* is one we have already encountered in *The Ethics of Ambiguity*: The transformation from the assertion of pure freedom to the recognition of the reciprocity of freedom is a "conversion," one that must constantly be made.

47. Note that I am interpreting her use of the master–slave dialectic quite differently from most critics, such as Ferguson, *The Man Question*, and O'Brien, *Politics of Reproduction*. Both argue that Beauvoir is accepting the Hegelian masterful subject uncritically, and that the Hegelian subject is a masculine subject predicated on domination (Ferguson) or alienation from the birth process (O'Brien). Whether or not these are persuasive accounts of Hegel's subject, my point is that Beauvoir doesn't accept the Hegelian subject uncritically at all, but appropriates and transforms Hegel's dialectic for her own ends.

48. Beauvoir, *The Second Sex*, 139.

49. Beauvoir, *The Second Sex*, 141.

50. Beauvoir, *The Second Sex*, 140, TA; *Deuxième sexe I*, 238. Parshley's translation here unintentionally obscures both the philosophical import of Beauvoir's writing and the connections between her analysis in *The Ethics of Ambiguity* and *The Second Sex*. He translates "conversion" as transformation.

51. Beauvoir, *The Second Sex*, 140.

52. Beauvoir, *The Second Sex*, 141.

53. Beauvoir, *The Second Sex*, 141, 144.

54. Butler, *Subjects of Desire: Hegelian Reflections in Twentieth Century France* (New York: Columbia, 1987), 44.

55. Butler, *Subjects of Desire*, 45.

56. Beauvoir, *The Second Sex*, 36.

57. Beauvoir, *The Second Sex*, 267.

58. Much of Beauvoir's writing on the aging body and the body in illness and pain highlights the immanence of the body and suggests the difficulty of maintaining an orientation to the future while in that condition. However, her writing on illness and aging is also notable for its nuance and for the suggestion that the experience of illness may lead us to an assumption of our ambiguity. I address this further later in the chapter.

59. Beauvoir, *The Second Sex*, 269. And see Bergoffen, *The Philosophy of Simone de Beauvoir: Gendered Phenomenologies, Erotic Generosities* (New York: State University of New York Press, 1997), 147.

60. Beauvoir, *The Second Sex*, 370–71.

61. Beauvoir, *The Second Sex*, 32.

62. Beauvoir, *The Second Sex*, 26–30, 31, 34–35.

63. See, for example, Mackenzie, "Simone de Beauvoir: Philosophy and/or the Female Body," in *Feminist Challenges: Social and Political Theory*, ed. Carole Pateman and Elizabeth Gross (Boston: Northeastern University, 1987), 144–56, and Charlene Haddock Seigfried, "'Second Sex': Second Thoughts," in *Hypatia Reborn*, ed. Azizah al-Hibri and Margaret Simons (Bloomington: Indiana University Press, 1990), 305–22.

64. Beauvoir, *The Second Sex*, 29–30.

65. This is also Merleau-Ponty's claim in *The Structure of Behaviour*, trans. Alden L. Fisher (Boston: Beacon Press, 1963) and in *The Phenomenology of Perception*, trans. Colin Smith (London: Routledge, 1962).

66. Beauvoir, *The Second Sex*, 36, TA; *Deuxième sexe*, 76. "*Se reflètent des désirs et des craintes qui traduisent leur attitude ontologique.*" Parshley translates "*attitude ontologique*" as "essential nature," which obscures Beauvoir's point here: Humans have no essential nature.

67. This central insight of *The Second Sex* has been taken up and developed in, for example, Dorothy Dinnerstein, *The Mermaid and the Minotaur: Sexual Arrangements and the Human Malaise* (New York: Harper & Row, 1976) and Jessica Benjamin, *The Bonds of Love* (New York: Pantheon, 1988).

68. Beauvoir, *The Second Sex*, 144.

69. Beauvoir, *The Second Sex*, 144: "He well knows that he exists only in so far as he lives."

70. Beauvoir, *The Ethics of Ambiguity*, 9.

71. Beauvoir, *The Second Sex*, 144.

72. Beauvoir, *The Second Sex*, 148.

73. Beauvoir, *The Second Sex*, 146.

74. Beauvoir, *The Second Sex*, 146.

75. Beauvoir, *The Second Sex*, 180–81.

76. Beauvoir, *The Second Sex*, 165–66.

77. Beauvoir, *The Second Sex*, 196.

78. Beauvoir, *The Second Sex*, 196.

79. Beauvoir, *The Second Sex*, 146.

80. Beauvoir, *The Second Sex*, 146.

81. This is one of Zirilli's central arguments in "A Process without a Subject: Simone de Beauvoir and Julia Kristeva on Maternity," *Signs* 18, no. 1 (1992): 111–35, 126

82. Beauvoir, *The Second Sex*, 154.

83. Beauvoir, *The Second Sex*, 163.

84. Beauvoir, *The Second Sex*, 164.

85. Beauvoir, *The Second Sex*, 165.

86. Beauvoir, *The Second Sex*, 168.

87. In chapter 2 of this book.

88. Beauvoir, *The Second Sex*, xxxv.

89. Beauvoir, *The Second Sex*, 267.

90. Beauvoir, *The Second Sex*, 280, 282.

91. Beauvoir, *The Second Sex*, 298.

92. Beauvoir, *The Second Sex*, 306.

93. Beauvoir, *The Second Sex*, 307.

94. Beauvoir, *The Second Sex*, 307.

95. Beauvoir, *The Second Sex*, 308. See also 312.

96. This sense of the reproductive body as threatening to the girl or woman is repeated through the text, reappearing in the context of sexual initiation. The threat of a impregnation, Beauvoir writes, makes the man appear a threat and the sperm seem like "injurious germs" or "offensive matter": the young girl becomes "terrified by the threat that lurks in her lover's body" (Beauvoir, *The Second Sex*, 387). The reproductive body as a threat to the self arises most infamously in Beauvoir's depiction of pregnancy (see chapter 5).

97. Beauvoir, *The Second Sex*, 315. As we see in chapter 5, it is in this context that her analysis and her horrifying images of pregnancy make sense: They describe the subjective experience of pregnancy in a situation that turns it into a destiny and turns the pregnant woman into the passive recipient of a species destiny: In the current social context, Beauvoir is saying, pregnancy cannot be lived as a human endeavor—a strange echo of the situation of the primitive nomads.

98. Beauvoir, *The Second Sex*, 386, TA; *Deuxième sexe II*, 167. "*Le rut feminin, c'est la molle palpitation d'un coquillage.*" *Molle*, soft, also has connotations of sluggish, flaccid, or weak.

99. Beauvoir, *The Second Sex*, 386, TA; *Deuxième sexe II*, 167. "*elle guette comme la plante carnivore, le marécage ou insectes et infants s'enlisent; elle est succion, ventouse, humeuse, elle est poix et glu, un appel immobile, insinuant et visqueux: du moins est-ce ainsi que sourdement elle se sent.*" Parshley has "passive influx" for "*appel immobile*"; I have rendered this more literally as "motionless appeal." He mistranslates "*sourde-ment*" as "vaguely"; I have substituted "silently."

100. Beauvoir, *The Second Sex*, 386.

101. Beauvoir, *The Second Sex*, 386, TA; *Deuxième sexe II*, 166. "*le sexe féminin est mystérieux pour la femme elle-même, caché, tourmenté, muqueux, humide; il saigne chaque mois, il est parfois souillé d'humeurs, il a une vie secrète et dangereuse. C'est en grande partie parce que la femme ne se reconnaît pas en; ui qu'elle n'en reconnaît pas comme siens les désirs.*" Parshley inserts "even" in "mysterious . . . to the woman her-self" and omits "*tourmenté*," or tormented.

102. Beauvoir, *The Second Sex*, 391, TA; *Deuxième sexe II*, 176. "*la femme . . . subit une veritable alienation,*" "*tant celle-ci apparait absente d'elle-meme, en proie a l'egare-ment.*" Parshley has woman "really los[ing] her mind" and being "more profoundly be-side herself than is man" where the text refers to alienation: This is one of the more serious inadequacies of his translation since it obscures Beauvoir's consistent use of this term. Where Parshley has "so beside herself she seems, a prey to her aberration" I have substituted the more literal "absent from herself," and in the same line "her turmoil" is a better rendition of "*égarement*" (close in meaning to the French "*trou-ble*") than is "aberration," implying, as it does, deviation or abnormality.

103. Beauvoir, *The Second Sex*, 397, TA; *Deuxième sexe II*, 183. "*Plus profondément aliénée que l'homme, du fait qu'elle est désir et trouble dans sons corps tout entier.*" A se-rious inconsistency in Parshley's translation is his inattention to the difference be-tween the French terms "*désir*" and "*trouble*" as Beauvoir uses them, translating them both indiscriminately as "desire" or "sexual excitement." I flag these terms in the text, as the distinction is crucial to my argument later in the section titled Generos-ity: The Erotic as Risk and Gift of Self.

104. Moi, for example, argues that Beauvoir's own obsessions and horror show through here in her metaphors, and that her metaphors link femininity with im-manence and masculinity with transcendence (though she also argues that Beau-voir's metaphors are separate from her argument per se, and we could jettison them while retaining the core notions of responsibility, freedom, and liberation from her text). Beauvoir's metaphoric language about sexuality seems even more disturbing when we note the coincidence of her language with Sartre's, with his now infamous "holes and slime." (See, for example, Collins and Pierce, Greene, Le Doeuff, and Moi.) Many people have argued that this is a blind spot in Beau-voir's analysis, but I'd like to suggest that, seen in the broader context of her work, there is something more subversive, transgressive, and even transformative at work in Beauvoir's echoing of Sartre's metaphors. She seems to be saying that— given the current conditions of inequality—you may desire a woman, Sartre, but what you're going to get is a bog, a sucking mollusk. Beauvoir's argument about

the meaning of the penis is also more complex than this passage would suggest, as I note below at note 111.

105. Beauvoir, *The Second Sex*, 386, TA; *Deuxième sexe II*, 166. "*La femme est imbue des representations collectives qui donnent au rut masculin un charactere glorieux, et qui font du trouble feminin une abdication honteuse.*"

106. Beauvoir, *The Second Sex*, 402.

107. Beauvoir, *The Second Sex*, 402: "This conflict has a more dramatic shape for woman because at first she feels herself to be an object and does not at once realize a sure independence in sex enjoyment."

108. Terry Keefe, "Simone de Beauvoir and Sartre on Mauvaise Foi," *French Studies* 34 (July 1980): 300–14.

109. Beauvoir, *The Second Sex*, 688, TA; *Deuxième sexe II*, 608.

110. Beauvoir, *The Second Sex*, 402.

111. Beauvoir's argument about the social meaning of the penis is actually rather complex. It is important in the development of the young boy's sense of himself as a subject because it can be experienced as active (Beauvoir, *The Second Sex*, 273). The little boy can identify himself with it and invest it with his subjectivity. The boy can experience the penis as an expression of his will/transcendence and feel pride in it; its capacities can become for him "the measure of his own worth" (Beauvoir, *The Second Sex*, 278). But it is also the source of such ambiguously voluntary/involuntary bodily experiences as urination and ejaculation, and is a "capricious and foreign" source of a pleasure that is experienced subjectively (Beauvoir, *The Second Sex*, 48). This means, Beauvoir argues, that the young boy can bring the "life that overflows" from his penis—his connection to the species, the involuntary—"into integration with his subjective individuality." He is able to feel and experience his penis as at once himself and other than himself (Beauvoir, *The Second Sex*, 48). However, the social power invested in the penis as a symbol of male transcendence "keep[s] alive the tradition that identifies the phallus and the male idea"—or rather, identifies the penis and the phallus (Beauvoir, *The Second Sex*, 271; see also 281, 48). As it becomes the symbol of the social power vested in males (i.e., becomes a phallus), it becomes the incarnation of male transcendence. Beauvoir's argument implies that the anatomical penis can only be conflated with the symbol of male power, the phallus, as long as it is the incarnation of activity and drive, that is, as long as the penis is only imagined as the erect penis. Patriarchal myths thus conflate the penis and the phallus, creating a mythical male anatomy. However, while the penis as phallus can symbolize transcendence, the penis partakes of the ambivalence of the body generally: It incarnates the human condition of ambiguity of immanence/transcendence. The penis symbolizes masculine transcendence but also undermines this sense of transcendence, because it connects man to species-life: "in his sex organ he finds himself again beset with life, nature and passivity"; the penis "denies the proud singularity of the subject" (Beauvoir, *The Second Sex*, 162–63). For this reason, patriarchal mythology (the imaginary) must valorize the erection/ejaculation and "forget" the flaccid penis, the connection with life/death, if it is to sustain the illusion of pure transcendence.

112. See chapter 3.

113. Beauvoir, *The Second Sex*, 475.

114. Beauvoir, *The Second Sex*, 456. Beauvoir insists that "marriage must be prohibited as a career for women." Beauvoir, *The Second Sex*, 482.

115. See Catherine Keller, *From a Broken Web*, ch. 1; Michèle Le Doeuff, "Simone de Beauvoir and Existentialism," *Feminist Studies* 6, no. 2 (1980): 277–89; ; Ferguson, *The Man Question*; and Andrea Nye, "Preparing the Way For a Feminist Praxis," *Hypatia* 1, no. 1 (1986). Nye also argues, however, that there are tensions in Beauvoir's thought that indicate a move beyond hostility and toward reciprocity, but that this ideal is not assimilated theoretically into Beauvoir's existentialism. Nye, "Preparing the Way," 105, 111.

116. See Beauvoir, *The Ethics of Ambiguity*, 96–97.

117. See earlier in this chapter.

118. Beauvoir, *The Second Sex*, 333, 726.

119. Beauvoir, *The Second Sex*, 331–32, 724.

120. Beauvoir, *The Second Sex*, 332.

121. Lundgren-Gothlin argues in *Sex and Existence* that the central claim of *The Second Sex* is that women must demand recognition by entering into the master–slave dialectic, risking through violence, concrete projects in the world, sport, and art. See 73, 114, and 222–26.

122. Beauvoir, *The Second Sex*, 540. This is a sense of subjectivity that is only hinted at in *The Second Sex*; it echoes Beauvoir's analysis of the *fête* or festival in *The Ethics of Ambiguity*, as a moment when the relentless projection of the self into the future is arrested in a moment of sensuous abandon with others. The festival, Beauvoir argues, marks a human need to celebrate existence in its immediacy and negativity. In drunkenness, eroticism, destruction there is an immediate communication with others. See Beauvoir, *The Ethics of Ambiguity*, 125.

123. Beauvoir, *The Second Sex*, 626.

124. Beauvoir, *The Second Sex*, 585–59, 721.

125. Beauvoir, *The Second Sex*, 402, TA; *Deuxième sexe II*, 189–90.

126. Beauvoir, *The Second Sex*, 402, TA; *Deuxième sexe II*, 190.

127. As I have noted before, Beauvoir's writings on illness and the aging body emphasize the ways in which these experiences make us aware of the ambiguity of our condition. In that sense, her depictions of illness and the aging body present some parallels with her account of the possibilities of the erotic. *Old Age*, trans. Patrick O'Brien (London: Andre Deutsch Ltd., 1972), a relatively neglected book, is particularly striking in this regard. The argument that we must recognize the other within ourselves is, if anything, made more directly in that text than in *The Second Sex*. Writing about the aged as Other, she compares the Buddha's recognition that he is the future dwelling place of old age with our general refusal to assume this otherness within: "in the old person that we must become, we refuse to recognize ourselves . . . let us recognize ourselves in this old man or that old woman" (4–5).

128. Beauvoir, *The Second Sex*, 728, TA; *Deuxième sexe II*, 658.

129. Beauvoir, *The Second Sex*, 401, TA; *Deuxième sexe II*, 189.

130. Beauvoir, *The Second Sex*, 401, TA; *Deuxième sexe II*, 189.

131. See chapter 3.

132. Note that this is an explicitly heterosexual vision. Though Beauvoir's chapter entitled "The Lesbian" was ahead of its time as an analysis of lesbianism that didn't pathologize it, arguing instead that it could be an authentic choice, she stopped short of seeing it as part of the ideal.

133. Beauvoir, *The Second Sex*, 401.

134. This point is also made by Debra Bergoffen in *Philosophy of Simone de Beauvoir*, 160–63. That the erotic for Beauvoir makes possible a new ethic based on the gift is one of her central claims.

135. Beauvoir, *The Second Sex*, 728, TA; *Deuxième sexe II*, 658–59.

136. Beauvoir, *The Second Sex*, 402.

137. Beauvoir, *The Second Sex*, 59.

138. Beauvoir, *The Ethics of Ambiguity*, 125. Rosalyn Diprose, "Generosity: Between Love and Desire," *Hypatia* 13, no. 1 (1998), argues that erotic generosity is a means of extending existence through others without entrapment or possession.

139. Beauvoir, "Must We Burn Sade?" 33.

140. Beauvoir, "Must We Burn Sade?" 32. Beauvoir's writing on illness, aging, and death reveals some parallels with her discussion of sexuality here. She suggests that the lived experience of the body in aging and death undermines the illusion of the Absolute Subject, and the fantasy of the controlled, contained, impermeable body on which it is founded. In her accounts of Sartre's and her mother's illness and death, Beauvoir figures the body in terms of abandon, loss of control, loss of boundary and self-possession—that is, in the same way that she depicts women's experience of sexuality in *The Second Sex* and the transformation into flesh in "Must We Burn Sade?" This suggests to me that Beauvoir's work on aging could give us some insight into the cultural connections between aging, sexuality, passivity, and the construction of femininity.

141. Beauvoir, "Must We Burn Sade?" 32.

142. Beauvoir, "Must We Burn Sade?" 32.

143. Beauvoir, "Must We Burn Sade?" 33.

144. Beauvoir, "Must We Burn Sade?" 34.

145. Beauvoir, "Must We Burn Sade?" 39.

146. Beauvoir, *The Second Sex*, 191.

147. As Zerilli argues in *A Process without a Subject*, 130–31.

~

CHAPTER FIVE

Bodies at Risk:
The Meanings of Maternity

Can we understand Beauvoir's portrayal of maternity in the light of the analysis of her ethics that I have made in the last two chapters? Beauvoir analyzes patriarchy as an institution that allows men to avoid seeing themselves as flesh, by reducing women to their bodies as flesh. Beauvoir's philosophical essays, and indeed the whole structure of *The Second Sex*, lead to the conclusion that ethical conversion—avoiding mastery and subservience in our relations with others—requires us to assume our ambiguity as freedom and flesh, to fully assume our embodiment. But her critics have argued that her analysis of maternity, and, particularly, the images she employs to portray the pregnant body, suggest that the flesh will always be a prison for women, and that there is no way to live it in freedom.[1]

One of Beauvoir's central arguments in *The Second Sex* is that the body is not simply a biological object. While it may have objective structures and limitations, these only take on meaning in a complex situation. We cannot ever say definitively what the body is, but only explore its meaning as it is lived. An argument that the pregnant body simply *is* limitation belies this central tenet of Beauvoir's. But beyond this, the body has, as I have argued, a central part in Beauvoir's ethics. We are freedom-in-situation, and thus our condition is always one of a profound tension between freedom and facticity. Though the body is an important aspect of our facticity, Beauvoir doesn't argue that it signifies pure constraint or necessity. Rather, she argues that the body partakes of the ambiguity that characterizes the human condition more generally. Our body is both our grasp on the world, and it is an object in the world, flesh that subordinates us to species demands. In her brief portrayal of the erotic relation, Beauvoir also suggests that the body, assumed as both freedom and flesh, can be the basis for a deep connection, communication, and ethical relation with others.

In the light of this, the question becomes whether Beauvoir's treatment of pregnancy is consistent with her ethical aims throughout *The Second Sex* and the essays. If we read Beauvoir's account of maternity in the light of her ethics we can see that she does remain consistent with her argument in *The Second Sex*. It is not reproductive biology itself that is a problem for women, but what has been made of women's biology, the meanings that it carries in patriarchal society.[2] Beauvoir argues that maternity is not a destiny and that the patriarchal myths that posit women as one with nature, fulfilled and completed through maternity, are part of a structure of enforced maternity that limits and constrains women's freedom. The images of invasion and resistance that mark Beauvoir's account of maternity should thus be seen as a graphic depiction of this enforced maternity. Beauvoir shows, in her analysis and her imagery, what it is like for women to experience maternity when it has been constructed as a destiny and as a submission to species demands that is not animated by human intention. Her imagery of invasion and resistance portrays the experience of maternity when the mother's subjectivity is not recognized and when women are given no concrete choices or opportunities in the world. Her discourse of war and horror serves to break the links between the natural process of reproduction and the reproductive destiny that is constructed in patriarchal societies.

Beauvoir further argues for the conditions that would make "free maternity," or *maternité libre*, possible: choice and involvement in the public world. This is an argument both for maternity as an engagement or a project and for mothers as subjects. For Beauvoir free maternity is an engagement, an obligation and a responsibility, and an opening onto the future; a mother must have concrete opportunities to shape the world because she is taking on responsibility for the world her child will enter. In reconceiving maternity in this way, Beauvoir asserts that maternity is not simply an immersion in the cyclical time of the species, but is an essential connection with the future through the other, the child-to-be. Motherhood is thus an engagement with the world: Citizenship and subjectivity are not only compatible with motherhood, but free maternity actually requires them.

In her account of maternity, Beauvoir doesn't articulate explicitly the ambiguity of immanence and transcendence at once that is so striking in her account of the erotic. She presents a feminist account of free maternity and the social and political conditions it would require. However, her description of free maternity is of the mother's relation with her child and not the experience of pregnancy itself. In that sense, her account of maternity remains implicated in the distinction between the body as instrument and the body-as-flesh that seems to break down at other points in her text. Women will live out a tension and ambiguity, but there is little, in Beauvoir's descriptions of pregnancy, to suggest that the flesh itself may be a source of joy or mode of communication with the other, as it can be in the erotic embrace.

However, read in the context of Beauvoir's ethics of ambiguity and embodied subjectivity, the possibilities of maternal subjectivity can be seen to be much richer. In what follows, I develop an account of pregnant subjectivity that builds on Beauvoir's ethics of otherness within, going beyond what is explicit in *The Second Sex*. I argue, as Linda Zerilli suggests, that Beauvoir's rhetoric both reveals how the patriarchal mythology of motherhood denies women's subjectivity and discloses how this is lived out by women in maternity. Zerilli argues that Beauvoir's rhetoric restages maternity as "unnatural" in order to unsettle the patriarchal myth of blissful fusion and allow for a feminist rewriting of maternal desire that takes into account the many individual experiences of pregnancy and maternity.[3] However, Zerilli also argues that Beauvoir was too fearful of reinstating patriarchal myths of motherhood as destiny to actually begin to articulate a feminist interpretation of maternal subjectivity.[4] While it is true that Beauvoir doesn't fully articulate maternal subjectivity, the ethics that she developed throughout both the essays and *The Second Sex* allow us to think with her about the direction it might take. Beauvoir's discussion of conversion, risk, and generosity reveals the way in which mothers as subjects and pregnancy as a project undermine the absolute subject and point toward a new vision of subjectivity as immanence and transcendence at once. A chosen pregnancy is a risk—both physical and ontological—and Beauvoir's analysis of pregnancy thus also reveals how the risk that founds subjectivity has changed through *The Second Sex*. As in the erotic encounter, here risk is not simply projecting oneself out into the world as a freedom, but also most graphically assuming otherness within the self.

Beauvoir's Rhetorical War

The images Beauvoir uses to describe reproduction throughout *The Second Sex* are horrifying, as so many critics have noticed. Most often, this is explained as a sign of Beauvoir's own fear or disgust of her body or her internalization of a masculine fear of the female body.[5] The fact that Beauvoir was never herself pregnant is sometimes taken as proof of her psychological problem with it.[6] As with my discussion of her language about sexuality, with its strange and disturbing images of mollusks and bogs, I want to shift our attention away from speculation about Beauvoir as the source of the excessive imagery and explore instead the effects of that imagery when it is considered as a rhetorical strategy. Beauvoir's language *is* excessive, in the sense that many women would probably not recognize themselves and their experience of maternity in it; it is unfamiliar, strange, and disturbing. The question I bring to a consideration of Beauvoir's language, then, is what might be gained—both by Beauvoir and her readers—by her recasting of the maternal experience in an unfamiliar light.

What is striking in Beauvoir's portrayal of maternity are the metaphors of control and loss of control, boundary and boundaries breached. The images of confrontation, invasion, and resistance mark pregnancy in *The Second Sex* as the site of a struggle. These images make up a narrative about subjectivity or agency, through the symbolism of the pregnant body, and are part of Beauvoir's struggle over the terms of subjectivity itself.

In the chapter on biology, Beauvoir's language is explicitly that of war and invasion. Beauvoir's survey of various species presents reproduction as the primary battlefield in a war between the individual and the species. As Beauvoir presents it, the species is an invader, which overtakes the individual female organism in order to ensure its own survival. In the lower species, the individual organism is "devoured," or "consumed," by the species.[7] Beauvoir presents horrifying images of females "almost entirely reduced to [their] reproductive apparatus," subservient and dedicated to the needs of the species, even "sacrificed" to the species.[8] Here "the female is hardly more than an abdomen, her existence entirely devoured by the work of a monstrous ovulation."[9] Indeed, the invasion of the species seems to turn the female herself into a kind of monster. Beauvoir describes a female who is reduced to a receptacle for fulfilling the needs of the species: She is a shapeless pudding (*boudin blanchâtre*) of "giant proportions . . . her appendages only stumps, her body a shapeless sac, all her organs degenerated to profit the eggs."[10]

When Beauvoir describes human conception and reproduction her language also portrays the female as attacked and invaded by a hostile other. Copulation itself is a "violation"[11]; the female is "an enclosure that is broken into" (*intériorité violée*), her body a "resistance to be broken through" (*résistance brisée*).[12] Repeatedly, Beauvoir describes this invasion as alienating the female from her own body. Once the egg is penetrated by a foreign gamete, she writes, "the female is then alienated . . . inhabited by an other who feeds upon her substance."[13] Women experience "a more profound alienation" as the fertilized egg develops in the uterus.[14] "It is as if she is possessed by foreign forces—alienated."[15] Her body becomes an "obscure, alien thing . . . the prey of a stubborn and foreign life."[16] Finally Beauvoir names this hostile other, who, having invaded, lives off the female as a parasite: "it is true that [women] have within them a hostile element: it is the species which eats away at them" (*qui les ronge*).[17] "From birth the species has taken possession of woman."[18]

The theme of the female individual as enslaved to the invading species runs throughout the chapter. The female ant is "enslaved to the species" (*asservie à l'espèce, esclave*)[19]; the worker bee "has a sad destiny" (*triste destinée*), "a life entirely consecrated to raising the larvae," while the queen bee is "enslaved to the hive."[20] Reproduction for these females is a destiny.[21] In mammals as well, Beauvoir writes, the whole female organism is adapted for "the servitude of maternity."[22] The female is the "victim" (*proie*)[23] or slave[24] of a species that "demands this abdication"[25]; she "escapes its grasp" and is "delivered from her servitude"[26] only after menopause.

As Beauvoir describes the physiology of reproduction in increasingly complex species, the language of invasion and enslavement builds. The war reaches its crisis point when Beauvoir describes reproduction in human females. Woman is the most individualized female in all the species, and in humans the struggle and tension between individual aims and species demands is the most pronounced of any species. But Beauvoir's language also changes slightly as she begins to discuss human females. She begins to write not only of invasion, but also of women's resistance to that invasion.[27] Precisely because in the human female individual aims are more developed, Beauvoir argues, her alienation is the most profound of any species, and she resists the invasion of the species most intensely:

> Woman is of all mammalian females at once the one who is most profoundly alienated, and the one who most violently refuses this alienation; in no other is the enslavement of the organism to reproduction more imperious or more unwillingly accepted.[28]

The final picture of reproduction is thus of a desperate struggle in which women must fight for their very survival as individuals.

It is clear, then, that Beauvoir's language throughout the chapter on biology is curiously heightened and emotionally laden.[29] And this quality of the language seems strangely at odds with the argument of the chapter. Beauvoir's aim in the chapter titled "The Facts of Biology" is to dispassionately assess the significance of biological givens for women's position. She argues explicitly that the humans are distinct from other species and that we cannot draw any conclusions about women from her survey of animal reproduction.[30] What is more, her ultimate conclusion is that biological givens are not meaningful in the abstract and do not determine women's position.[31] Citing Merleau-Ponty, she writes that "man is not a natural species: he is an historical idea" since humans are not fixed or defined but make themselves what they are.[32] She also mocks those who would draw conclusions about women's proper place from the relationship between egg and sperm and who would make a play of doubtful analogies from egg to woman, sperm to man.[33] The drama of the struggle between individual and species, which builds through the whole chapter, is suddenly undercut by her conclusion that biology does not determine the meaning of reproduction for humans. In the context of this explicit argument, why would Beauvoir portray reproduction as a crisis and struggle in this way? And what effect does the discourse of invasion and resistance have?

The picture becomes more complex as the disturbing images are echoed in the chapter devoted to "The Mother" in the second book of *The Second Sex*. Here Beauvoir's stated intent is not to describe biological facts in the abstract, but to portray how women experience a complex human situation.[34] While Beauvoir argues that as a biological function, reproduction is enslaving to the individual female, she also explicitly argues that the body is never lived as a biological given, but in the context of an entire situation. There is no one meaning of reproduction; rather, its meaning varies with the way nature is "taken up" in human society through history.[35] As Beauvoir presents many narratives of pregnancy, the images of war and struggle recur. Beauvoir describes pregnancy as a mutilation, annihilation, and assault; in her text women are overwhelmed, ensnared, and possessed, fed upon by parasites, and the prey of the species.[36] In what follows, I want to suggest that it is in this echoing that we should look for Beauvoir's message. In the echoing of images Beauvoir suggests that the enslavement to the species that women experience on a biological level, and in the situation of early nomadic societies, is reproduced illegitimately within patriarchy.

One passage from the chapter on biology that is explicitly echoed in Beauvoir's depiction of the experience of pregnancy is her description of morning sickness as "the revolt of the organism against the invading species."[37] Responding to this passage, Mary Evans exclaims in exasperation that pregnancy should be "regarded as fundamentally active, and normal (!)"[38] Is it possible, however, that Beauvoir didn't understand that pregnancy is a normal process? Surely we should give her more credit than that. But she is not writing about what pregnancy is but what pregnancy means. What concerns her is not whether pregnancy is a biologically normal process, but the way in which it is constructed as socially normal. Read in context, her reference to morning sickness makes her critical aims clear:

Certainly gestation is a normal process, which, if it takes place under normal conditions of health and nutrition, is not harmful to the mother . . . however, contrary to [this] optimistic view whose social utility is all too evident, gestation is a tiring task of no individual benefit to the woman which demands on the contrary heavy sacrifices. It is often accompanied in the first months with lack of appetite and vomiting, which are not observed in any other female domestic animal and which express the revolt of the organism against the species which takes possession of it.[39]

In this, we can see Beauvoir's point. It is not very far from a normal to a natural process, to an inevitability and a destiny. These are the links in the public imagination, and in the culture, "whose social utility is all too evident."[40] Beauvoir's discourse of invasion, war, and horror breaks these links. Why was it so important to do this? We have to think back to the context of Beauvoir's writing. She was writing in France, in 1949, at a time when legislation forbade the buying, selling, or use of contraception and even the distribution of information about it. She was writing at a time when abortion was illegal and both laws and mores promoted marriage and childrearing as women's vocation.[41] What Beauvoir gives us as readers of The Second Sex is a dramatic restaging of "normal" pregnancy as "enforced maternity."[42] The "social utility" she refers to here is really utility for men: Woman as mother, subordinate to a reproductive species destiny, is a crucial support for the masculine Absolute Subject. In this context of enforced maternity, Beauvoir suggests, pregnancy is an invasion, and a mother is engaged in a struggle for her subjectivity. The physiological event of pregnancy blurs with the social imposition of femininity; the fetus merges with the patriarchy. As Zerilli forcefully argues, in this sense the invasion of matter is also the invasion of norms and values, and thus the woman resisting the pregnancy through morning sickness is a woman fighting her "fate" of femininity and submission.[43] Beauvoir articulates the separateness of the mother from the fetus in order to rewrite the destiny of the woman.[44]

In this context, the disturbing echoing of the images in the chapter on biology become intelligible. They portray the subjective experience of pregnancy in a situation which turns it into a destiny and turns the pregnant woman into the passive recipient of a species destiny. Within patriarchy, Beauvoir is arguing, it is very difficult to live pregnancy as a human endeavor, animated by human intention. When these images and metaphors recur in Beauvoir's chapter on maternity within patriarchal society, we should see not Beauvoir's personal horror but a graphic depiction of this enforced maternity. If in her chapter on biology Beauvoir describes the species as enslaving and sacrificing individual females, in the chapter on motherhood she describes the way in which women are sacrificed to uphold a masculine illusion of pure freedom. The first chapter sets up the species as an invader and a parasite, while the chapter on mother-hood reveals the real invader to be the norms and values of patriarchy.[45] The effect of the repetition of the images is to suggest that the enslavement of the female of the species on a biological level is reproduced illegitimately as a des-tiny in patriarchal society.

As we saw in the last chapter, Beauvoir assumes that biology effectively was destiny in the context of early nomadic life. She argues that reproduc-tion couldn't be undertaken in freedom, because of the economic and tech-nological constraints of early nomadic societies. It couldn't be experienced as a human project or engagement because no choice and therefore no risk was involved.[46] Within patriarchal society, in contrast, biology is not destiny; rather, it is constructed as such. Beauvoir's repetition and echoing of images suggests the way in which patriarchy, by constructing a situation in which maternity is lived as a destiny, illegitimately repeats the experience of the no-mad horde. In this situation, the constraints are not economic or technolog-ical but ideological and social.

Beauvoir begins her chapter on maternity by analyzing the way in which, because of the unavailability of legal abortion or adequate contraception, maternity could not be considered a free choice in the context of postwar France.[47] As Beauvoir writes, in this context, "a woman often finds herself compelled to reproduce against her will."[48] All Beauvoir's description in this chapter—all the many narratives of pregnancy and motherhood it relates—are of what she explicitly terms "enforced maternity."[49] Enforced maternity describes more than just the inadequacy of contraception, however. It refers to the way in which patriarchy constructs motherhood as a destiny more generally. Even when a woman is not directly compelled to reproduce, Beau-voir writes, she is often "enclos[ed] in situations where maternity is for her the sole outcome—the law or the mores enjoin marriage, birth control and abortion are prohibited, divorce is forbidden."[50] By denying women eco-nomic independence and concrete opportunities in the world, patriarchal society makes marriage and motherhood their only possibility while con-structing it as their "marvellous privilege."[51] As Beauvoir writes, "from in-fancy woman is told over and over that she is made for childbearing, and the splendours of maternity are forever being sung to her."[52] Part of the con-struction of maternity as destiny within patriarchy is a pervasive myth about woman as close to nature, fulfilled and completed through reproduction. This is what Zerilli has called the "eternal maternal": the myth of the mother as one with the earth and the cyclical rhythm of life and fused in blissful union with the fetus.[53]

With her imagery Beauvoir aims to show how such a dubious privilege is lived. Throughout the second book of *The Second Sex*, Beauvoir makes it clear that in the context of this socially imposed destiny, maternity takes on the character of invasion.[54] Of the young girl just beginning to grasp the concrete limitations that will be placed on her, Beauvoir writes, "marriage and motherhood involve her entire destiny, and from the time when she begins to glimpse their secrets her body seems to her to be odiously threatened."[55] When she becomes aware of the destiny, the closed future, lowering onto her, Beauvoir suggests, what once seemed wondrous will instead horrify her: "often it no longer seems marvellous but rather horrible that a parasitic body should proliferate within her body, the very idea of this monstrous swelling terrifies her."[56] If the changes of puberty take on the character of a "struggle" and a "laceration,"[57] a "threat to her integrity,"[58] it is because they signify the closing of her future. While a boy sees in the changes of puberty vague promises of an open future, for the girl they are the bodily signs that "she has been caught, there is no escape": Her fate, that "brutal and prescribed drama" (*brutal et clos*) now "lurks in her belly."[59] Thus where patriarchal ideology presents a blissful fusion of mother and fetus, Beauvoir substitutes annihilation; where patriarchy sees union, Beauvoir sees a woman whose subjectivity has been obliterated by her reproductive destiny.

Free Maternity

Beauvoir is therefore critical of patriarchal societies for constructing motherhood as a destiny and as the natural culmination and fulfillment of a woman's life. What follows from this? If maternity isn't a natural destiny, then it isn't something that will fulfill all women. Rather, the experience of it will vary depending on situation and individual circumstance. As she writes, a child is not a universal panacea, and maternity is not "enough in all cases to crown a woman's life."[60] Maternity doesn't necessarily give meaning to a woman's existence. Rather, the meaning of maternity depends on the situation. If the subject is truly embodied—that is, if the body is not simply a site of biological processes but, as Susan Bordo writes, "must be treated as invested with personal meaning, history and value," as "suffused with subjectivity"[61]—then the meaning of a pregnancy can only be determined by the pregnant woman and will vary depending on her situation and individual perspective. Beauvoir recognizes the complex interaction of situation and individual freedom in her account of pregnancy. She argues that the meaning of pregnancy will vary depending on the situation and attitude of the mother-to-be and that some will experience it as a mutilation and some as an enrichment. However, given the ideology and social conditions of patriarchal societies, it is almost impossible to live it in freedom or to undertake it authentically.[62] If the patriarchal script of blissful fusion is the only one available, then the many meanings of maternity cannot be heard.

It is important to distinguish here between the pleasure women may take in maternity and the possibility of undertaking maternity ethically. Beauvoir does not deny that in the limited and constrained situations many women live out, maternity will be experienced positively and as a source of joy.[63] However, she does argue that given the constraints of those situations, it is very difficult to undertake it authentically, as a project and as an ethical relation with an other. This is partly because women's situations often lead them into the inauthentic path of devotion, of living through the other. But more importantly, to the extent that they themselves lack an open future, women cannot open up the future for their children and to that extent their powerlessness undermines the potential of the relationship.[64]

If pregnancy, and maternity more broadly, isn't a natural destiny, then it is rightly—or should be—a choice, an engagement, and an undertaking. This is the meaning behind Beauvoir's insistence that there is no such thing as maternal instinct and nothing natural about maternal love.[65] There are no natural mothers, and no unnatural mothers. Rather, there are women embarking on a complex undertaking. Lived authentically, maternity is not a natural function but a human achievement. Her argument against motherhood as destiny, far from being a rejection of maternity, is a plea that it be recognized as a complex human endeavor and not simply as a natural function. She asks us, in fact, to take maternity or motherhood far more seriously than we currently do. To have a child, she writes, is to take on a solemn obligation and a relationship with a free other, with all the risks and difficulties that this implies. Approvingly citing William Stekel, she writes: "children are not mere material to fill out an empty existence. Children are a responsibility and a heavy obligation."[66] Beauvoir is insistent that the decision to have a child is a moral choice. For this reason the relation between parent and child must be freely willed: "there is nothing natural in such an obligation: nature can never dictate a moral choice; this implies an engagement."[67]

Maternity, then, could be a positive engagement, if undertaken in a social and political context that would allow it to be freely assumed. Beauvoir argues for the social conditions that would make maternity free. The first among these is choice: "contraception and legal abortion would permit woman to freely assume her maternities."[68] Beauvoir assumes that as reproductive technology develops, the extent of choice available to women will only grow. She suggests that women's growing interest in artificial insemination shows a hope that freedom of maternity will be accepted at last.[69]

Maternité libre, for Beauvoir, means pregnancy that could be a real choice. Choice, however, means not only the ability to refuse an unwanted pregnancy through contraception and legal abortion, but also the real possibility of choosing other paths. She insists that free maternity requires that women have a wide range of work and career paths.[70] It would also require that the woman have the economic independence to raise a child outside of traditional marriage, because, to Beauvoir, traditional marriage implies the economic and emotional dependence of the wife.[71]

But more than this, pregnancy undertaken in freedom implies motherhood as an engagement, a project: "The child is an enterprise to which one can validly give oneself . . . to have a child is to take on an engagement."[72] Beauvoir describes maternity undertaken authentically as an engagement, an obligation and a responsibility, a relationship with a free other and an opening onto the future: as, in a word, a project. The conditions for authentic maternity are even more far reaching and transformative. A free woman-subject-mother would have to have chosen her pregnancy, of course, desired it, and assumed the situation, but also would have to have some involvement in the world that her child is to enter. The child, Beauvoir writes, cannot represent the mother's whole horizon.[73] A mother should not be confined to a life entirely within the household, and not only because Beauvoir thinks that such mothers, in their frustration, could be damaging to their children, seeking tyrannically to attain through their devotion to their children a self-realization that they are unable to achieve through activities in the world.[74] A mother must have some involvement in the world because being in the world, acting as a citizen, and being a mother are not only not incompatible, but they positively demand each other. Motherhood as an engagement and a human undertaking demands also an engagement in the world one's child will inherit:

> She can only consent to bring forth life if life has meaning; she cannot be a mother without endeavoring to play a role in the economic, political, and social life of the times. It is not the same thing to produce cannon fodder, slaves, victims, or on the other hand, free men.[75]

This means that maternity—seen as an engagement—is an orientation to the future and thus also demands an engagement in projects that open onto a future and create new meanings in a shared, human world.[76] A mother, in taking on the responsibility of the relationship with that free other, the child, must also be a free subject who can help shape the situation that the child will enter and the possibilities that the child will be afforded. Free maternity is thus an ethical engagement with another that immediately also implies political tasks and responsibilities: The mother, engaging in an ethical relation with the child, must also take on the task of helping to create a world in which the child can experience his or her subjectivity. She must, as it were, help to create a world in which the child can one day experience the promises of adolescence rather than the frustrations of the eternal child, a world of "free men" rather than "cannon fodder." Here we see most clearly in Beauvoir's work the way in which an ethical engagement with another also implies a political engagement in the world. Free maternity demands that a mother, in opening herself to another, also open herself to the world. If motherhood is "usually a strange mixture of narcissism, altruism, idle daydreaming, sincerity, bad faith, devotion and cynicism,"[77] it is because women who are denied "an independent grasp on the world or on the future"[78] can hardly enter into an ethical relation with another. Beauvoir is clear: Only when women have the concrete opportunities to express their subjectivity in the world will they be able to undertake maternity freely.

She further argues that it is only when maternity is undertaken in freedom that it can be undertaken generously. Motherhood, authentically engaged in as a project, requires generosity on the part of the mother, rather than devotion. Beauvoir's disdain is not for motherhood itself, but for the expectation that it is a woman's destiny to live through her devotion to another. She targets the cultural ideal of the selfless mother who lives for and through her child as both one of the supports of patriarchy and, on the woman's part, as an evasion of her own freedom.[79] In this sense her critique of maternity parallels her critique of the other ways in which women within patriarchy are tempted into bad faith. For Beauvoir, devotion is a submerging of the self, in bad faith pursuing transcendence and freedom by proxy, by living through the object of one's devotion and setting up that object as one's end. This is also the main danger of romantic love for women in the context of patriarchy.[80] In a situation in which women have no way to project themselves into the world on their own account, the myths of romantic love entice them to justify themselves and gain their transcendence through a great love, through their devotion to a great man. The cultural creation of a maternal destiny for women is structurally the same as the promise of romantic love: the promise to women that they can fulfill themselves through devotion to another, the child, whose freedom and future will justify their life. When a mother is trapped in a situation of dependence, living out her maternity as a destiny, she lives through her child rather than on her own account.

But Beauvoir distinguishes the bad faith of evading freedom through devotion from authentic maternal generosity. True maternal devotion—rare

within patriarchy—is valuable: It is a form of generosity that consists in taking the other's freedom as your object.[81] The relationship of mother to child
is unique: When it is undertaken authentically, as a human endeavor and obligation, it is one of pure, nonreciprocal generosity.[82] Beauvoir recognizes
that this kind of mothering (and we should also add, though she didn't, par-
enting) is difficult, and its achievement is a real virtue.[83] This means that she
takes maternity seriously and holds mothers to a high standard.

It is clear that maternity can be undertaken in bad faith or authentically.
Nomad life didn't give women the opportunity to undertake it as a human
activity at all. Because of the conditions of nomadic life, maternity was not
something that opened onto a future, and it was not something animated by
human intention. But patriarchy also makes it very difficult to undertake maternity authentically (that is, ethically), because it perverts the bond into devotion and makes true generous maternal love almost impossible.

Maternal Subjects?

Clearly Beauvoir's description of free maternity indicates that maternity can
be an authentic and free undertaking. Maternity isn't necessarily enslaving.
When women are engaged in the world and have access to concrete opportunities in it, they will be able to live out their maternity as a human endeavor rather than as a purely animal function, as something that reaches out
into the future through others rather than as something simply trapped in the
cyclical time of the species. This much is clear in Beauvoir's text. However,
Beauvoir is clearer about the project of motherhood in terms of the mother's
relationship with the child than she is about the physiological process of
pregnancy itself. Mothers can and must be subjects for Beauvoir, but it is less
obvious in her text how really considering pregnant women subjects—at the
moment at which they are split, doubled, both one and not one—will change
the meaning of subjectivity.

I want to suggest that Beauvoir's ethical project points toward the change
that must take place in our notion of subjectivity. When we read Beauvoir's
account of free maternity in the context of her ethics of ambiguity and conversion, the maternal subject directly challenges the conception of subjectivity as pure transcendence. While Beauvoir presents no one narrative of
pregnancy and motherhood, but many different voices, she reveals pregnancy
as, above all, an intense experience of the ambiguity of the human condition.
When we consider the imagery of alien invaders and parasites in this light,
we can see in the ambiguity that characterizes the experience of maternity
the potential to point us toward the ethical conversion that I have traced

through Beauvoir's work. In this context, Beauvoir's images of threatened boundaries and invasion can work in a different way. Rather than expressing a cultural (or Beauvoir's personal) horror of the maternal body, they can lead to the assumption of otherness within. As Beauvoir reveals with her imagery of invasion, pregnancy is an intense experience of otherness within, and it can point us to the need to assume our own otherness rather than project it outside ourselves.[84] It is a kind of creation that we cannot mistake for control, a process that we cannot completely master, and a relationship with an other that calls for risk and generosity. In what follows I discuss each of these aspects of pregnant subjectivity in turn.

Ambiguity

If we reconsider Beauvoir's imagery of alien invaders and parasites, we should see that its meaning, and the lived experience of pregnancy, will change once maternity is freely undertaken. Pregnancy need not be a struggle for subjectivity, but it will still be an intense experience of the ambiguity of the human condition, an intense experience of otherness within. Indeed ambiguity could be said to be the keynote of Beauvoir's chapter on the mother.[85] A pregnant woman is caught in the cycle of the species, affirming life against time and death, but the birth of the child is also a foreshadowing of her own death, a reminder of her mortality.[86]

In this chapter, Beauvoir describes the experiences of many women. No one coherent narrative emerges from her survey: Because the lived experience of maternity will depend on the individual situation, one woman may experience it as an enrichment while another experiences a threat to her self.[87] Overall, however, Beauvoir presents women's experience as one of profound ambiguity:

> But pregnancy is above all a drama that is acted out within the woman herself. She experiences it as at once an enrichment and a mutilation; the fetus is a part of her body, and is a parasite that feeds on it; she possesses it and is possessed by it; it represents the future and, carrying it, she feels herself vast as the world; but this very opulence annihilates her, she feels that she herself is no longer anything. A new existence is going to manifest itself and justify its own existence, she is proud of it; but she also feels herself to be the plaything of dark forces, she is torn, assaulted.[88]

The pregnant woman is at once self and not self: "the female during the whole period of gestation is at once herself and other than herself; after the birth she feeds the new-born from the milk of her breasts."[89] She is undertaking a project, and reaching out to the future, but doing so in a way that underlines her lack of control over the process and undermines any attempt at mastery: "she lends herself to this mystery [of the Incarnation] but she does not control it: the ultimate truth of this being which makes itself in her womb escapes her."[90] This ambiguity, Beauvoir writes, the ambiguity of being part of a process but not master of it, leads to two fantasies: of giving birth to a hero, a free being, or a defective monster, contingent flesh, suggesting again how pregnancy partakes of both immanence and transcendence.[91]

This sense of undertaking a project without being sovereign over it suggests how Beauvoir's conception of the project has changed. Giving birth and suckling are natural activities and not projects in the sense that they are not entirely under our control, but rather are part of a great reproductive cycle by which we are subsumed as individuals to the species. But Beauvoir's idea of conversion suggests that we don't have full control over any of our projects, and that aiming at such control is a way of denying ambiguity and dominating others. This means that perhaps pregnancy (or rather, pregnancy as part of a free maternity) can be seen as a kind of project that tests the limits of what a project can be. This becomes clearer as we think about the relation between creativity and pregnancy.

Creativity

Beauvoir's critics have claimed that she argues that gestation and pregnancy can't be considered creative acts. Michelle Boulous Walker, for example, argues that Beauvoir makes a clear distinction between production as "active, masculine culture" and reproduction as "static feminine nature," and that her argument constitutes a "damning denial of women's creative potential,"[92] condemning women to an endless repetition of the same.

Beauvoir does write, in the context of nomadic life, that pregnancy isn't a creative activity but a function: "giving birth and suckling are not activities, they are natural functions; no project is involved."[93] She also writes in the chapter on the mother that pregnancy isn't a creative act: "Life is usually only a condition of existence; in gestation it appears creative, but it is a strange creation which is realized in contingence and facticity."[94] She explicitly contrasts the subjectivity of men engaged in activities in the world with the more doubtful subjectivity of the pregnant woman:

> The transcendence of the artisan, of the man of action, is inhabited by a subjectivity, but in the mother-to-be the opposition of subject and object ceases to exist; she and the child with whom she is swollen form an ambiguous couple that life engulfs.[95]

However, again we need to attend to the context of her argument. Part of the masculine myths that make up the structure of enforced maternity is the idea that maternity is a special kind of female creativity, that women are natural mothers, and that all women are fulfilled by maternity. Society gives to women as mothers a dignity that it refuses to women on their own terms.[96] Beauvoir describes the illusory sense of subjectivity that the pregnant woman experiences because of the social valorization of her role as mother:

> [The pregnant woman] is a link in the endless chain of generations, flesh that exists for and by [through] an other flesh. . . . [S]he is no longer an object subservient to a subject, nor is she a subject anguished by her freedom, she is this ambiguous reality: life. Her body is at last her own because it is for the infant that belongs to her. Society recognises her right of possession and invests it, moreover, with a sacred character. . . . Alienated in her body and in her social dignity, the mother enjoys the pacifying illusion of feeling that she is a being in-itself, a value completely given.[97]

Society's valorization of motherhood encourages this sense of subjectivity-as-creativity the pregnant woman gets through a feeling of oneness with her bodily processes. However, as we have seen, the social valorization of motherhood as a destiny in fact undermines a woman's subjectivity by enclosing her in a child's world, a world of values already given, or as Beauvoir writes, a serious world. This plays upon women's nostalgia for the certainties of childhood and the illusion of the desire to be.

> But it is only an illusion. For she does not really make the baby, it makes itself within her; her flesh engenders flesh only, she is incapable of establishing an existence that will have to establish itself. . . . A mother can have her reasons for wanting a child, but she cannot give to this other, who will exist tomorrow, his own reasons for being; she engenders him in the generality of his body, not in the singularity of his existence.[98]

It is when she is describing the situation of women in this situation—taken in by the masculine myths, living out maternity as a destiny—that Beauvoir describes a kind of compensatory fantasy of creativity that they experience. Her point is clear. When maternity is not undertaken in conditions of freedom—when it cannot be considered to be a choice and therefore a risk—it is a mystification, a "pacifying illusion," to construct it as women's special and unique mode of creativity.

We should be attentive, however, to her description of the "strange kind of creativity"[99] that is pregnancy, because it clearly describes the vision of subjectivity as the ambiguity of immanence and transcendence that her work as a whole is moving toward. Gestation is a strange kind of creativity that is undertaken without full control of the process or outcome. Thus, it reveals most sharply the limits of the subject's sovereignty and allows for a new conception of embodied subjectivity.

Risk

Moreover, pregnancy as a project, and the pregnant woman as subject, reveals how Beauvoir's text alters the risk that founds subjectivity. As we have seen, for Beauvoir subjectivity is founded on the risk of self. Thinking about pregnancy as risk shows most clearly how Beauvoir has appropriated and changed the meaning of risk from Hegel's text. Beauvoir describes pregnancy among the early nomads as not a risk because in her view it was not chosen; in that sense it could only be a danger that was undergone rather than a risk consciously chosen.[100] A chosen pregnancy, however, is certainly a risk. Moreover, a chosen pregnancy reveals more than one dimension of risk. It is a risk of life in the Hegelian sense: In any pregnancy, a woman puts her health and even life at risk. But a chosen pregnancy also risks the mother's sense of self, integrity, and boundary. A chosen pregnancy is a risk both physical and ontological: It is the generous gift of oneself as flesh to create, yet not control, a potential new freedom. Thought of in this way, pregnant subjectivity has some parallels with the erotic relation as Beauvoir describes it at the end of *The Second Sex*. It is an act of bodily generosity, a gift of the self as flesh, and an abandonment to the flesh to reach out to the other.

This is a reading of Beauvoir that is against the grain, in a sense, because there is much in Beauvoir's text to support the idea that for Beauvoir, pregnancy, and reproduction more generally, is something to be mastered and controlled. At the end of her extensive survey of the history of birth control and reproductive rights (in which she is explicit about the link between reproductive rights and feminist struggle) she argues that finally women are in a position to complete the mastery of their bodies.[101] She is also in favor of reproductive technologies such as artificial insemination, in part because they, too, promise to "enable humanity to master the reproductive function."[102] But this emphasis on the ways in which women need to gain more control over reproduction coexists, perhaps uneasily, with her ethical project, which recognizes that mastery and control are harmful illusions and that the attempt to master others undermines free subjectivity by not recognizing the freedom of others.

Conclusion

The process of pregnancy radically undermines some fundamental assumptions we make about ourselves as subjects: that we exercise rational self-determination and self-control, that we are independent rather than interdependent, and that we are in fact one, unitary, with clear and discrete bodily boundaries. Beauvoir's depiction of maternity suggests that subjectivity as boundedness and mastery is a fiction based on a masculine idealization of the body—and that this is an idealization or illusion that is difficult to maintain.

Our concept of subjectivity is based on an individualism that ignores, and cannot comprehend, the pregnant body. Our ideas of subjectivity and individualism are based on a symbolism of the body as a bounded and ideally impermeable system. Like the erotic encounter, the situation of the pregnant woman is, in the context of this ordering, an anomaly: Not only is the body's permeability highlighted, but our essential interdependence is also underlined—both boundedness and oneness are undermined.

The pregnant body, as symbol or metaphor, has a profoundly unsettling potential to blur boundaries and to threaten received notions of independence and autonomy. However, it also has the potential to symbolize social relations, relations of self and other, and of the interdependence of the individual and the political community. If we consider the situation of pregnancy, we find many of our theoretical constructions—of the individual as a bounded, separate, independent, self-sovereign individual—are inadequate. Pregnancy, this astoundingly complex yet entirely commonplace process of creation, dissolves bodily boundaries, undermines the possibility of distinguishing self from other, and ruptures the connections we commonly make between creativity and conscious manipulation and control. Thus, there are two aspects of modern subjectivity that a consideration of pregnancy disturbs: our sense of ourselves as closed, bounded individuals (as one) and our sense of mastery or self-control.[103]

What is shown by the "problem" of pregnancy is that the existentialist project proves somewhat resistant to Beauvoir's probing and in some ways tentative attempts to transform it from a masculine preserve to a human capacity. She is, I think, led into some difficulty when she tries to describe subjectivity lived out in feminine form because the project retains some of its associations with the body-as-instrument. Beauvoir's portrayal of pregnancy reveals most strikingly the way in which her text leads us toward a vision of subjectivity different from the one with which she begins.

If freedom or subjectivity is defined as pure transcendence, pregnancy becomes an obstacle to women's freedom and subjectivity. However, if we read

The Second Sex in the light of Beauvoir's ethical essays and recognize the centrality of ambiguity and conversion, the equation of subjectivity with pure transcendence is revealed as a masculine illusion founded on Woman/Other as symbolic of immanence. *The Second Sex* transforms the meaning of subjectivity and human freedom. Beauvoir isn't valorizing a masculine model of subjectivity. Rather, in the process of shifting subjectivity from a masculine preserve to a human capacity she in fact alters the meaning of subjectivity and the project and the relationship of risking to subjectivity.

I have argued that we need to be attentive to the political and social context Beauvoir was writing in to understand her imagery about pregnancy and to comprehend the intentions and effects of her portrayal of pregnancy as invasion and struggle. In *The Second Sex*, Beauvoir concentrates on how pregnancy has been lived in patriarchy. Beauvoir is, because of the context she is writing in, understandably more concerned to articulate the ways in which pregnancy can be made a choice, be brought to some extent under women's control, than to think about the ways in which it always remains somewhat resistant to that control. But is her account limited to its time? In many ways, the possibilities for women have changed quite dramatically in the five decades since Beauvoir wrote *The Second Sex*. Many more women have the concrete opportunities in the world that Beauvoir argued were the preconditions of choice and thus free maternity.[104] Is it possible that Beauvoir's plea for mothers to be recognized as subjects is no longer necessary?

I would argue that Beauvoir's message is still timely. The political, social, and rhetorical context has changed dramatically, but in some respects is now even less amenable to women's subjectivity. The dominant ideology may no longer be one of the blissful fusion of mother and child-to-be, in which, as Beauvoir argued, the subjectivity of the woman is submerged in a reproductive imperative. However, if the dominant ideology is no longer blissful fusion and reproductive destiny, it often still fails to recognize the mother as subject. Ironically, an increasingly dominant conception of pregnancy is of two parties, mother and fetus, with separate, and often conflicting interests.[105] In contrast, however, to Beauvoir's picture of women threatened by the hostile invader lurking in their wombs, in the contemporary imagination and in contemporary fetal rights discourse it is most likely to be the fetus that is seen to be at risk and at the mercy of a hostile or inadequate mother.[106] Though the rhetoric seems very different on the surface, there are deeper similarities. Underlying both the myth of blissful fusion and the current fetal rights rhetoric is the ideology of motherhood as self-sacrifice and selfless devotion. The current social and legal discourse of pregnancy also fails to recognize the mother's subjectivity: The language of fetal rights reduces women to fetal containers as effectively as did the myth of blissful fusion.

Thus a conception of subjectivity that can account for the uniqueness of the pregnant woman's subjectivity—neither one nor two, open to otherness within—is still to be worked toward. The key question for law and policy still is how to take the subjectivity of the pregnant woman seriously while recognizing that this subjectivity can't be conceived as one body housing two sets of rights or as one set of rights, bounded and discrete. Beauvoir's analysis helps us to see that while pregnant subjectivity is unique it is also simply an extreme example of the relational aspect of all subjectivity.[107]

Beauvoir's reconceptualization of subjectivity allows us to think about subjectivity not as something held in isolation, as liberal accounts of subjectivity would have it, but as enabled by a social situation and always experienced in relation with another and with otherness. Subjectivity in this sense can't be separated from the ethical and political demands it makes on us to ensure that our actions enlarge the freedom of others. Pregnant subjectivity is perhaps then the extreme case that reveals the bad faith of the Absolute Subject, because we can't think of the pregnant woman as one, bounded, independent, and separate any more than we should think of her as two at war.

Notes

1. See, for example, Mary Lowenthal Felstiner, "Seeing The Second Sex through the Second Wave," *Feminist Studies* 6, no. 2 (1980): 247–76; Toril Moi, "Existentialism and Feminism: The Rhetoric of Biology in 'The Second Sex,'" *Oxford Literary Review* 8 (1986): 88–95; Naomi Greene, "Sartre, Sexuality and *The Second Sex*," *Philosophy and Literature* 4, no. 2 (1980): 190–211. See also my discussion in chapter 2, the section titled The "Body Problem" in *The Second Sex*.

2. My argument here will differ from that of Bergoffen, who argues that Beauvoir was "taken in" by the patriarchal myths about reproduction. Bergoffen finds that Beauvoir "accepts the idea that ovaries and uteri are marks of immanence" (Bergoffen, *The Philosophy of Simone de Beauvoir: Gendered Phenomenologies, Erotic Generosities* [New York: State University of New York Press, 1997], 151) and for this reason misses the possibilities of pregnant subjectivity (Bergoffen, *Simone de Beauvoir*, 209). See also Bergoffen's discussion in "Simone de Beauvoir: Disrupting the Metonymy of Gender," in *Resistance, Flight, Creation: Feminist Enactments of French Philosophy*, ed. Dorothea Olkowski (Ithaca: Cornell, 2000), 97–110. On page 105 of that text, Bergoffen writes that "[Beauvoir] is not willing to consider the natural process of childbirth as amenable to inscriptions of subjectivity." As will become clear later, I argue that Beauvoir does indeed consider pregnancy and maternity "amenable to in-

scriptions of subjectivity": I find the seeds of a feminist account of pregnant subjectivity within Beauvoir's rhetoric on the maternal body.

3. Linda Zerilli, "A Process without a Subject: Simone de Beauvoir and Julia Kristeva on Maternity," *Signs* 18, no. 1 (1992): 111–35. Zerilli's argument about the restaging of maternity is made in the context of her comparison between Beauvoir's and Kristeva's accounts of maternal subjectivity. I am indebted to Zerilli for her incisive analysis of Beauvoir's rhetorical strategy of defamiliarization ("Process," 121), though, as will become apparent later, my sense of the vision of maternal subjectivity that is implicit in *The Second Sex* differs from Zerilli's in several respects.

4. Zerilli, "Process," 132.

5. Mary Evans, *Simone de Beauvoir: A Feminist Mandarin* (London: Tavistock, 1985); Carol Ascher, *Simone de Beauvoir: A Life of Freedom* (Boston: Beacon, 1981), and see my discussion in chapter 2.

6. In fact, it is not clear whether Beauvoir was ever pregnant or not. In 1971 she signed "The Manifesto of the 343," a statement signed by 343 French women declaring that they had had illegal abortions and demanding abortion rights. However, in 1982 she told her biographer, Deirdre Bair, that she had never been pregnant and had never had an abortion, and had signed the manifesto simply in order to "take the risk on behalf of those who could not." Bair, *Simone de Beauvoir, A Biography* (New York: Summit Books, 1990), 547.

7. Simone de Beauvoir, *The Second Sex*, trans. and ed. H. M. Parshley (New York: Vintage, 1989), 17, 18; *Deuxième sexe I*, 51–52, 54.

8. Beauvoir, *The Second Sex*, 17, 21; *Deuxième sexe I*, 52, 57.

9. Beauvoir, *The Second Sex*, 17; *Deuxième sexe I*, 51.

10. Beauvoir, *The Second Sex*, 17; *Deuxième sexe I*, 51.

11. Beauvoir, *The Second Sex*, 24; *Deuxième sexe I*, 58.

12. Beauvoir, *The Second Sex*, 21; *Deuxième sexe I*, 57.

13. Beauvoir, *The Second Sex*, 24–25, TA; *Deuxième sexe I*, 58.

14. Beauvoir, *The Second Sex*, 33; *Deuxième sexe I*, 67.

15. Beauvoir, *The Second Sex*, 25; *Deuxième sexe I*, 62.

16. Beauvoir, *The Second Sex*, 29; *Deuxième sexe I*, 67.

17. Beauvoir, *The Second Sex*, 34, TA; *Deuxième sexe I*, 68.

18. Beauvoir, *The Second Sex*, 26; *Deuxième sexe I*, 63.

19. Beauvoir, *The Second Sex*, 17; *Deuxième sexe I*, 52.

20. Beauvoir, *The Second Sex*, 18; *Deuxième sexe I*, 53.

21. Beauvoir, *The Second Sex*, 19; *Deuxième sexe I*, 54.

22. Beauvoir, *The Second Sex*, 20, 31; *Deuxième sexe I*, 56, 69.

23. Beauvoir, *The Second Sex*, 20; *Deuxième sexe I*, 56.

24. Beauvoir, *The Second Sex*, 27; *Deuxième sexe I*, 64.

25. Beauvoir, *The Second Sex*, 23; *Deuxième sexe I*, 59.

26. Beauvoir, *The Second Sex*, 31; *Deuxième sexe I*, 69.

27. Beauvoir, *The Second Sex*, 36; *Deuxième sexe I*, 70.

28. Beauvoir, *The Second Sex*, 36; *Deuxième sexe I*, 70.

29. See Moi's commentary on Beauvoir's rhetoric and metaphors in *Simone de Beauvoir: The Making of an Intellectual Woman* (Oxford: Basil Blackwell, 1994), 150–55, and in "Existentialism and Feminism." In contrast to Moi, who reads Beauvoir's rhetoric as a sign of her unconscious fear or ambivalence about the body, Zerilli argues that it is a conscious rhetorical strategy, a discursive deployment of horror. Zerilli, "Process," 125–26.

30. Beauvoir, *The Second Sex*, 33.

31. Beauvoir, *The Second Sex*, 32–33, 34.

32. Beauvoir, *The Second Sex*, 34.

33. Beauvoir, *The Second Sex*, 12, 13–14. Zerilli identifies mimicry as one of Beauvoir's rhetorical strategies to mock and undermine the authoritative masculine discourses on biology. Zerilli, "Process," 118.

34. Beauvoir, *The Second Sex*, xxxvi (introduction to the second book).

35. Beauvoir, *The Second Sex*, 37, TA; *Deuxième sexe I*, 77. And see Karen Vintges, "The Second Sex and Philosophy," in *Feminist Interpretations of Simone de Beauvoir*, ed. Margaret Simons (University Park: Pennsylvania State University Press, 1995), 45–58, 55.

36. Beauvoir, *The Second Sex*, 495, 498.

37. Beauvoir, *The Second Sex*, 30, 498.

38. Evans, *Feminist Mandarin*, 63.

39. Beauvoir, *The Second Sex*, 29–30, TA; *Deuxième sexe I*, 67.

40. Beauvoir, *The Second Sex*, 29, TA; *Deuxième sexe I*, 67.

41. See Claire Duchen, *Women's Rights and Women's Lives in France, 1944 to 1968* (London: Routledge, 1994), and Eva Lundgren-Gothlin, *Sex and Existence: Simone de Beauvoir's The Second Sex*, trans. Linda Schenck (London: Athlone Press, 1996), 14–17, for accounts of the social and legal restrictions on reproductive rights in France in the post–World War II period. Beauvoir would become active in the struggle for abortion rights in the 1970s. See Bair, *Simone de Beauvoir*, 543–57, for an account of Beauvoir's feminist activism.

42. Beauvoir, *The Second Sex*, 485; *Deuxième sexe II*, 331.

43. Zerilli, "Process," 122.

44. Ann Snitow notes the "shamelessness" with which Shulamith Firestone and other radical feminists of the 1970s followed up on this political task and "celebrated the idea of separating women from fetuses." See Snitow, "The Paradox of Birth Technology," *Ms* 15 (December 1986): 46. While this is certainly one of Beauvoir's aims, this strategy doesn't do justice to her full argument about pregnancy, as I argue later.

45. See Zerilli, "Process," 122.

46. This is certainly, on the face of it, a strange claim, since pregnancy in the context of early nomadic societies must have posed great dangers to the life and health of the women undergoing it. However, as I discuss in chapter 4, Beauvoir distinguishes between danger and risk. As she defines it, risk only arises from a freely undertaken activity. See chapter 4, the section titled Masters and Slaves, Men and Women: Hegel Rewritten.

47. Beauvoir, *The Second Sex*, 484–92.

48. Beauvoir, *The Second Sex*, 492.

49. Beauvoir, *The Second Sex*, 485; *Deuxième sexe II*, 331.

50. Beauvoir, *The Second Sex*, 59.

51. Beauvoir, *The Second Sex*, 328–29, 491; *Deuxième sexe II*, 89–90, 341.

52. Beauvoir, *The Second Sex*, 491; *Deuxième sexe II*, 341.

53. Zerilli, "Process," 132.

54. Beauvoir, *The Second Sex*, 315; *Deuxième sexe II*, 75. Again, I should note that Beauvoir's language here, as in her chapter on biology, is excessive, in the sense that many mothers wouldn't recognize their experience in it and probably wouldn't describe themselves as being at war. Beauvoir does, throughout her chapter on the mother, indicate that women's experiences of maternity vary greatly, and that most mothers will experience their child as an enrichment and a source of joy (see later). In this sense Beauvoir's language is better understood as a dramatic restaging than as intended as a realistic depiction of maternity.

55. Beauvoir, *The Second Sex*, 298; *Deuxième sexe II*, 54.

56. Beauvoir, *The Second Sex*, 299; *Deuxième sexe II*, 54.

57. Beauvoir, *The Second Sex*, 307; *Deuxième sexe II*, 64.

58. Beauvoir, *The Second Sex*, 493.

59. Beauvoir, *The Second Sex*, 315; *Deuxième sexe II*, 75. See also my discussion in chapter 4, the section titled Lived Experience. Beauvoir argues explicitly that the meaning of puberty for both boys and girls is not determined by biology. She writes that the essential difference in boys' and girls' experiences of puberty isn't the result of physiology. Rather, "puberty takes on a radically different significance in the two sexes because it does not portend the same future to both of them."

60. Beauvoir, *The Second Sex*, 521.

61. Bordo, "Are Mothers Persons? Reproductive Rights and the Politics of Subject-ivity," in *Unbearable Weight: Feminism, Western Culture and the Body*, 10th anniversary edition (Berkeley: University of California Press, 2004): 71–98, 74.

62. Beauvoir, *The Second Sex*, 696.

63. Beauvoir, *The Second Sex*, 511.

64. Beauvoir, *The Second Sex*, 513–18 and 595–99.

65. Beauvoir, *The Second Sex*, 523.

66. Beauvoir, *The Second Sex*, 522, citing Stekel.

67. Beauvoir, *The Second Sex*, 522–23.

68. Beauvoir, *The Second Sex*, 492; *Deuxième sexe II*, 343.

69. Beauvoir, *The Second Sex*, 696; 618. This assumption is a troubling one in the current context of reproductive technology, in which rapidly expanding technological control of the processes of pregnancy and birth have not necessarily allowed women more control over the process. See, for example, Cynthia Daniels, *At Women's Expense* (Boston: Harvard University Press, 1993), and Anna Lowenhaupt Tsing, "Monster Stories: Women Charged with Perinatal Endangerment," in *Uncertain Terms: Negotiating Gender in American Culture*, ed. Faye Ginsberg and Anna

Lowenhaupt Tsing (Boston: Beacon Press, 1990), 282–99. I discuss this further later in the section titled Risk.

70. Beauvoir, *The Second Sex*, 524–25.

71. Beauvoir, *The Second Sex*, 430, 469, 480.

72. Beauvoir, *The Second Sex*, 522, TA; *Deuxième sexe II*, 385, 386. Beauvoir uses the verb "*se destiner*" here rather than "*se devouer*": "*Certes, l'enfant est un enterprise a laquelle on peut valablement se destiner*"(*Deuxième sexe II*, 385). Parshley translates this as "to devote oneself," which is misleading, since, as I argue elsewhere, devotion has a very specific meaning for Beauvoir: She uses it to describe the bad faith of seeking justification through the freedom of another (see my text later in this chapter). In contrast, "*se destiner*," translated as "to give oneself," suggests the generosity of self that Beauvoir argues is central to authentic motherhood.

73. Beauvoir, *The Second Sex*, 524.

74. Beauvoir, *The Second Sex*, 513–14, 524.

75. Beauvoir, *The Second Sex*, 525; *Deuxième sexe II*, 388.

76. Contrary to the critics who argue that maternity in Beauvoir's text is simply repetition and immersion in the cyclical time of the species, such as Michelle Walker, *Philosophy and the Maternal Body: Reading Silence* (New York: Routledge, 1998).

77. Beauvoir, *The Second Sex*, 513.

78. Beauvoir, *The Second Sex*, 513.

79. Beauvoir, *The Second Sex*, 513–18, 585–89.

80. Beauvoir, *The Second Sex*, 642–69, and Kathryn Pauly Morgan, "Romantic Love, Altruism and Self-Respect: An Analysis of Simone de Beauvoir," *Hypatia* 1, no. 1 (Spring 1986): 117–48.

81. Beauvoir, *The Ethics of Ambiguity*, 141–42.

82. See Beauvoir, *The Second Sex*, 513. That maternal generosity is nonreciprocal is perhaps a curious claim. Beauvoir argues that generous maternal love is all the more laudable because at least at first, the mother cannot expect anything in return for her generosity from the infant, in the sense that the infant is not able to respond rationally or give her recognition. As developmental theorists such as Jessica Benjamin (in *The Bonds of Love*, 11–50) would argue, the mother–child relation does develop into one of mutual recognition.

83. Beauvoir, *The Second Sex*, 513.

84. Here, and in what follows, my reading of maternity in Beauvoir diverges somewhat from Zerilli's. Zerilli argues that Beauvoir's main claim is that women must be recognized as subjects, as having a place "within discourse," in order to undermine the mother as mute subject or eternal maternal ("Process," 131). This entails, Zerilli argues, maintaining a "symbolic border" within the maternal body, between the mother and the child-to-be ("Process," 113, 132). On my reading, in contrast, Beauvoir's work is open to undermining the boundaries between self and other in the maternal subject.

85. Beauvoir, *The Second Sex*, 497. The significance of pregnancy is ambiguous, Beauvoir asserts.

86. Beauvoir, *The Second Sex*, 497.

87. Beauvoir, *The Second Sex*, 492, TA; *Deuxième sexe II*, 343: "pregnancy and motherhood are very variously experienced according to whether they unfold in revolt, in resignation, in satisfaction or in enthusiasm." Zerilli notes the many conflicting narratives and voices in "Process," 123.

88. Beauvoir, *The Second Sex*, 495; *Deuxième sexe II*, 349.

89. Beauvoir, *The Second Sex*, 22; *Deuxième sexe I*, 58.

90. Beauvoir, *The Second Sex*, 497; *Deuxième sexe II*, 351–52.

91. Beauvoir, *The Second Sex*, 497; *Deuxième sexe II*, 351–52.

92. Walker, *Philosophy and the Maternal Body*, 165–6.

93. Beauvoir, *The Second Sex*, 63.

94. Beauvoir, *The Second Sex*, 495, TA; *Deuxième sexe II*, 350.

95. Beauvoir, *The Second Sex*, 495, TA; *Deuxième sexe II*, 350.

96. Beauvoir, *The Second Sex*, 496.

97. Beauvoir, *The Second Sex*, 496, TA; *Deuxième sexe II*, 351.

98. Beauvoir, *The Second Sex*, 496, TA; *Deuxième sexe II*, 351.

99. Beauvoir, *The Second Sex*, 495.

100. Beauvoir, *The Second Sex*, 62–64. See also chapter 4, the section titled Masters and Slaves, Men and Women: Hegel Rewritten.

101. Beauvoir, *The Second Sex*, 121.

102. Beauvoir, *The Second Sex*, 121.

103. Emily Martin in *The Woman in the Body: A Cultural Analysis of Reproduction* (Boston: Beacon Press, 1987), documents the many ways in which women try to gain control of the process, or feel in control. See especially 139–155.

104. This is not to ignore, of course, the fact that many women still lack significant concrete opportunities for action in the world and that many do not exercise what Beauvoir would recognize as free choice in their reproductive lives and cannot be said to be undertaking maternity freely, in Beauvoir's terms.

105. See, for example, Sarah Franklin, "Fetal Fascinations: New Dimensions to the Medical-Scientific Construction of Fetal Personhood," in *Off-Centre: Feminism and Cultural Studies*, ed. Sarah Franklin, Celia Lury, and Jackey Stacy (London: Harper Collins Academic, 1991), 190–205; and Susan Bordo, "Are Mothers Persons?" in *Unbearable Weight: Feminism, Western Culture and the Body* (Berkeley: University of California Press, 1993), 71–97.

106. Our conceiving of the fetus as separate is primarily, I would argue, the outcome of technology that allows us to visualize the fetus as a separate being earlier than ever before, such as ultrasound imaging (see Barbara Duden, *Disembodying Women* [Boston: Harvard University Press, 1993]) and also technology that allows us to intervene more directly in its functioning (i.e., operations in which the fetus is the patient). See Cynthia Daniels, "The Pregnant Citizen: Pregnancy, Self-Sovereignty and Citizenship for Women," paper presented to the APSA, September, 1993, for an account of legal cases in which the fetus is conceived of as the victim of a hostile mother.

107. See Daniels, "Pregnant Citizen," 17.

~

CHAPTER SIX

Conclusion: Others Within— From Ethics to Politics

Refiguring Subjectivity

I have aimed to reinterpret the argument and language of *The Second Sex* by reading it in light of the broader ethical and political project in Beauvoir's writing that develops out of her early ethical and philosophical essays. The objections I have countered are that in *The Second Sex* Beauvoir valorizes a masculine conception of freedom and that she denigrates the female body for philosophical and psychological reasons. I have considered the reception of Beauvoir and *The Second Sex* by feminist critics to show how the politics of the feminist movement has influenced the reading of *The Second Sex* and how Beauvoir's status as a feminist model has often caused her work to be read, reductively, in terms of her life. My aim, in my own reading of Beauvoir, is to read *The Second Sex* in the context of the development of Beauvoir's thought and not to reduce her ideas or language to an expression of her personal life, but to understand and read her own textual representation of her life in terms of her overall ethical project.

Reading *The Second Sex* in this way highlights what I argue is the central ethical claim of Simone de Beauvoir's writing: that the acceptance of otherness within the self is necessary for a mutual recognition of others as equals. In contrast to most Western ethics, which is premised on finding the self in the other, Beauvoir demands that we acknowledge the other in the self. At the core of *The Second Sex* lies an ethical demand to her readers: that we end the oppressive dynamic of the masculine Absolute Subject and the feminine Other by reciprocal recognition of the other as subject and the self as other. And at the end of *The Second Sex*, the erotic embrace is portrayed as a privileged moment for this reciprocal recognition of "otherness within."

This ethical demand, I have argued, should be read as a demand for a new way of understanding our freedom as human subjects. Beauvoir reveals the illusion of absolute freedom to be complicit in relations of domination and asks us instead to recognize ourselves as embodied and relational subjects: conscious individuals who are at the same time constituted through our relationship to others and through the generality of the body, in its relationship to time, history, society, and to the species. We are, Beauvoir suggests, both individual free subjects and in a sense other to ourselves in our inevitable subjection to the frailties and demands of our bodies and our inability to control and master the most important features of our existence.

In my account, I have tried to show how Beauvoir's portrayal of the body can thus be seen as more nuanced than many of her feminist critics would grant. The body is not simply that which excludes us from the human world by enclosing us in solitary sensation; it is not purely immanent. The female body has, within patriarchy, been made into flesh, the sign of pure immanence, but this is illegitimate and has served to uphold and maintain oppressive relations between men and women. In fact the body is itself ambiguous: As embodied we can reach out to the future through others, but as embodied we can also be reduced to an object by others. The body both gives us a world populated by other freedoms and encloses us in solitude. Beauvoir argues that our human condition is ambiguous in this sense, and she presents the assumption of this ambiguity as a conversion, a moral coming of age. Her writing is both a plea that we accept the tension of our human embodiment and a claim that equality and freedom require the lucid acceptance of this tension.

In Beauvoir's brief passages on the erotic encounter, I have argued, we can see the conversion that Beauvoir is demanding as a bodily conversion. Beauvoir presents the erotic moment, this "strange ambiguity of existence made body"[1] as a privileged moment that can reveal our ambiguity to us. In the erotic encounter, we can see the possibility of reciprocal recognition, lived concretely and carnally. Beauvoir is presenting, here, the erotic as a form of authentic subjectivity founded on the risk of assuming otherness within the self and the generous gift of self as flesh. We can see how Kristeva, and Beauvoir's other feminist critics, have missed the significance of Beauvoir's analysis of sexuality when we examine the erotic as a particularly revealing aspect of embodiment in Beauvoir's work, as a moment at which the ambiguity of embodiment is heightened. This analysis shows us that Beauvoir is not repudiating sexuality, or the female body, but rather challenging a particular form of male–female relations that have been structured by patriarchy.

In the light of Beauvoir's ethical demand I have undertaken a creative re-reading of Beauvoir's writing about pregnancy, which has been the target of much feminist criticism of her work. Many readings of Beauvoir interpret the pregnant body in her text as inescapably mired in immanence. However, I have tried to show that Beauvoir's analysis of maternity may be much more complex and transformative than her critics allow. Beauvoir makes us aware that it is as mother that women have been most definitively cast as Other, as immanence, and as flesh. She reveals how women's many possibilities are reduced by masculine myth to reproduction as destiny and how the many ways in which maternity is experienced by women are effaced by the myth of blissful fusion and oneness with nature. I have argued that Beauvoir's figuration of the pregnant body should be read as a response to this patriarchal myth, which she identifies as a crucial support for the masculine Absolute Subject. In Beauvoir's retelling of them, the myths of blissful fusion and maternal devotion become instead the story of a sociocultural destiny being lowered onto women, a story of the sacrifice of individual women to a species destiny. Her rhetoric of struggle and resistance, which casts fetuses as hostile invaders and women as embattled defenders, undermines maternity-as-destiny by separating women from fetuses in order to articulate women's claim to subjectivity.

On my account, Beauvoir's portrayal of free maternity suggests a new conception of pregnant subjectivity that is neither the "fetal container" of patriarchal discourse nor the bounded and unitary masculine subject. This conception of subjectivity that can account for the uniqueness of the pregnant woman's subjectivity—neither one nor two, open to the other within—is, in the current climate of increasing insistence on fetal rights, increasing surveillance, and even incarceration of pregnant women, very timely.

Beauvoir's imagery of pregnancy can be reinterpreted in the light of her ethics of ambiguity. Her portrayal of pregnancy as an intense experience of otherness within points toward a new conception of pregnant subjectivity: free maternity as a generous gift of self. Beauvoir presents free maternity, a chosen pregnancy, as a risk of self, integrity, and bodily boundaries and as an intense experience of otherness within. Beauvoir not only dramatically portrays the horrors of maternity as destiny, she also writes about what maternity has the potential to become: a real choice, a real risk, and an engagement with the future. It is both an assumption of otherness within the self, and a generous opening of the self to the other. In this sense, Beauvoir's representation of the pregnant body can also be seen as a refiguration of ourselves as embodied subjects. The pregnant body is in a sense simply the extreme case of the interdependence and ambiguity of all embodied subjects. In her depiction of the pregnant body, she graphically figures the tension of "existence made body."

From Ethics to Politics

How, then, might Beauvoir's refiguration of the embodied subject and ethics of the other within inform our understanding of Beauvoir as a political thinker, or indeed inform our own political practice and thinking? Would it be hopelessly naive to think that the ambiguous body, as Beauvoir depicts it in the experiences of the erotic encounter and free maternity, might provide an alternative understanding of our relationships with otherness, with others, and with our communities? I want to take my cue here from Debra Bergoffen, who, in her work on the erotic in Beauvoir, suggests that it can. She argues that for Beauvoir the erotic carries within it "a paradigm for an alternative understanding of the other, the couple, the 'we' and the world."[2] It is not, Bergoffen argues, that the erotic of itself can create the conditions of a just society, but that the significance of the erotic—the communicative possibilities of the ambiguous embodied subject—must be taken into account if we are to create such conditions. As she writes: "this is not to say that thinking through the disruptions of the erotic can, by itself, create the conditions for a just society, but rather to say that I do not think a just community can come into being if the ethical import of the erotic event is not brought to bear on the realities of social, political and ethical life."[3]

In what follows, I want to think about the ethical import of the ambiguous, embodied self—the self at once freedom and flesh—and speculate about how the insights we have gained in rethinking subjectivity with Beauvoir might be brought to bear on our political lives. Can the ethics of otherness within give us any kind of political guide? I believe that it can. Beauvoir's conception of freedom as intersubjective, developed in her early ethical essays, gives us reason to work for the freedom of others, to engage in political liberation struggles. However, her analysis of women's oppression in *The Second Sex* implicitly warns us of the dangers of projects of political liberation that are based on a model of freedom as pure transcendence. Thus, Beauvoir's writing suggests the dangers of a liberationist politics that, finding the self in the other, effaces difference in the name of equality and freedom and assimilates the other. Her ethic of otherness within, instead, can provide the foundation for a politics that is committed to the freedom of others while respecting the ways in which they differ from us.

Oppression and the Body-as-Flesh

As I have argued throughout this book, Beauvoir's analysis of women's oppression in *The Second Sex* makes clear the ways in which patriarchal societies are founded upon a denial of the body's ambiguity. The masculine Absolute Subject—the self as pure transcendence—is maintained only at the
cost of projecting the body-as-flesh onto women and identifying women with
immanence. Beauvoir's analyses of inequality and oppression in other contexts also suggest this central dynamic. Her account of the social marginal-
ization and oppression of the aged in *Old Age*, for example, highlights the
way in which it is an effect of our refusal to recognize ourselves as "the future
dwelling place of old age," as bodies subject to the inevitability of aging and
decay.[4] And her account of tyranny also reveals the way in which it rests on
the denial of bodily ambiguity: The tyrant limits the embodied possibilities
of the subjugated population in order to maintain the illusion of pure transcendence for himself. While Beauvoir's examples of the tyrant and the Nazi
concentration camps are extreme examples of the denial of the other's freedom by the reduction of the other to abject flesh, we can see the same dynamic at work in other situations of structural inequality. This is to say that
such inequality relies on the projection of difference, the projection of what
we fear onto the other, which transforms difference into otherness and the
other into an absolute Other. Imperialist politics constructs difference as otherness: In this, tyrannical regimes are different in degree but not in kind from
patriarchal and other inegalitarian societies. Just as woman as Other is a way
for men to avoid the demands of reciprocity and the real risks of freedom, any
relationship in which we project onto others what we most fear turns difference into otherness and protects us from the real risks of freedom.

Beauvoir analyzed both totalitarianism and colonialism as structures of inequality that rest on the denial of the others' freedom, on the other as flesh.
The politics of colonialism, in Beauvoir's analysis, is based on projecting otherness, creating an inessential Other of the colonized, or, in other words, on
reducing the colonized to immanence or flesh while maintaining the illusion
of pure transcendence for the self. Beauvoir saw the French public, and herself as a French woman, as complicit in this. Beauvoir's writing on the Algerian war can be seen as an attempt to make French citizens less able to
maintain this projection of otherness, by bringing the body, the embodied
subject, into the discourse surrounding the Algerian war and French colonial
policy.

Beauvoir's actions against French colonial policy in Algeria took a number of forms, but primarily her activism took the form of publicizing the case
of Djamila Boupacha, a young Algerian woman and member of the resistance

who was raped and tortured by French soldiers while being held for interrogation in Algeria.[5] Boupacha's trial revealed the ubiquity of torture on the part of the French authorities in Algeria. Beauvoir became involved in Boupacha's case through Boupacha's lawyer, Gisele Halimi, who realized that making her case public would be the only way to overturn the verdict, given that there were no witnesses save other soldiers. In one sense, Beauvoir's article for *Le Monde* and the foreword that she cowrote with Halimi to a book on the case were simply an exercise in getting the facts of the case out to the French public. However, Beauvoir's intervention in the war can also be seen as arising out of her analysis of the ethical subject and our relation to otherness. Beauvoir had already referred to colonial regimes in her ethical writings, if only briefly. In *The Ethics of Ambiguity*, she writes of the way in which the grinding poverty and hopelessness in an Algerian village serves the colonial regime by dehumanizing the Algerians in the eyes of their oppressors, the colonizers:

> All oppressive regimes become stronger through the degradation of the oppressed. In Algeria I have seen any number of colonists appease their conscience by the contempt in which they held the Arabs who were crushed with misery: the more miserable the latter were, the more contemptible they seemed, so much so that there was never any room for remorse.[6]

But Beauvoir's claim isn't simply that an effect of poverty is to dehumanize the poor, but that this kind of degradation is a central tactic of oppressive regimes. Beauvoir explicitly analyzed the French colonial regime in Algeria by drawing parallels with the Nazi's dehumanization of the Jews. In both cases, oppression was sustained by an "absolute evil": the systematic reduction of the other to abject flesh.[7]

In this context, the effect of Beauvoir's writing on Djamila Boupacha—a focus on one individual, graphically and passionately describing her torture and rape—was not to reinscribe Boupacha as abject flesh, but to reveal the way in which the French army, government, and citizenry were all complicit in the attempt to reduce Algerians to flesh. By portraying Boupacha's individuality and identity at the same time as she insists on her embodiment, Beauvoir undermines the colonizers' tactic of reserving pure transcendence for the self and projecting immanence as flesh onto the other. She presents Boupacha as an embodied subject rather than either a mysterious other or simply abject flesh.[8] In addition, her insistence on the complicity of all French citizens in the actions of the torturers emphasizes our responsibility for the situations of others and thus our obligation to involve ourselves in struggles for political liberation.

Ethics and Political Liberation: The Limits of Liberation

Beauvoir's ethics, then, immediately imply certain political commitments: They demand that we involve ourselves in liberation struggles. Ethical engagements with others also imply a political engagement in the world. Our moral coming of age involves the realization that our freedom is linked to the freedom of others. We need others to take up our projects and give them a future by using them as their own points of departure. As she writes, we need others who can be our "peers." We need peers, or free others, to confirm our freedom, but we also need free others to create a world with and for us, to create a situation in which we can experience our adolescence, or our capacity to put the given world in question. Others cannot take up our projects or respond to the appeal of our freedom if they are "ground down with illness and want," and so Beauvoir's ethics immediately imply a commitment to struggles against economic oppression. Others also cannot take up our projects if they cannot recognize themselves as free actors in the world, if they do not have the capacity to mark the world with their meanings, and so Beauvoir's ethics also immediately implies a commitment to struggle against political and social oppression.[9] This is certainly true of the oppression of women, and it is no less true of other oppressed groups.

However, a politics of liberation risks reinscribing an imperialist politics, in the form of assimilating the other. In the name of liberation, we risk projecting sameness onto others in the name of freeing them. We risk imposing our own vision of freedom and our own values. If, in Beauvoir's model, the tyrant refuses to acknowledge the other as a subject and instead, in his drive to master the other, constructs the other's difference as otherness, one who aims to liberate others faces a similar temptation of mastery and control. How can we decide for others what their freedom is and what their actions should be? How can we act to liberate those who are unaware of their oppression, unable or unwilling to see it? Beauvoir's answers to this dilemma in *The Ethics of Ambiguity* are rather tentative. She argues that we can bring to the other the "seed of his liberation": All that our action can do is "to put the oppressed in the presence of his freedom: then he will decide positively and freely."[10] But she is also explicitly critical of Hegel for practicing a form of recognition politics that is imperialist and assimilationist in the ways I am describing: The Hegelian self, Beauvoir writes, recognizes the other as substantially the same as the self. This form of recognition achieves harmony only at the expense of real individuality and real differences.

This criticism of Hegel is key, I would argue, to understanding the political implications of Beauvoir's work. If we take her conception of embodied freedom and her ethic of otherness within seriously, then we are faced with the difficult political work of assuming otherness within the self rather than projecting the self onto the other.

Otherness Within

In contrast to the imperialist politics of the oppressor, and the assimilationist politics of liberation, the politics emerging from an ethic of otherness within would mean recognizing others in their differences without projecting or turning those differences into otherness: recognizing others as subjects in their difference from us. It would mean not only recognizing that others must be given the opportunity to define themselves, but also accepting that this self-definition may be experienced by us as a challenge to our own identity and sense of self. This, I think, is part of what Beauvoir means when she writes about the "risks and inevitable element of failure involved in any engagement in the world."[11] When we act with others, we must accept that they may take up our acts in ways that will challenge us, even challenge us quite fundamentally.

Clearly it would be naive to think that the ethics of assuming otherness within, as I have identified it in Beauvoir's work (in the erotic encounter, in free maternity) translates directly into what we think of as the political sphere. And certainly it would be naive to think that oppressors will suddenly assume the otherness they have founded their identity on projecting. Beauvoir argues as much in *The Ethics of Ambiguity*: We cannot wait and hope for a collective conversion of the oppressors. Conflict among freedoms and the inescapable possibility of violence are facts we must live with as we decide how to act. But is it naïve to think that the generosity of giving the self as flesh can have a counterpart in the political arena? That risking otherness within the self can be seen as a political risk?

We can certainly take from Beauvoir the point that structures, institutions, and societies that allow some to minimize the sense of their own embodied ambiguity (because they are sheltered from mundane tasks of bodily maintenance, for example) at the expense of others who are closely tied to or identified with the body are unethical. As we would condemn colonial regimes for reducing the colonized to the body-as-flesh, we should condemn any political communities or identities that depend on this structure of projected otherness.[12] It is not a matter of finding a parallel so much as insisting that any political structure that enables some to project flesh at the expense of others who are identified with the flesh is unjust and that political equality or freedom will be difficult to establish in conditions that allow some to maintain the illusion of pure transcendence at the expense of others.

What then would an ethical political community be? What would a just society look like? It would be one in which we ensured as much as possible every member's capacity to act freely, and one in which receptive generosity—an openness to the foreignness of the other—is the guiding principle of our encounters with others. This, I would argue, is the political implication of an ethics of ambiguity, an ethics of otherness within.

The political import of the embodied subject, then, is that we can reach the other, and communicate with the other, by generously assuming and ourselves as flesh, and by accepting the ways in which we are not sovereign over and cannot remain master of our free acts. Our attempts to master others and the external world inevitably end in failure, but it is a failure we should joyously assume. In political terms, surely, that means that we have to welcome the ways in which our actions, our projects, are taken up by others—ways we may not have predicted or even desired. We need to practice a receptive generosity to those others whose understandings and undertakings contest ours. As Beauvoir insists, though this might be difficult politically, it will also have its rewards: It is only through our failure to master others and in our acceptance of our failure to impose our own meaning on the world to the exclusion of others' that we will be able to delight in a world now rich in intersubjective meanings—a world revealed through multiple freedoms.

When we ask if assuming our embodied subjectivity might give rise to a more egalitarian political life, we should not separate Beauvoir's ethics of liberation from her ethics of ambiguity:[13] To will others free must mean to help create the conditions in which they can act freely, but it must also mean to cease projecting otherness upon them, to approach them as subjects, and to see them as subjects whose projects can contest ours. In that sense, acting with others is a risk of self. Beauvoir's political project is a project of generosity, of giving the gift of the self as other. The politics that arises from Beauvoir's ethics of otherness within is akin to the passionate engagement, or the generous passion that she describes in the *Ethics of Ambiguity*: a relationship in which the other is revealed as an other, recognized in her difference, in that by which she escapes our control.

Beauvoir's understanding of the dynamic of patriarchy is relevant to our political situation today, which continues to be marked by structural inequalities and by the construction and projection of otherness. As Beauvoir reminds us, the identity or subjectivity we achieve by turning difference into otherness is always precarious. That which we project will continue to haunt us as what is unacknowledged within, the "enemy within" that threatens our security while remaining crucial to our identity, our sense of self.[14] Beauvoir suggests that living with an enduring tension and risking the assumption of this otherness within the self is the price to be paid for nonoppressive social relations. Perhaps this will help us more generally politically: help us to see our political, and not only our personal boundaries as more permeable, and to stop securing our own borders by transforming difference into otherness and projecting it onto those we deem foreign, different, or strange.

Notes

1. Simone de Beauvoir, *The Second Sex*, trans. and ed. H. M. Parshley (New York: Vintage, 1989), 728.

2. Debra Bergoffen, "Simone de Beauvoir: Disrupting the Metonymy of Gender," in *Resistance, Flight, Creation: Feminist Enactments of French Philosophy*, ed. Dorothea Olkowski (Ithaca: Cornell, 2000), 108.

3. Bergoffen, "Disrupting the Metonymy of Gender," 110.

4. Simone de Beauvoir, *Old Age*, trans. Patrick O'Brien (London: Andre Deutsch Ltd., 1972), preface.

5. There is relatively little feminist analysis of Beauvoir's activism and political writing on Algeria, which is surprising given that the Algerian war figures prominently in Beauvoir's memoirs, and Beauvoir herself identified it as a crucial catalyst for her political involvement. See Julien Murphy, "Beauvoir and the Algerian War: Toward a Postcolonial Ethics," in *Feminist Interpretations of Simone de Beauvoir*, ed. Simons (University Park: Pennsylvania State University Press, 1995), 263–97, for a full account of Beauvoir's political activism in the conflict.

6. Simone de Beauvoir, *The Ethics of Ambiguity*, trans. Bernard Frechtman (New York: Philosophical Library, 1948), 101.

7. Beauvoir, *The Ethics of Ambiguity*, 100–102. In *Oeil pour oeil* (*An Eye for an Eye*) *Les Temps Modernes* 1 (1946): 813–30. Beauvoir justifies using violence against Nazis and collaborators on the basis that they have reduced others to immanence and denied their transcendence; reducing them to flesh in turn will make them realize that they share this dimension of human ambiguity with their former victims. See also Kristiana Arp's discussion of *Oeil pour oeil* in *The Bonds of Freedom*, 38–40, and 138. As she argues, Beauvoir recognizes that this kind of vengeful punishment is unlikely to achieve its aim of inducing the victimizer to recognize his victim's existence as an ambiguous subject (as well as his own), since this kind of moral conversion cannot be forced.

8. Simone de Beauvoir and Gisele Halimi, *Djamila Boupacha* (Paris: Gallimard, 1962).

9. Though it is less clear in Beauvoir's work how we should make individual decisions to act in different contexts. While her ethics immediately imply political commitments, Beauvoir is careful to distinguish between the ethical and the political: In *The Ethics of Ambiguity* she writes that the ethical imperative is to will oneself free by willing others free, but also that precisely what actions are to be taken is a political question that will depend on specific circumstances. Ethics, she writes, "does not furnish recipes" for political action. Beauvoir, *The Ethics of Ambiguity*, 134.

10. Beauvoir, *The Ethics of Ambiguity*, 85, 87.

11. Beauvoir, *The Ethics of Ambiguity*, 67.

12. Though it is important not to assume that all structures of inequality depend on this identification of the oppressed with the body-as-flesh—and there would certainly be reason to condemn inequalities even in the absence of this pattern.

13. As both Kristana Arp and Debra Bergoffen suggest that we should (though Arp focuses on the ethics of liberation, while Bergoffen finds more promise in Beauvoir's ethics of generosity). See Kristana Arp, *The Bonds of Freedom* (Chicago: Open Court, 2001), and Debra Bergoffen, *The Philosophy of Simone de Beauvoir* (New York: State University of New York Press, 1997).

14. See William Connolly, *Political Theory and Modernity* (Ithaca: Cornell University Press, 1993), 179, and Julia Kristeva, *Strangers to Ourselves*, trans. Leon S. Roudiez (New York: Columbia University Press, 1991).

~

Bibliography

Adamowski, T. H. "Death, Old Age and Femininity: Simone de Beauvoir and the Politics of 'La Vieillesse.'" *Dalhousie Review* 50, no. 3 (1970): 394–401.

Allen, Jeffner. "A Response to a Letter from Peg Simons." In *Feminist Interpretations of Simone de Beauvoir*, edited by Margaret Simons, 113–35. University Park: Pennsylvania State University Press, 1995.

Amery, Jean. "Torture." In *Art from the Ashes: A Holocaust Anthology*, edited by Lawrence Langer, 121–37. New York: Oxford University Press, 1995.

Appignanesi, Lisa. *Simone de Beauvoir*. London: Penguin, 1988.

Arendt, Hannah. *The Human Condition*. Chicago: University of Chicago Press, 1958.

Aristotle. *The Politics*. Translated by Ernest Barker. London: Oxford, 1958.

Armogathe, Daniel. *Le deuxième sexe, Simone de Beauvoir: Analyse critique*. Paris: Hatier, 1977.

Arp, Kristana. *The Bonds of Freedom: Simone de Beauvoir's Existentialist Ethics*. Chicago: Open Court, 2001.

Ascher, Carol. *Simone de Beauvoir: A Life of Freedom*. Boston: Beacon, 1981.

Audet, Jean-Raymond. *Simone de Beauvoir face à la mort*. Lausanne: Editions l'Age d'Homme S.A., 1979.

Bair, Deirdre. "Simone de Beauvoir: Politics, Language and Feminist Identity." *Yale French Studies* 72 (1986): 149–62.

———. "'Madly Sensible and Brilliantly Confused': From 'Le Deuxième Sexe' to 'The Second Sex.'" *Dalhousie French Studies* 13 (1987): 23–35.

———. *Simone de Beauvoir, A Biography*. New York: Summit Books, 1990.

Barnes, Hazel. *The Literature of Possibility: A Study in Humanistic Existentialism*. Lincoln: University of Nebraska, 1959.

Bataille, Georges. *The Inner Experience*. Translated by Leslie Anne Boldt. Albany: State University of New York Press, 1988, reprinted.

Bauer, Nancy. *Simone De Beauvoir, Philosophy and Feminism*. New York: Columbia University Press, 2001.

Beauvoir, Simone de. *Pyrrhus et Cinéas*. Paris: Gallimard, 1944; reprinted in *Pour une morale de l'ambiguïté, suivi de Pyrrhus et Cinéas*, 233–370. Paris: nrf, Gallimard, 1965.

———. "La phénoménologie de la perception de Maurice Merleau-Ponty." *Les Temps Modernes* 2 (1945): 363–67.

———. "Oeil pour Oeil." *Les Temps Modernes* 1 (1946): 813–30.

———. *Pour une morale de l'ambiguïté*. Paris: Gallimard, 1947; reprinted in *Pour une morale de l'ambiguïté, suivi de Pyrrhus et Cinéas*, 9–230. Paris: nrf, Gallimard, 1965.

———. *The Ethics of Ambiguity*. Translated by Bernard Frechtman. New York: Philosophical Library, 1948.

———. *Le deuxième sexe I: les faits et les mythes*. Paris: Gallimard, 1949; reprint, Paris: Gallimard, 1976.

———. *Le deuxième sexe II: l'expérience vécue*. Paris: Gallimard, 1949; reprint, Paris: Gallimard, 1976.

———. *Privilèges*. Paris: nrf, Gallimard, 1955.

———. *Memoirs of a Dutiful Daughter*. Translated by James Kirkup. London: Penguin, 1959.

———. "Must We Burn Sade?" In *The Marquis de Sade: An Essay by Simone de Beauvoir, with Selections from his Writings Chosen by Paul Dinnage*, 11–82. Translated by Annette Michelson. London: John Calder Publishers, Ltd., 1962.

———. *Djamila Boupacha* (foreword, with Gisele Halimi). Paris: Gallimard, 1962.

———. *Force of Circumstance*. Translated by Richard Howard. London: Penguin, 1964.

———. *Pour une morale de l'ambiguïté, suivi de Pyrrhus et Cinéas*. Paris: nrf, Gallimard, 1965.

———. *The Prime of Life*. Translated by Peter Green. London: Penguin, 1965.

———. *Old Age*. Translated by Patrick O'Brien. London: Andre Deutsch Ltd., 1972. Originally published as *La Vieillesse*. Paris: Gallimard, 1970.

———. *All Said and Done*. Translated by Patrick O'Brian. London: Penguin, 1974.

———. *She Came to Stay*. Translated by Yvonne Moyse and Roger Senhouse. London: Fontana, 1984.

———. "Women and Creativity." In *French Feminist Thought*, edited by Toril Moi, 17–32. Oxford: Blackwell, 1987.

———. *The Second Sex*. Translated and edited by H. M. Parshley. New York: Alfred A. Knopf, 1953; reprint, with an introduction by Deirdre Bair, New York: Vintage Press, 1989.

———. *Journal de Guerre: Septembre 1939–Janvier 1941*. Edited by Sylvie Le Bon de Beauvoir. Paris: Gallimard, 1990.

———. *Letters to Sartre*. Translated and edited by Quintin Hoare. New York: Little, Brown and Company, 1992. (Originally published as *Lettres à Sartre, 1940–1963*. Edited by Sylvie Le Bon de Beauvoir. Paris: Gallimard, 1990.)

Beiber, Konrad. *Simone de Beauvoir*. Boston: Twayne, 1979.

Benhabib, Seyla. "On Hegel, Women and Irony." In *Situating the Self: Gender, Community and Postmodernism in Contemporary Ethics*, 242–59. New York: Routledge, 1992.

Benhabib, Seyla, and Drucilla Cornell. *Feminism as Critique*. Minneapolis: University of Minnesota, 1987.

Benjamin, Jessica. *The Bonds of Love: Psychoanalysis, Feminism and the Problem of Domination*. New York: Pantheon Books, 1988.

Bergoffen, Debra. "Out from Under: Beauvoir's Philosophy of the Erotic." In *Feminist Interpretations of Simone de Beauvoir*, edited by Margaret Simons, 179–92. University Park: Pennsylvania State University Press, 1995.

———. *The Philosophy of Simone de Beauvoir: Gendered Phenomenologies, Erotic Generosities*. New York: State University of New York Press, 1997.

———. "Simone de Beauvoir: Disrupting the Metonymy of Gender." In *Resistance, Flight, Creation: Feminist Enactments of French Philosophy*, edited by Dorothea Olkowski, 97–110. Ithaca: Cornell, 2000.

Best, Sue. "Sexualizing Space." In *Sexy Bodies: The Strange Carnalities of Feminism*, edited by Elizabeth Grosz and Elspeth Probyn, 181–94. London: Routledge, 1995.

Bock, Gisela, and Susan James. *Beyond Equality and Difference*. London: Routledge, 1992.

Bordo, Susan. *Unbearable Weight: Feminism, Western Culture and the Body*, 10th anniversary ed. Berkeley: University of California Press, 2004.

Bordo, Susan. "Are Mothers Persons? Reproductive Rights and the Politics of Subject-ivity." In *Unbearable Weight: Feminism, Western Culture and the Body*, 10th anniversary ed., 71–98. Berkeley: University of California Press, 2004.

Braidotti, Rosi. *Patterns of Dissonance*. Translated by Elizabeth Guild. Cambridge: Polity, 1991.

Brosman, Catherine Savage. *Simone de Beauvoir Revisited*. Boston: Twayne, 1991.

Brown, Wendy. *Manhood and Politics*. Lanham, Md.: Rowman & Littlefield, 1988.

Bryson, Valerie. *Feminist Political Theory: An Introduction*. New York: Paragon, 1992.

Butler, Judith. "Sex and Gender in Simone de Beauvoir's 'Second Sex.'" *Yale French Studies* 72 (1986): 35–50.

———. *Subjects of Desire: Hegelian Reflections in Twentieth Century France*. New York: Columbia, 1987.

———. "Variations on Sex and Gender: Beauvoir, Wittig and Foucault." In *Feminism as Critique*, edited by Seyla Benhabib and Drucilla Cornell, 128–42. Minneapolis: University of Minnesota, 1987.

———. "Sexual Ideology and Phenomenological Description." In *The Thinking Muse: Feminism and Modern French Philosophy*, edited by Jeffner Allen and Iris Marion Young, 85–100. Bloomington: Indiana University, 1989.

———. *Gender Trouble: Feminism and the Subversion of Identity*. New York: Routledge, 1990.

Butler, Judith, and Joan Scott. *Feminists Theorize the Political*. New York: Routledge, 1992.

Caputi, Mary. "Beauvoir and the New Criticism: Humanist Premises, Postmodernist Assaults." *Women & Politics* 11, no. 1 (1991): 109–21.

Cavarero, Adriana. "Equality and Sexual Difference: Amnesia in Political Thought." In *Beyond Equality and Difference*, edited by Gisela Bock and Susan James. London: Routledge, 1992.

Chanter, Tina. *Ethics of Eros: Irigaray's Rewriting of the Philosophers*. London: Routledge, 1995.

Coles, Romand. *Rethinking Generosity: Critical Theory and the Politics of Caritas*. New York: Cornell University Press, 1997.

Collins, Margery, and Christine Pierce. "Holes and Slime: Sexism in Sartre's Psychoanalysis." In *Women and Philosophy: Toward a Theory of Liberation*, edited by Carol Gould and M. Wartofsky, 112–27. New York: Putnam, 1976.

Connolly, William. *Politics and Ambiguity*. Madison: University of Wisconsin, 1987.

———. *Political Theory and Modernity*. Ithaca: Cornell University Press, 1993.

Coole, Diana. *Women in Political Theory: from Ancient Misogyny to Contemporary Feminism*, 2d ed. Boulder, Colo.: Lynne Reinner, 1993.

Cottrell, Robert. *Simone de Beauvoir*. New York: Frederick Unger, 1975.

Crosland, Margaret. *Simone de Beauvoir: The Woman and Her Work*. London: Heinemann, 1992.

d'Eubonne, Françoise. *Une femme nommée Castor: mon amie Simone de Beauvoir*. Paris: Encre, 1986.

Dallery, Arleen. "Sexual Embodiment: Beauvoir and French Feminism." In *Hypatia Reborn*, edited by Azizah al-Hibri and Margaret Simons, 270–79. Bloomington: Indiana University, 1990.

Dallmayr, Fred. *Twilight of Subjectivity: Contributions to a Post-Individualist Theory of Politics*. Amherst: University of Massachusetts, 1981.

———. *Language and Politics*. Notre Dame: University of Notre Dame, 1984.

———. *Critical Encounters: Between Philosophy and Politics*. Indiana: University of Notre Dame, 1987.

———. *Margins of Political Discourse*. New York: State University of New York, 1989.

———. *G. W. F. Hegel: Modernity and Politics*. London: Sage, 1993.

Daniels, Cynthia. *At Women's Expense*. Boston: Harvard University, 1993.

———. "The Pregnant Citizen: Pregnancy, Self-Sovereignty and Citizenship for Women." Paper presented at the meeting of the American Political Science Association, Washington, DC, 1993.

Dayan, Josée. *Simone de Beauvoir: un film de Josée Dayan et Malka Ribowska, réalisé par Josée Dayan avec la participation de Jean-Paul Sartre et. al.* Paris: Gallimard, 1979.

de Lauretis, Teresa. *Feminist Studies/Critical Studies*. Bloomington: Indiana University, 1986.

Delphy, Christine. "L'Invention du 'French Feminism': une démarche essentielle." *Nouvelles Questions Feministes* 17, no. 1 (1996).

Descartes, René. *Meditations on First Philosophy with Selections from the Objections and Replies*. Translated by John Cottingham. Cambridge: Cambridge University Press, 1986.

Descombes, Vincent. *Modern French Philosophy*. Cambridge: Cambridge University Press, 1980.

Di Stefano, Christine. *Configurations of Masculinity*. Ithaca: Cornell University Press, 1991.

Dietz, Mary. "Introduction: Debating Simone de Beauvoir." *Signs* 18, no. 1 (1992): 74–88.

Dijkstra, Sandra. "Simone de Beauvoir and Betty Friedan: The Politics of Omission." *Feminist Studies* 6, no. 2 (1980): 290–303.

Dinnerstein, Dorothy. *The Mermaid and the Minotaur: Sexual Arrangements and the Human Malaise*. New York: Harper & Row, 1976.

Diprose, Rosalyn. "Generosity: Between Love and Desire." *Hypatia* 13, no. 1 (1998).

Douglas, Mary. *Purity and Danger*. London: Arc, 1966.

Duchen, Claire. *Feminism in France: From May '68 to Mitterand*. London: Routledge & Kegan Paul, 1986.

———. *Women's Rights and Women's Lives in France, 1944 to 1968*. London: Routledge, 1994.

Duden, Barbara. *Disembodying Women*. Boston: Harvard University, 1993.

Eisenstein, Hester. *Contemporary Feminist Thought*. Boston: G. K. Hall, 1984.

———. "Encountering Simone de Beauvoir." *Women & Politics* 11, no. 1 (1991): 61–74.

Eisenstein, Zillah. *The Female Body and the Law*. Berkeley: University of California, 1988.

Evans, Mary. *Simone de Beauvoir: A Feminist Mandarin*. London: Tavistock, 1985.

Fallaize, Elizabeth. *The Novels of Simone de Beauvoir*. London: Routledge, 1988.

Farganis, Sondra. "On Re-Reading 'The Second Sex': Thoughts on Contingency and Responsibility." *Women & Politics* 11, no. 1 (1991): 75–91.

Felstiner, Mary Lowenthal. "Seeing The Second Sex through the Second Wave." *Feminist Studies* 6, no. 2 (1980): 247–76.

Ferguson, Kathy E. *Self, Society and Womankind*. Westport, Conn.: Greenwood Press, 1980.

———. *The Man Question: Visions of Subjectivity in Feminist Theory*. Berkeley: University of California, 1993.

Firestone, Shulamith. *The Dialectic of Sex*. New York: William Morrow, 1970.

Forster, Penny, and Imogen Sutton. *Daughters of de Beauvoir*. London: Women's Press, 1989.

Fraisse, Geneviève. *Reason's Muse: Sexual Difference and the Birth of Democracy*. Translated by Jane Marie Todd. Chicago: University of Chicago, 1994.

Francis, Claude, and Fernande Gontier. *Les ecrits de Simone de Beauvoir*. Paris: Gallimard, 1979.

———. *Simone de Beauvoir: A Life, A Love Story*. Translated by Lisa Nesselson. New York: St. Martin's Press, 1987.

Francis, Claude, and Janine Niepce. *Simone de Beauvoir et le cours de Monde*. Paris: Klincksieck, 1978.

Franklin, Sarah. "Fetal Fascinations: New Dimensions to the Medical-Scientific Construction of Fetal Personhood." In *Off-Centre: Feminism and Cultural Studies*, edited by Sarah Franklin, Celia Lury, and Jackey Stacey, 190–205. London: Harper Collins Academic, 1991.

Friedan, Betty. *The Feminine Mystique*. London: Penguin, 1963; reprinted 1986.

Fullbrook, Kate, and Edward Fullbrook. *Simone de Beauvoir and Jean-Paul Sartre: The Remaking of a Twentieth Century Legend*. Hertfordshire, U.K.: Harvester Wheatsheaf, 1993.

Fullbrook, Edward, and Kate Fullbrook. *Simone de Beauvoir, A Critical Introduction*. Cambridge: Polity, 1998.

Gatens, Moira. "Toward a Feminist Philosophy of the Body." In *Crossing Boundaries: Feminisms and the Critique of Knowledges*. Edited by B. Caine, E. Grosz, and M. de Lepervanche. Sydney: Allen & Unwin, 1988.

———. *Feminism and Philosophy: Perspectives on Difference and Equality*. Bloomington: Indiana University Press, 1991.

Genari, Genevieve. *Simone de Beauvoir*. Paris: Éditions Universitaires, 1958.

Green, Karen. "Femininity and Transcendence." *Australian Feminist Studies* 10 (1989): 85–96.

Greene, Naomi. "Sartre, Sexuality and *The Second Sex*." *Philosophy and Literature* 4, no. 2 (1980): 190–211.

Grosz, Elizabeth. *Volatile Bodies: Toward a Corporeal Feminism*. Bloomington: Indiana University Press, 1994.

———. "Animal Sex: Libido as Desire and Death." In *Sexy Bodies: The Strange Carnalities of Feminism*, edited by Elizabeth Grosz and Elspeth Probyn, 278–99. London: Routledge, 1995.

Grosz, Elizabeth, and Elspeth Probyn, eds. *Sexy Bodies: The Strange Carnalities of Feminism*. London: Routledge, 1995.

Hatcher, Donald. *Understanding "The Second Sex."* New York: Peter Lang, 1984.

Heath, Jane. *Simone de Beauvoir*. New York: Harvester Wheatsheaf, 1989.

Hegel, G. W. F. *Philosophy of Right*. Translated by T. M. Knox. London: Oxford University Press, 1967.

———. *Phenomenology of Spirit*. Translated by A. V. Miller. London: Oxford University Press, 1977.

Heinämaa, Sarah. "What is a Woman? Butler and Beauvoir on the Foundations of the Sexual Difference." *Hypatia* 12, no. 1 (Winter 1977): 20–39.

Hekman, Susan. "Reconstituting the Subject: Feminism, Modernism and Postmodernism." *Hypatia* 6, no. 2 (1991): 44–63.

Hobbes, Thomas. *The Leviathan*. Edited by C. B. Macpherson. London: Penguin, 1985.

Hodge, Joanna. "Subject, Body and the Exclusion of Women from Philosophy." In *Feminist Perspectives in Philosophy*, edited by Morwenna Griffiths and Margaret Whitford, 152–68. London: MacMillan, 1988.

Huston, Nancy. "Castor and Poulou: The Trials of Twinship." *L'éspirit Créateur* 29, no. 4 (1989): 8–20.

Hyppolite, Jean. *Studies on Marx and Hegel*. Translated by John O'Neill. London: Basic Books, 1969. (Originally published as *Études sur Marx et Hegel*. Paris: Marcel Rivière et Cie., 1955.)

Idt, Geneviève. "Simone de Beauvoir's 'Adieux': A Funeral Rite and a Literary Challenge." In *Sartre Alive*, edited by Ronald Aronson and Adrian van den Hoven, 363–84. Detroit: Wayne State University, 1991.

Irigaray, Luce. *Speculum of the Other Woman*. Translated by Gillian Gill. Ithaca: Cornell University, 1985.

———. *This Sex Which is not One*. Translated by Catherine Porter. Ithaca: Cornell University, 1985.

———. *An Ethics of Sexual Difference*. Translated by Carolyn Burke and Gillian Gill. Ithaca: Cornell University, 1993.

———. *je, tu, nous: Toward a Culture of Difference*. Translated by Alison Martin. New York: Routledge, 1993.

———. *To Be Two*. Translated by Monique M. Rhodes and Marco F. Cocito-Monoc. New York: Routledge, 2001.

Jacobus, Mary, Evelyn Fox Keller, and Sally Shuttleworth, eds. *Body/Politics: Women and the Discourses of Science*. New York: Routledge, 1990.

Jaggar, Alison, and Susan Bordo. *Gender/Body/Knowledge*. London: Rutgers, 1989.

Jaggar, Alison, and William McBride. "'Reproduction' as Male Ideology." In *Hypatia Reborn*, edited by Azizah al-Hibri and Margaret Simons, 249–69. Bloomington: Indiana University, 1990.

Jardine, Alice. "Death Sentences: Writing Couples and Ideology." In *Critical Essays on Simone de Beauvoir*, edited by Elaine Marks, 207–17. Boston: G.K. Hall, 1987.

Jeanson, Francis. *Simone de Beauvoir ou l'Enterprise de Vivre, suivi de deux entretiens avec Simone de Beauvoir*. Paris: Editions de Seuil, 1966.

Jordanova, Ludmilla. *Sexual Visions: Images of Gender in Science and Medicine Between the 18th and 20th Centuries*. Madison: University of Wisconsin, 1989.

Joseph, Gilbert. *Une si douce occupation: Simone de Beauvoir, Jean-Paul Sartre, 1940–1944*. Paris: Albin Michel, 1991.

Julienne-Caffé, Serge. *Simone de Beauvoir*. Paris: Gallimard, 1966.

Kaufmann, Dorothy. "Simone de Beauvoir, 'The Second Sex' and Jean-Paul Sartre." *Signs* 5 (1979): 209–33.

———. "Politics of Difference: The Women's Movement in France from May 1968 to Mitterand." *Signs* 9, no. 2 (1983): 282–93.

———. "Simone de Beauvoir: Questions of Difference and Generation." *Yale French Studies* 72 (1986): 121–31.

Keefe, Terence. "Simone de Beauvoir and Sartre on Mauvaise Foi." *French Studies* 34 (July 1980): 300–14.

Keller, Catherine. *From a Broken Web: Separation, Sexism and Self.* Boston: Beacon, 1986.

Kojève, Alexandre. *Introduction to the Reading of Hegel.* Translated by James H. Nichols, Jr. and edited by Allan Bloom. New York: Basic Books, 1969. (Originally published as *Introduction à la lecture de Hegel; leçons sur La phénoménologie de l'espirit professées de 1933 à 1939 à l'École des hautes-etudes.* Réunies et publiées par Raymond Queneau. Paris: Gallimard, 1947.)

Kristeva, Julia. "Women's Time." Translated by Alice Jardine. *Signs* 7, no. 1 (1981): 13–35. (Originally published as "Le Temps des femmes" in *34/44: Cahiers de recherche de sciences des textes et documents,* no. 5 (1979), 5–19.)

———. "Motherhood According to Giovanni Bellini." In *Desire in Language: A Semiotic Approach to Literature and Art,* edited by Leon S. Roudiez, 237–70. New York: Columbia University Press, 1980.

———. "Stabat Mater." In *Tales of Love,* translated by Leon S. Roudiez, 234–63. New York: Columbia University Press, 1987.

———. *Strangers to Ourselves,* translated by Leon S. Roudiez. New York: Columbia University Press, 1991.

Kruks, Sonia. "Simone de Beauvoir and the Limits to Freedom." *Social Text* 17 (1987): 111–22.

———. "Simone de Beauvoir entre Sartre et Merleau-Ponty." *Les Temps Modernes* 45, no. 520 (1989).

———. *Situation and Human Existence: Freedom, Subjectivity and Society.* London: Unwin Hyman Ltd., 1990.

———. "Introduction: A Venerable Ancestor? Re-reading Simone de Beauvoir." *Women & Politics* 11, no. 1 (1991): 53–60.

———. "Simone de Beauvoir: Teaching Sartre about Freedom." In *Sartre Alive,* edited by Ronald Aronson and Adrian van den Hoven, 285–300. Detroit: Wayne State University, 1991.

———. "Gender and Subjectivity: Simone de Beauvoir and Contemporary Feminism." *Signs* 18, no. 1 (1992): 89–110.

Lamblin, Bianca. *A Disgraceful Affair: Simone de Beauvoir, Jean-Paul Sartre and Bianca Lamblin.* Translated by Julie Plovnick. Boston: Northeastern University Press, 1966.

Landes, Joan. *Women and the Public Sphere in the French Revolution.* Ithaca: Cornell University Press, 1988.

———. "The Performance of Citizenship: Democracy, Gender and Difference in the French Revolution." In *Democracy and Difference,* edited by Seyla Benhabib. Princeton: Princeton University Press, 1996.

Langer, Monika. "A Philosophical Retrieval of Simone de Beauvoir's *Pour une morale de l'ambiguïté.*" *Philosophy Today* 38 (Summer 1994): 181–90.

Laubier, Claire, ed. *The Condition of Women in France: 1945 to the Present, A Documentary Anthology.* London: Routledge, 1990.

Lazaro, Reyes. "Feminism and Motherhood: O'Brien vs. Beauvoir." *Hypatia* 1 (1986): 87–102.

Le Doeuff, Michèle. "Simone de Beauvoir and Existentialism." *Feminist Studies* 6, no. 2 (1980): 277–89.

———. "Women and Philosophy." In *French Feminist Thought*, edited by Toril Moi, 181–209. Oxford: Blackwell, 1987.

———. *Hipparchia's Choice: An Essay Concerning Women, Philosophy, etc.* Oxford: Blackwell, 1991.

———. "Simone de Beauvoir: Falling into (Ambiguous) Line." In *Feminist Interpretations of Simone de Beauvoir*, edited by Margaret Simons, 59–66. University Park: Pennsylvania State University Press, 1995.

Leighton, Jean. *Simone de Beauvoir on Woman*. London: Associated University Press, 1975.

Léon, Céline. "Beauvoir's Woman: Eunuch or Male?" In *Feminist Interpretations of Simone de Beauvoir*, edited by Margaret Simons, 137–59. University Park: Pennsylvania State University Press, 1995.

Levi, Primo. *The Drowned and the Saved*. New York: Random House, 1989.

Lilar, Suzanne. *Le Malentendu du deuxième sexe*. Paris: Presse Universitaire de France, 1970.

Lloyd, Genevieve. "Masters, Slaves and Others." *Radical Philosophy* 34 (1983).

———. "Selfhood, War, and Masculinity." In *Feminist Challenges: Social and Political Theory*, edited by Carole Pateman and Elizabeth Gross, 63–76. Boston: Northwestern University Press, 1986.

———. "Woman as Other: Sex, Gender and Subjectivity." *Australian Feminist Studies* 10 (1989): 13–21.

———. *Man of Reason: Male and Female in Western Philosophy*, 2d ed. London: Routledge, 1993.

Locke, John. *Second Treatise of Government*. Edited by C. B. Macpherson. Indianapolis: Hackett, 1980.

Lowenhaupt Tsing, Anna. "Monster Stories: Women Charged with Perinatal Endangerment." In *Uncertain Terms: Negotiating Gender in American Culture*, edited by Faye Ginsburg and Anna Lowenhaupt Tsing, 282–99. Boston: Beacon, 1990.

Lundgren-Gothlin, Eva. *Sex and Existence: Simone de Beauvoir's The Second Sex*. Translated by Linda Schenck. London: Athlone Press, 1996.

Mackenzie, Catriona. "Simone de Beauvoir: Philosophy and/or the Female Body." In *Feminist Challenges: Social and Political Theory*, edited by Carole Pateman and Elizabeth Gross, 144–56. Boston: Northeastern University, 1987.

MacNabb, Elizabeth. *The Fractured Family: The Second Sex and its (Dis)connected Daughters*. New York: Peter Lang, 1993.

Madsen, Axel. *Hearts and Minds: The Common Journey of Simone de Beauvoir and Jean-Paul Sartre*. New York: Morrow, 1977.

Mahon, Joseph. *Existentialism, Feminism and Simone de Beauvoir*. New York: St. Martin's Press, 1997.

Marks, Elaine. *Simone de Beauvoir: Encounters with Death*. New Brunswick: Rutgers, 1973.

———. "Transgressing the (In)cont(in)ent Boundaries: The Body in Decline." *Yale French Studies* 72 (1986): 181–202.

———. *Critical Essays on Simone de Beauvoir*. Boston: G.K. Hall, 1987.

Marks, Elaine, and Isabelle de Courtivron, eds. *New French Feminisms*. Brighton: Harvester, 1979.

Martin, Emily. *The Woman in the Body: A Cultural Analysis of Reproduction*. Boston: Beacon, 1987.

———. "The Ideology of Reproduction: The Reproduction of Ideology." In *Uncertain Terms: Negotiating Gender in American Culture*, edited by Faye Ginsburg and Anna Lowenhaupt Tsing, 300–14. Boston: Beacon, 1990.

Matthews, Eric. *Twentieth Century French Philosophy*. Oxford: Oxford University Press, 1996.

Merleau-Ponty, Maurice. *The Phenomenology of Perception*. Translated by Colin Smith. London: Routledge, 1962.

———. *The Structure of Behaviour*. Translated by Alden L. Fisher. Boston: Beacon Press, 1963.

Mill, John Stuart. *The Subjection of Women*. Edited by Susan M. Okin. Indianapolis: Hackett, 1988.

Millet, Kate. *Sexual Politics*. New York: Avon, 1970.

Mills, Patricia. *Woman, Nature and Psyche*. New Haven: Yale University Press, 1987.

Miskowiec, Jay. "Selections from *Towards a Morals of Ambiguity, According to Pyrrhus and Cinéas*." *Social Text* 17 (Fall 1987): 135–42.

Moi, Toril. "Existentialism and Feminism: The Rhetoric of Biology in 'The Second Sex.'" *Oxford Literary Review* 8 (1986): 88–95.

———. *French Feminist Thought*. Oxford: Basil Blackwell, 1987.

———. *Feminist Theory and Simone de Beauvoir*. Oxford: Basil Blackwell, 1990.

———. *Simone de Beauvoir: The Making of an Intellectual Woman*. Oxford: Basil Blackwell, 1994.

Morgan, Kathryn Pauly. "Romantic Love, Altruism and Self-Respect: An Analysis of Simone de Beauvoir." *Hypatia* 1, no. 1 (Spring 1986): 117–48.

Murphy, Julien. "Beauvoir and the Algerian War: Toward a Postcolonial Ethics." In *Feminist Interpretations of Simone de Beauvoir*, edited by Margaret Simons, 263–97. University Park: Pennsylvania State University Press, 1995.

Nye, Andrea. *Philosophia*. New York: Routledge, 1994.

———. "Preparing the Way for a Feminist Praxis." *Hypatia* 1, no. 1 (1986): 101–16.

O'Brien, Mary. *The Politics of Reproduction*. London: Routledge & Kegan Paul, 1981.

Okely, Judith. *Simone de Beauvoir: A Re-reading*. London: Virago, 1986.

Oliver, Kelly. *Reading Kristeva: Unraveling the Double-bind*. Bloomington: Indiana University Press, 1993.

Pagès, Irène. "Simone de Beauvoir and the New French Feminism." *Canadian Women's Studies* 6, no. 1 (1984): 60–62.

Pateman, Carole. *The Sexual Contract*. Stanford: Stanford University, 1988.

Pateman, Carole, and Elizabeth Gross. *Feminist Challenges: Social and Political Theory*. Boston: Northeastern University Press, 1987.

Patterson, Yolanda. "Simone de Beauvoir and the Demystification of Motherhood." *Yale French Studies* 72 (1986): 87–106.

Pilardi, Jo-Ann. "Female Eroticism in the Works of Simone de Beauvoir." In *The Thinking Muse: Feminism and Modern French Philosophy*, edited by Jeffner Allen and Iris Marion Young, 18–34. Bloomington: Indiana University, 1989.

———. "Philosophy Becomes Autobiography: The Development of the Self in the Writings of Simone de Beauvoir." In *Writing the Politics of Difference*, edited by Hugh Silverman, 145–64. Albany: State University of New York, 1991.

———. "The Changing Critical Fortunes of 'The Second Sex.'" *History and Theory* 32, no. 1 (1993): 51–73.

———. *Simone de Beauvoir Writing the Self: Philosophy Becomes Autobiography*. London: Greenwood Press, 1999.

Plato. *The Republic*. Translated by G. M. A. Grube. Indianapolis: Hackett Publishing Co., 1974.

———. *Symposium*. Translated with introduction and notes by Alexander Nehamas and Paul Woodruff. Indianapolis: Hackett Publishing Co., 1989.

Poster, Mark. *Existential Marxism in Postwar France: From Sartre to Althusser*. Princeton: Princeton University Press, 1975.

Rapp, Rayna. "Constructing Amniocentesis: Maternal and Medical Discourses." In *Uncertain Terms: Negotiating Gender in American Culture*, edited by Faye Ginsburg and Anna Lowenhaupt Tsing, 28–42. Boston: Beacon, 1990.

Riesenberg, Peter. *Citizenship in the Western Tradition*. Chapel Hill: University of North Carolina Press, 1992.

Rodgers, Catherine. *Le Deuxième Sexe de Simone de Beauvoir: Un héritage admiré et contesté*. Paris: L'Harmattan, 1998.

Rorty, Amelie Oksenberg. "Descartes on Thinking with the Body." In *The Cambridge Companion to Descartes*, edited by John Cottingham, 371–92. Cambridge: Cambridge University Press, 1992.

Saccani, Jean-Pierre. *Nelson et Simone*. Paris: Éditions du Rocher, 1994.

Sapiro, Virginia. *A Vindication of Political Virtue: The Political Theory of Mary Wollstonecraft*. Chicago: University of Chicago Press, 1992.

Sartre, Jean-Paul. *Existentialism and Humanism*. Translated by Philip Mairet. London: Methuen and Co., 1948.

———. *Being and Nothingness*. Translated by Hazel Barnes. New York: Philosophical Library, 1956.

———. *Cahiers pour une morale*. Paris: Gallimard, 1983.

———. *Witness to My Life: The Letters of Jean-Paul Sartre to Simone de Beauvoir, 1926–1939*. Translated by Lee Fahnestock and Norman MacAfee. Edited by Simone de Beauvoir. New York: Scribner, 1992.

Scarry, Elaine. *The Body in Pain: The Making and Unmaking of the World*. New York: Oxford University Press, 1985.

Schwarzer, Alice. *Simone de Beauvoir Today: Conversations 1972–1982*. Translated by Marianne Howarth. London: Chatto and Windus, Hogarth Press, 1984.

Seery, John. *Political Theory for Mortals: Shades of Justice, Images of Death*. Ithaca: Cornell University Press, 1996.

Seigfried, Charlene Haddock. "'Second Sex': Second Thoughts." In *Hypatia Reborn*, edited by Azizah al-Hibra and Margaret Simons, 305–22. Bloomington: Indiana University Press, 1990.

Shanley, Mary Lyndon. "Marital Friendship and Slavery: John Stuart Mill's 'The Subjection of Women.'" In *Feminist Interpretations and Political Theory*, edited by Mary Lyndon Shanley and Carole Pateman, 164–80. University Park: Pennsylvania State University Press, 1991.

Shanley, Mary Lyndon, and Carole Pateman, eds. *Feminist Interpretations and Political Theory*. University Park: Pennsylvania State University Press, 1991.

Simons, Margaret A. "The Silencing of Simone de Beauvoir: Guess What's Missing from 'The Second Sex.'" *Women's Studies International Forum* 6 (1983): 559–64.

———. "Beauvoir and Sartre: The Philosophical Relationship." *Yale French Studies* 72 (1986): 165–79.

———. "Sexism and the Philosophical Canon: On Reading Beauvoir's 'The Second Sex.'" *Journal of the History of Ideas* 51 (1990): 487–504.

———. "Lesbian Connections: Simone de Beauvoir and Feminism." *Signs* 18, no. 1 (1992): 136–61.

———. "*The Second Sex*: From Marxism to Radical Feminism." In *Feminist Interpretations of Simone de Beauvoir*, edited by Margaret Simons, 243–62. University Park: Pennsylvania State University Press, 1995.

———. *Beauvoir and The Second Sex: Feminism, Race and the Origins of Existentialism*. Lanham, Md.: Rowman & Littlefield, 2000.

Simons, Margaret, ed. *Feminist Interpretations of Simone de Beauvoir*. University Park: Pennsylvania State University Press, 1995.

Simons, Margaret, and Jessica Benjamin. "Simone de Beauvoir: An Interview." *Feminist Studies* 5, no. 2 (1979): 330–45.

Singer, Linda. "Interpretation and Retrieval: Rereading Beauvoir." In *Hypatia Reborn*, edited by Azizah al-Hibri and Margaret Simons, 323–36. Bloomington: Indiana University, 1990.

Slama, Béatrice. "Simone de Beauvoir: Feminine Sexuality and Liberation." In *Critical Essays on Simone de Beauvoir*, edited by Elaine Marks, 218–34. Boston: G.K. Hall, 1987.

Snitow, Ann. "The Paradox of Birth Technology." *Ms* 15 (December 1986): 46.

Spelman, Elizabeth. "Woman as Body: Ancient and Contemporary Views." *Feminist Studies* 8, no. 1 (1982): 109–31.

———. *Inessential Woman: Problems of Exclusion in Feminist Thought*. Boston: Beacon Press, 1988.

———. "Simone de Beauvoir and Women: Just Who Does She Think 'We' Is?" In *Feminist Interpretations and Political Theory*, edited by Mary Lyndon Shanley and Carole Pateman, 199–216. University Park: Pennsylvania State University Press, 1991.

Stone, Robert. "Simone de Beauvoir and the Existential Basis of Socialism." *Social Text* 17 (1987): 123–33.

Strickling, Bonnelle Lewis. "Simone de Beauvoir and the Value of Immanence." *Atlantis* 13, no. 2 (1988): 36–43.

Suleiman, Susan, ed. *The Female Body in Western Culture.* Harvard: Harvard University Press, 1986.

Taylor, Harriet. "The Enfranchisement of Women." In *Essays on Sex Equality: John Stuart Mill and Harriet Taylor Mill,* edited by Alice Rossi. Chicago: University of Chicago Press, 1970.

Tong, Rosemary. *Feminist Thought: A Comprehensive Introduction.* Boulder, Colo.: Westview, 1989.

Tristan, Anne, and Annie de Pisan. "Tales from the Women's Movement." In *French Feminist Thought,* edited by Toril Moi, 33–69. Oxford: Blackwell, 1987.

Vintges, Karen. "The Second Sex and Philosophy." In *Feminist Interpretations of Simone de Beauvoir,* edited by Margaret Simons, 45–58. University Park: Pennsylvania State University Press, 1995.

———. *Philosophy as Passion: The Thinking of Simone de Beauvoir.* Translated by Anne Lavelle. Bloomington: Indiana University Press, 1996.

Waldby, Catherine. "Destruction: Boundary Erotics and Refigurations of the Heterosexual Male Body." In *Sexy Bodies: The Strange Carnalities of Feminism,* edited by Elizabeth Grosz and Elspeth Probyn, 266–77. London: Routledge, 1995.

Walker, Michelle Boulous. *Philosophy and the Maternal Body: Reading Silence.* New York: Routledge, 1998.

Ward, Julie. "Beauvoir's Two Senses of 'Body' in The Second Sex." In *Feminist Interpretations of Simone de Beauvoir,* edited by Margaret Simons, 223–42. University Park: Pennsylvania State University Press, 1995.

Wenzel, Hélène. "An Interview with Simone de Beauvoir." *Yale French Studies* 72 (1986): 5–32.

Whitford, Margaret, ed. *The Irigaray Reader.* Oxford: Blackwell, 1991.

Whitmarsh, Anne. *Simone de Beauvoir and the Limits of Commitment.* Cambridge: Cambridge University Press, 1981.

Winegarten, Renee. *Simone de Beauvoir: A Critical View.* Oxford: Berg, 1988.

Wollstonecraft, Mary. *A Vindication of the Rights of Women (1792).* New York: Whitson Publishing Co., 1982.

Woodward, Kathleen. "Simone de Beauvoir: Aging and Its Discontents." In *The Private Self: Theory and Practice of Women's Autobiographical Writings,* edited by Shari Benstock, 90–113. Chapel Hill: University of North Carolina Press, 1988.

Young, Iris Marion. *Throwing Like a Girl and Other Essays in Feminist Philosophy and Social Criticism.* Bloomington: Indiana University Press, 1990.

Zephir, Jacques, and Louise Zephir. *Le Néo-féminisme de Simone de Beauvoir. Trente ans après Le deuxième sexe: un postsciptum.* Paris: Editions Denoël/Gonthier, 1982.

Zerilli, Linda. "'I am a Woman': Female Voice and Ambiguity in 'The Second Sex.'" *Women & Politics* 11, no. 1 (1991): 93–108.

———. "A Process without a Subject: Simone de Beauvoir and Julia Kristeva on Maternity." *Signs* 18, no. 1 (1992): 111–35.

Index

~

About the Author

Fredrika Scarth received her Ph.D. in political theory from the University of Toronto in 2002. She has taught in political theory and women's studies at the University of Toronto and Waterloo University.